THE SEARCH FOR ONENESS

THE SEARCH FOR ONENESS

LLOYD H. SILVERMAN
FRANK M. LACHMANN
ROBERT H. MILICH

INTERNATIONAL UNIVERSITIES PRESS, INC.

NEW YORK

Library of Congress Cataloging in Publication Data

Silverman, Lloyd H.
  The search for oneness.

  Bibliography: p.
  Includes index.
  1. Intimacy (Psychology) 2. Psychoanalysis.
3. Mental health. 4. Psychology, Pathological. 5. Mahler,
Margaret S. 6. Kohut, Heinz. I. Lachmann, Frank M.
II. Milich, Robert, 1945-   . III. Title.
BF575.I5S54 1982   616.89'14   82-4658
ISBN 0-8236-6013-3

Grateful acknowledgment is made to the publishers for per-
mission to use material from:
Effective Psychotherapy—The Contribution of Hellmuth Kaiser, ed-
ited by Louis J. Fierman. Copyright © 1965 by The Free Press,
a division of Macmillan Publishing Co., Inc.
"The Role of the Heartbeat in the Relations between Mother
and Infant," by Lee Salk, *Scientific American,* 28:24-31. Copyright
© 1973 by Scientific American Incorporated. All rights reserved.
"An Experimental Approach to the Study of Dynamic Propositions in Psychoanalysis: The Relationship between the Aggressive Drive and Ego Regression—Initial Studies," by Lloyd
H. Silverman, *Journal of the American Psychoanalytic Association,*
15:376-403. Copyright © 1967 by the American Psychoanalytic
Association.

Manufactured in the United States of America

We affectionately dedicate this book to

Gillian, Ilena, Mara, and Stef
Peter and Suzie
Sara
And their Mommies

CONTENTS

ACKNOWLEDGMENTS

Of the many psychoanalytic writings that have influenced our thinking, we feel most indebted to the seminal contributions of Margaret Mahler and Heinz Kohut.

We have found extremely helpful the discussions of presentations of our work at meetings of the American Psychoanalytic Association, the Division of Psychoanalysis of the American Psychological Association, the American Academy of Psychoanalysis, the Institute for Psychoanalytic Training and Research, the George Klein Research Forum, the Postgraduate Center for Mental Health, the Rapaport-Klein Study Group, the Society for Cross-Cultural Research, the New York and Western New England Psychoanalytic Societies, and the Departments of Psychology at Adelphi, Brown, Long Island, New York, Northwestern, Pennsylvania, St. John's, and Yale Universities.

Valuable ideas related to different facets of this work have been offered through the years by Robert Bak, Martin Bergmann, Abbot Bronstein, Hartvig Dahl, Henry Edelheit, Susan Farber, Charles Fisher, Susan Frank, Norbert Freedman, Leo Goldberger, Nancy Goldberger, Stanley Grand, Robert Holt, Marvin Hurvich, George Klein, Robert Langs, Peritz Levinson, Lester Luborsky, Eric Mendelsohn, Fred Pine, Harold Sackeim, Doris Silverman,

Robert Sollod, Roseanne Ungaro, Paul Wachtel, and David Wolitzky.

The doctoral dissertations referred to throughout our discussions of the research have been crucial sources of data, without which this book could not have been written. We owe a great debt to the psychologists who carried these out as well as to Anne Fishel, Raoul Rosenberg, and Nancy Schwartz who, as research volunteers, contributed substantial portions of their time to various facets of the work presented.

We are also deeply indebted to Leo Goldberger, Robert Holt, and the late George Klein who, as present and past directors of the Research Center for Mental Health at New York University, generously provided laboratory space for many of the experiments herein reported and to the Veterans Administration and the Liss Foundation, both of which supported the research program on which most of the book is based.

Finally, we have found invaluable the constructive criticisms and suggestions of Nicholas Cariello in the preparation of successive versions of the manuscript.

1

INTRODUCTION

There are certain adult wishes and fantasies, typically unconscious, that are directed toward a state of oneness with another person; in the terminology of psychoanalysis, a state in which, to varying degrees, representations of self and object are merged. This search for oneness is, we believe, a psychological phenomenon implicated in a striking variety of adaptive and maladaptive behaviors. In this book we shall undertake (1) to demonstrate the ubiquity of oneness wishes in a variety of human activities, and (2) to explore the therapeutic implications of fantasies of having attained a state of oneness in a variety of treatment and non-treatment contexts. We view the latter task as the raison d'être of the book and we shall subsequently address it in terms of the following specific hypothesis: *Unconscious oneness fantasies can enhance adaptation if, simultaneously, a sense of self can be preserved.*

What is the range of activities in which wishes for oneness are implicated? Consider the following passages culled from various pages of this book, pertaining, respectively, to love, jogging, and meditation.

> ... the intense yearning which each of them has towards the other does not appear to be the desire of lover's intercourse, but of something else which the soul of either evidently desires and cannot tell, and of which she has only a dark and doubtful presentiment. Suppose Hephaestus, with his instruments,

[was] to come to the pair who are lying side by side ... and [say] to them ... "Do you desire to be wholly one: always day and night to be in one another's company? for if this is what you desire, I am ready to melt you into one and let you grow together ..." there is not a man who when he heard the proposal would deny that this meeting and melting into one another, this becoming one instead of two, was the very expression of his ancient need [Plato, *Symposium*, 192, as quoted by Bergmann, 1971].

I felt at the beginning of the run ... a peak feeling. ... I take the universe around me and wrap myself in it and become one with it [Sheehan, 1978, pp. 227, 229].

"I really began to feel, you know, almost as though the blue and I were perhaps merging—or that the vase and I were [merging]—it was as though everything was sort of merging" [unknown meditator, quoted by Deikman, 1973, p. 223].

Consider now two less adaptive expressions of the search for oneness, the first in a drug-induced "high" and the second in an experience of surrender to a religious cult:

"There was a feeling of oneness with this other person and a oneness with all the world" [unnamed drug user, quoted by Bowers, Chipman, Schwartz, and Dann, 1967, p. 561].

As I clapped and shouted, I could feel my tension slipping away, my sense of involvement growing. In spite of myself, I felt a desire to merge into this family. ... I began to sing louder and louder until I was putting one hundred percent—"One-oh-oh!" as the Family called it. Ecstatically I merged into the mass, tasting the glorious pleasure that accompanies the loss of ego [Edwards, 1979, pp. 31, 41].

Finally, some examples of the manifestations of a distorted search for oneness from patients in treatment.

"How can I live my own life and still love my mother?. . . I see myself bound to her forever. . . . I am trying to get away. . . . She is not holding onto me but I feel . . . [that] if I am my own person, I won't feel real anymore" [unnamed patient, quoted by Beskind, 1972, p. 54].

"It's only a short dream. It's of my mother bleeding right down the middle and I'm rolling over on top of her . . . like Siamese twins together. . . ." [unnamed patient, quoted by Socarides, 1969, pp. 182-183].

In discussing these phenomena, psychoanalytic clinicians commonly refer to the wishes being expressed as "symbiotic"; that is to say, they are viewed as directed toward the "good mother" of infancy or, in more technical language, toward the gratifying maternal figure of what has been termed the symbiotic and separation-individuation phases of development (Mahler, Pine, and Bergman, 1975).

Through meditation . . . a profound but temporary and controlled regression occurs. This deep experience helps the individual regress to the preoedipal level . . . to the somato-symbiotic phase of the mother-child relationship. The re-experience of this preverbal phase of union with mother and the environment rekindles temporarily the phase of "basic trust" [Shafii, 1973, p. 442].

. . . love revives, if not direct memories, then feelings

and archaic . . . states that were once active in the symbiotic phase [Bergmann, 1971, p. 32].

In referring to the unconscious oneness wishes of adults, we think it preferable to characterize them as "symbiotic-like" rather than "symbiotic," a practice that we shall adhere to throughout this book. In our view, there is no certain way of knowing just how similar these adult wishes are to the symbiotic needs of the infant; we assume only that the former share with the latter certain significant qualities. Moreover, as we shall later discuss, oneness wishes may emanate from later developmental periods and may be used in the service of defense, particularly against oedipal conflict. Finally, we should state at the outset that regardless of the developmental level from which oneness wishes derive, or the psychological function they serve, we leave as an open question (to be discussed in Chapter 6) the degree to which they may involve memory traces of infancy and childhood experiences on the one hand, and adult "reconstructions" of early life on the other.

But while issues pertaining to the phenomenology, function, and derivation of oneness wishes are important, they occupy a subordinate place in the present work. Let us turn now to our central hypothesis that, under particular circumstances, fantasies of having *attained* a state of oneness can enhance adaptation. A number of anecdotes and citations from the psychoanalytic literature will help to illustrate this thesis.

> Many years ago Dr. Robert Spiro, currently a staff member at the Austen Riggs Foundation, related to one of the authors a talk he had had with a schizophrenic patient on a hospital ward. The patient, who possessed greater self-awareness than most schizophrenics, was describing how he helped himself when

out of the hospital. When he found himself "thinking crazily," he observed, he was sometimes able to interrupt the process by carrying out a particular ritual. He would visit a brothel, but instead of having sexual relations, he would pay a prostitute to lie in bed with him in a nude embrace. After a while, he reported, he would feel himself melting into her body, followed by a sense of calm and an abatement of his "craziness."

Another colleague, Dr. Girard Franklin, after listening to a presentation of our thesis, recalled a treatment session about which a patient recently had written him. The patient had made reference to merger feelings that were accompanied by the alleviation of a symptom. He wrote: "What did it feel like? . . . My skin felt highly sensitive, especially to your skin . . . as if you were in my skin. . . . No one else in the world had any importance. I wanted to become so together with you that we would melt into one. . . . [I became free] of the fear I'm so accustomed to—the fear of being hurt, humiliated, or otherwise made fun of."

A third colleague, Dr. Jerome Siller, also responding to a presentation of our thesis, suddenly recalled the Greek myth about Hercules wrestling Achelous, the son of Mother Earth. At first, Hercules looked as if he would easily be victorious. But on each occasion that his opponent was thrown to the ground, he hugged Mother Earth. As if by magic, his strength and vigor were restored and he arose to do battle with Hercules again.

And from the psychoanalytic literature:

Throughout life [a person] may temporarily suspend the distinction between self and others and thus momentarily experience a state of mind similar to the early unity with mother. . . . To merge in order to reemerge may be part of the fundamental process of psychological growth on all developmental levels. Although [such] fusion may dominate the most primitive levels, it contributes a richness of texture and quality to the others. Such operations may result in nothing more remarkable than normally creative adaptation to circumstance. At the least it affords what [William] James called "return from the solitude of individuation," refreshed to meet the moment. At the most, it may result in transcending the limitations of earlier stages . . . to simplify, unify anew and recreate an expanded reality [Rose, 1972, p. 185].

In schizophrenia fusion experiences may operate as a substitute for symptoms [Freedman, Cutler, Englehart, and Margolis, 1967, p. 32].

It seems necessary to me when this [symbiotic] need is too strong . . . that the [analysand] should be enabled to experience it at least fleetingly in analysis. . . . [If gratified] the patient will find . . . a new peace and strength which will prove valuable for achieving a normal relationship [Nacht, 1964, p. 301].

We will present further clinical and anecdotal evidence for the thesis that symbiotic-like oneness fantasies* can be ameliorative. But, as we shall elaborate in the next chapter, such evidence has its limitations. When presented alone, it is vulnerable to the argument that the observations referred to have been either selectively perceived or mis-

---

* It should be noted that our use of the term "symbiotic-like oneness fantasies" is designed to avoid the more cumbersome "fantasies of symbiotic-like oneness."

perceived by us or by those we are citing. Even more telling, such evidence is essentially "correlational": Showing that the two phenomena—oneness fantasies and improved adaptation—go together does not constitute a demonstration that the former has *produced* the latter. Thus, much of this book will be devoted to a presentation of another kind of evidence—that which emanates from a laboratory research method termed "subliminal psychodynamic activation" developed by one of us (L. H. Silverman) in research laboratories of the Veterans Administration and at New York University.

THE SUBLIMINAL PSYCHODYNAMIC ACTIVATION METHOD

The essence of this research method is captured by the following passage that prefaced an article that appeared in the *Journal of the American Psychoanalytic Association* in 1967:

> Consider the following situation. An individual looks into the eyepiece of a tachistoscope and sees a few flickers of light. He is aware of having seen nothing more, yet a picture has been exposed for four milliseconds. As brief as this exposure is, it is sufficient for the specific content of the picture to have registered in minute detail in the mind of the viewer. Thus, if he is asked to "form an image of whatever comes to mind," aspects of the structure or content of the picture can re-emerge. . . . This, of course, describes the now familiar "subliminal effect" that Charles Fisher brought to the attention of the contemporary scientific world eleven years ago.
>
> But let me continue. In a series of investigations . . . we have observed that if it is a picture with [con-

tent designed to stir up unconscious wishes] that registers and if a clinically sensitive instrument is used to assess the effect of this registration, much more appears than aspects of the original picture. One can then discern [derivatives of the unconscious wishes seeking expression,] defensive operations appearing in reaction to these derivatives, and the emergence of various kinds of psychopathological reactions. All this occurs on a small scale and lasts but a brief period of time, yet these changes in the individual's functioning have proved to be clearly discernible and even measurable. In short, we have found it possible to produce and study under controlled laboratory conditions microcosms of many of the phenomena that psychoanalysis has concerned itself with since its inception.

It has been reasoned that the occurrence of these phenomena is enhanced by, if not actually dependent on, the fact that the [wish-related] stimuli are presented *subliminally*. For the sudden press of [wish] derivatives that are triggered by the stimuli cannot be attributed to an external source, as they could be, for example, if the pictures were consciously perceived. Thus, clinical reactions ensue as they often do in real life when external events silently arouse [unconscious wishes] [Silverman, 1967, pp. 376-377].

Since the publication of this article, the use of the subliminal psychodynamic activation method has expanded in a number of directions. The main one was based on the discovery that just as subliminal stimuli with certain kinds of psychodynamic content (i.e., content related to unconscious wishes, defenses, anxieties, and fantasies) can *trigger* psychopathology, stimuli with other psychodynamic content can *dissipate* pathology or otherwise enhance adaptation. And among the latter stimuli, the one that most often has been shown to have this positive effect contains content designed to activate unconscious oneness fantasies.

An interesting illustration of this laboratory phenomenon was reported in the December, 1980 issue of the *Journal of Nervous and Mental Disease*. A treatment study had been carried out for a doctoral dissertation by Jay Palmatier, a graduate student at the University of Montana who had a joint interest in psychoanalysis and behavior therapy. His dissertation sponsor, Philip Bornstein, a well-known behaviorist, coauthored the article.

A group of 34 adults interested in giving up cigarette smoking volunteered for a behavior modification program that required the volunteers to be seen for 12 sessions over a three-week period. The key behavior modification technique that was used, "rapid smoking," called for the volunteers, during a number of the sessions, to smoke continuously and rapidly until they felt they could not continue. After a break, the procedure was repeated. The behaviorist rationale for this technique is that repeated saturation with nicotine and smoke constitutes an experience that is sufficiently noxious to "decondition" smokers to their habit.

Previous deconditioning studies of this sort had reported notable success in helping smokers quit their habit. However, these studies also highlighted the generally short-lived quality of the remissions generated by the behaviorist intervention. This characteristic of the remissions provided the rationale for Palmatier and Bornstein's study. They modified the experimental design of their deconditioning project by incorporating the method of subliminal psychodynamic activation and using the "oneness stimulus" devised in our Veterans Administration and New York University laboratories.

At the beginning of each behavior modification session, the volunteers were asked to look into a tachistoscope and were administered four successive exposures of a subliminal stimulus. Each exposure lasted four milliseconds and was perceived by the volunteers only as a flicker of light. The volunteers were informed that some researchers had previously found that a particular subliminal message was helpful in aiding individuals to alter a variety of behaviors. In the context of their own habit, the volunteers were told that the subliminal message they were to receive might help relieve the tension associated with resisting the urge to smoke.

The volunteers were randomly assigned to two different groups, each of which received under "double blind" conditions a different subliminal message. For the "control" group, the message was the phrase PEOPLE ARE WALKING. Earlier research had shown that this message typically had no impact on behavior and therefore constituted a kind of neutral, or "placebo," stimulus. The experimental group, on the other hand, received the oneness stimulus that earlier had been shown to have an ameliorative effect in a variety of treatment and non-treatment settings.

At the conclusion of the three-week study, all the volunteers in both control and experimental groups had quit smoking. But how long would this effect last? One month later, a follow-up revealed this striking finding: Whereas only 12.5 percent of the control group were not smoking at the time of the follow-up, 67 percent of the experimental group continued to abstain.

What was the subliminal stimulus that the experimental group had received? It was the printed message MOMMY AND I ARE ONE first used in our Veterans Administration and New York University laboratories. Palmatier and Bornstein's findings that the message had an ameliorative impact on cigarette smokers trying to quit their habit accorded with earlier research in which the subliminal presentation of this phrase had facilitated positive behavioral changes.

For the reader unacquainted with the method of subliminal psychodynamic activation, Palmatier and Bornstein's provocative finding surely raises more questions than it answers. How could a message of any kind exposed for four milliseconds affect the follow-up outcome of a behavioral study of this type? How can we account for the beneficial effect of the particular subliminal message MOMMY AND I ARE ONE? What is the relationship between this simple printed message and the unconscious oneness fantasies that are the subject matter of this book?

To answer these basic questions is to provide the rationale for the experimental program on the search for oneness that is reported in Chapters 4-6. Before providing this rationale, however, we must first consider both the issues surrounding the use of a laboratory method for assessing the impact of unconscious fantasies on behavior and the circumstances out of which the method of subliminal psychodynamic activation emerged. Accordingly, we turn to these tasks in Chapter 2.

2

PSYCHOANALYTIC PROPOSITIONS AND THE SUBLIMINAL PSYCHODYNAMIC ACTIVATION METHOD

It is rare in advancing psychoanalytic propositions to refer to "supporting research"; it is rarer still for the research to come, as does the research we shall review in this and subsequent chapters, from laboratory experimentation.[1] Thus, an explanation is called for.

If psychoanalytic clinicians were asked why laboratory experimentation has not influenced the clinical practice of psychoanalysis as it has influenced the clinical practice of medicine, there would probably be two kinds of responses. The first response would be that the development of psychoanalytic theory requires no other data than that which the clinical situation yields—in other words, that the productions of patients in treatment are quite sufficient for theory development. The second response would acknowledge the potential value of experimental data, but would maintain that a laboratory method does not presently exist that can do justice to the special subject matter of psychoanalysis—unconscious mental processes. We hope to illustrate shortly that this latter reaction involves a dated judgment. But first let us address the former response.

The view that clinical data (i.e., patients' verbal productions and nonverbal behavior in treatment sessions) are by themselves sufficient for the development of psychoanalytic theory is clearly vulnerable to the following argument.

Such data have not been able to resolve the many disagreements that have arisen among clinicians. Thus, not only have clinicians from different schools of therapy been unable to sway each other by calling attention to their "clinical evidence" (consider the fact that the number of schools of psychotherapy has increased rather than decreased through the years), but even within the "psychoanalytic community" the track record for adequate resolution of controversy has been far from encouraging. With few exceptions, controversies either have continued unabated or have been decided on the basis of such non-substantive considerations as the prevailing zeitgeist or the reputations of the adversaries more than on substantive grounds. Moreover, even the exceptions to this rule are vulnerable, as evidenced by instances in which a controversy had seemingly been resolved substantively, only to arise again years later as if nothing had been settled in the past.[2]

The reason why clinicians so often disagree and why these disagreements can remain unresolved is not difficult to understand. Clinical material, while providing splendid opportunities for therapists to *develop* hypotheses to account for a patient's behavior, has notable limitations when it comes to testing these hypotheses. These limitations are severe enough so that it is rare that one clinician can convince another of a clinical proposition about which the latter is skeptical. One of us has discussed these limitations in detail elsewhere (Silverman, 1975) and here they will simply be summarized.

First, the absence of a record of the patient's actual words leaves the therapist highly vulnerable to criticism by the skeptic that he or she has subtly (or not so subtly) distorted or selectively perceived the patient's behavior.

Second, even if the skeptic were to accept the therapist's rendition of the patient's behavior as accurate, it could be maintained that this behavior has itself been skewed in a particular direction by the therapist's theoretical bias and his or her resulting behavior toward the patient in the treatment situation.

Third, there are no agreed-upon criteria for evaluating the merit of a hypothesis derived from clinical data. More specifically, consensually agreed-upon criteria do not exist for deciding what observational data are pertinent to particular clinical concepts and what comprises adequate evidence to support a hypothesis. Thus, it is not surprising that in the few studies that have been carried out (e.g., Seitz, 1966) requiring different clinicians to make clinical judgments from transcripts of therapy sessions, the consensus reached has been notably low.

The limitations described thus far, while posing a serious problem for validating clinical hypotheses, may, to varying degrees, prove correctible in the future. Ways may be found to overcome these limitations without damaging the fiber of the treatment situation. There is, however, a fourth limitation of the treatment situation that we view as noncorrectible as far as theory validation is concerned: It is in the inherent nature of psychoanalytic treatment that it cannot allow for a *controlled test* of the relevance of a particular unconscious mental content for a particular piece of behavior. Let us explain.

In the psychoanalytic treatment situation the appearance of particular material in a patient's verbalizations allows the therapist to infer the presence of specific psychodynamic motives—i.e., unconscious wishes, anxieties, fantasies, and defensive operations. When the appearance of a psychodynamic motive is contiguous with the appearance of a particular kind of behavior, particularly when this contiguity repeats itself in treatment, the therapist can make the further inference that the psychodynamic motive and the behavior are linked in some way. But what the clinical data leaves ambiguous is the specific nature of the relationship between the two. To put matters simply, when two phenomena appear together, there is always ambiguity as to whether A has caused B, B has caused A, or whether both A and B are the result of C. Thus, for example, if a male patient's associations or dreams show a link between homosexual inclinations and unconscious fantasies of castration, this link could be understood in any of three ways. The castration fantasies could be seen as motivating the homosexual inclinations ("I can avoid castration by homosexually submitting to another male, the potential castrator."). Or the homosexual inclinations could be seen as stimulating the castration fantasies ("If I give vent to my homosexual feelings, I will feel like a woman—i.e., castrated."). Or both the homosexual inclinations and the castration fantasies could be viewed as a consequence of something else, a generalized defect in the sense of self, for example. As Schafer (1968) has put it, "clinical data at their best are primarily correlational and thus are hazardous evidence on which to base causal types of explanations" (p. 29).

In order to demonstrate the validity of a posited causal relationship, what is required is the setting in motion of the first step in the hypothesized sequence with observations made of the behavior that follows. Whereas the experimental laboratory allows for this type of "manipulation," the treatment situation does not. The closest approximation to this is the state of affairs in which the psychoanalytic therapist offers an interpretation which addresses a causal relationship that the therapist believes may be present, with the patient's response to the interpretation viewed as shedding light on the validity of the formulation. While this type of therapist-patient interaction has sometimes been viewed as quasi-experimental, it cannot be controlled for contaminating influences in the way that laboratory experimental procedures can be controlled.

The main problem is that one cannot assume that a patient's response to an interpretation is due to the interpretation's specific content, a necessary assumption if one is to view the response as reflecting the correctness of the therapist's understanding. In other words, a response that seems confirmatory may be less a reflection of the correctness of the interpretation than of the patient's unconscious gratitude for the therapist's "offering" (for example, the therapist's words = mother's milk); or it may reflect a need to placate the therapist out of an unconscious fear of him or her, to mention just two of a variety of motivations that could be at work in this kind of situation. Conversely, a response that seems non-confirmatory may follow an interpretation based on a correct theoretical inference when a contaminating influence has interfered with the rendering of the confirmatory response. For example, the timing of the interpretation may be off, the patient may be expressing an unconscious need to defeat the therapist, the acceptance of an interpretation may connote to the patient an unacceptable dependence on the therapist, etc.[3]

In the laboratory, contaminating variables such as these can be sorted out by introducing a control condition that is subject to the same influences as the experimental condition (examples will soon be given). One can then view the difference between what is elicited by the experimental and control manipulations as reflecting the special qualities of the former. The equivalent control in the treatment situation would be for the therapist deliberately to make interpretations that he or she views as incorrect, as well as interpretations that he or she views as correct, a practice that would be anti-therapeutic, unethical, and of dubious control value as well.[4]

The subliminal psychodynamic activation method, referred to in Chapter 1, with its double-blind controls, has proven capable of eliminating the contaminating variables of the clinical situation. It thereby allows for a new degree of scientific precision in testing psychoanalytic psychodynamic relationships. (See note 1 for the distinction between psychodynamic relationships and "genetic relationships" in psychoanalysis.) A variety of experiments were carried out in the process of developing this method. Since these early investigations provide the methodological foundation for the studies related to oneness fantasies discussed in Chapters 4-6, an account of this work should prove helpful to the reader. The following narrative describes the evolution of the subliminal psychodynamic activation method. This account has been written in the first person singular (by L. H. Silverman) because the experiments predate the authors' collaboration.

A RESEARCH ODYSSEY BEGINS

In 1961 I secured my first full-time research job at the University of Pennsylvania, Department of Psychiatry, on a project directed by Lester Luborsky on subliminal perception. In those days, "subliminal research" was focused on two questions: (1) Could one demonstrate in an unequivocal fashion that subliminal perception existed? (2) What characteristics of the "research participants"[5] and the situation in which the subliminal stimuli were delivered were most conducive to subliminal perception? With regard to the first question, there was, at that time, as much psychological literature attacking the validity of subliminal perception as there was literature supporting it. The skeptics maintained that there were very few replications of studies reporting positive results and none conducted in independent laboratories. Moreover, when positive results did emerge from a study, they could be more parsimoniously explained as the result of "partial cues" in awareness rather than "subliminal effects." (The latter can be defined as effects attributable to a stimulus, no elements of which can be consciously perceived.[6]) To give the reader a better sense of the status of the research during this time, let me describe a typical experiment from the period and the controversy that surrounded it.

In 1959 Eagle carried out a study in which he exposed to college students, with a slide projector, a picture of a neutral-looking face that was clearly visible. Superimposed on the face was a picture exposed subliminally. Under one condition, the subliminally exposed picture consisted of one boy stabbing another with their faces in distinct frowns; while under another condition, one smiling boy was handing another a birthday cake. The participants' task was to describe the face, with their descriptions then scored for positive and negative qualities.

Eagle (1959, 1962) reported two major findings from this experiment. First, he found that after the aggressive picture the descriptions were more unpleasant and otherwise negative than after the control (birthday cake) picture. (The descriptions were scored by judges who were blind to the stimulus condition under which each was given.) And second, he reported that there was a relationship between the degree to which this subliminal effect was in evidence and particular personality characteristics of the participants.

It was the first finding—interpreted as supporting the presence of subliminal perception—that came under fire. Critics (Wiener and Schiller, 1960) pointed out that the two subliminal stimuli differed in ways other than their content. The birthday cake scene, they maintained, contained more soft rounded lines than the knifing scene, which in turn contained more sharp angular lines. Thus, they suggested, the participant catching even a glimmer of each of the stimuli, while not being aware of their content, might well have been aware of these differential line qualities, which then led to the difference in how the supraliminal face was perceived. Since an objective analysis of the stimuli supported the claim that the line quality of the two stimuli differed in the way just described, the alternate explanation was a feasible one, particularly since Eagle had no convincing data to rule out the possibility that participants were conscious of small aspects of the stimuli.[7]

In the experiments being conducted by Luborsky at the time I came to work with him, the main objective was to rule out this alternative "partial cue" explanation for findings otherwise attributable to subliminal perception. First, verbal stimuli were introduced in place of pictures since it was easier to equate these for such structural characteristics as the angularity or roundness of lines. Second, what has come to be known as a "discrimination task" was given to the participants at the end of each experiment to demonstrate that to whatever degree the experimental and control stimuli still differed from each other structurally (despite efforts to equate them) participants were not aware of *any* stimulus aspects that would allow them consciously to tell them apart.[8]

In one of these experiments, the differential effect of the subliminal presentation of the words KNIFE and FENIK (a nonsense word with the same letters as knife) on participants' "free associations" was studied. These associations were scored blindly by judges for categories of associates to knife such as eating utensils (fork, spoon, plate, etc.), cutting instruments (saw, axe, etc.), and weapons (gun, blackjack, etc.). The major finding was that there were more knife associates after KNIFE than FENIK, but only to a degree that constituted a "statistical trend" rather than a "significant" finding.[9]

When I examined the data for each participant individually, an unexpected and interesting finding emerged. While for some participants (those in the majority) there were considerably more knife associates after the experimental stimulus than after the control, for others (a minority) there were many fewer knife associates than there were after the control. Thus when the participants were considered in toto, the difference in knife associates between the experimental and control conditions only constituted a statistical trend. In reflecting on this, the following explanation occurred to me. Perhaps the latter group of participants produced markedly fewer knife associates under the experimental condition because the word knife, when it registered subliminally, threatened them. That is, since one class of associates to knife was weapons, and since the idea of weapons could be threatening to people struggling with unconscious conflicts over aggression, the stirring of these aggressive ideas could have inhibited their ideational flow rather than facilitated it. If this understanding was correct, it would mean that subliminal stimuli with particular content could trigger unconscious conflict and activate defensive processes.

Supporting this possibility were occasional reports in the subliminal research literature of a group of participants responding in a way *opposite* to what had been expected, after being exposed to a subliminal stimulus with content related to the kinds of unconscious libidinal and aggressive wishes that psychoanalysis understands to be important motivators of behavior. For example, Pine (1961) used a subliminal stimulus related to nursing and dependence on mother and discovered a *decrease* in associates to the stimulus in subsequent Thematic Apperception Test (TAT) stories (compared to the number in TAT stories under a control condition). Similarly, in Eagle's (1959) study referred to above, there was one group of participants who responded to the highly charged aggressive stimulus by seeing the neutral face as more benign; and Klein, Spence, Holt, and Gourevitch (1958) reported that a group of their participants made very masculine drawings (relative to the drawings made at other times) after the subliminal exposure of a sketch of the lower half of a nude female.

Thus, evidence from several experiments was consistent with the hypothesis that the subliminal exposure of "wish-related" stimuli could trigger unconscious conflict and set in motion defensive processes. If this intriguing possibility were borne out, one could then subject to laboratory study the fascinating kinds of relationships that psychoanalysis has posited between conflict-laden unconscious wishes and overt behavior. The first order of business, then, was to subject this hypothesis to a carefully controlled test. I thus designed the following experiment that was carried out in Luborsky's laboratory.

College males responded to different sets of the Rorschach (inkblot) test after subliminal exposure to an experimental and a control stimulus. The former was of the same nude female torso that was used in the Klein, Spence, Holt, and Gourevitch (1958) experiment. This stimulus could be viewed as wish-related and thus capable of triggering unconscious conflict and eliciting defensive reactions. But how could it be demonstrated that the stimulus was, in fact, having this effect? The most convincing way, I reasoned, was to obtain information from each research participant that bore on the degree to which sexual content similar to that embodied in the stimulus was conflictual for *him;* and then to use this information to predict how he would respond after the subliminal exposure of the torso. This classifying information was obtained (see Silverman and D. K. Silverman, 1964, pp. 162-163), permitting the predictions to be made. Thus, where the independently collected information for one group suggested that its members would be comfortable thinking about the female body, the prediction was made that after subliminal exposure of the torso they would produce images directly related to the stimulus—e.g., vagina, ovary, a female figure, etc. For the members of another group, who revealed themselves to be somewhat inhibited in having such thoughts, the expectation was that they would respond with indirect or symbolic associates of the stimulus rather than direct ones (e.g., flowers, an ornate box, etc.). And for a third group of participants, who gave evidence of notable inhibition in thinking about the female body, the expectation was that there would be a reduction in female associates and an increase in responses associated with males (indicating flight from the presumably frightening content to its opposite).

For each of the above-described groups, responses after the subliminal exposure of the torso were consistent with the predictions made, and strong statistical support was found for the basic premise of the study. Thus, for the first time, an a priori hypothesis was supported demonstrating that responses to the subliminal exposure of a wish-related stimulus could be influenced by the degree to which defensive needs were present (Silverman and D. K. Silverman, 1964). In addition, other evidence for the activation of psychodynamic processes emerged unexpectedly from five participants who responded in the experimental session (but not in the control) with reactions that could be described as psychopathological. Two of these participants started to express paranoid ideas, a third began vigorously to scratch different parts of his body, a fourth reported feeling strangely dizzy, and the fifth became verbally aggressive.

My reaction to these unexpected findings was twofold. First, they opened up the possibility that the newly developed method not only could be used to study general reactions to unconscious conflict, but psychopathological reactions specifically. Second, precisely because of this, these same findings raised ethical questions. While it was my impression, as the experimenter in this first investigation, that these unanticipated pathological reactions were both mild and transient, any future work with the experimental method would have to test this impression in a systematic manner.

THE RESEARCH MOVES TO NORTHPORT

Two years later, when I took the position of research psychologist at the Northport Veterans Administration Neuropsychiatric Hospital, I was able to test both the promise and the risks of studying psychopathology with what I then began to refer to as the "subliminal psychodynamic activation method." The testing involved schizophrenic patients (by far the largest group of patients at Northport), and the hypothesis to be tested was one that viewed psychopathology in schizophrenia as related to unconscious conflict over aggressive impulses. This hypothesis had been suggested by a number of psychoanalytic clinicians (e.g., Pious, 1949; Bak, 1954) who had posited that schizophrenic symptoms were *most immediately* the result of this particular conflict. This seemed like a particularly worthwhile psychodynamic relationship to address since there were many other clinicians, psychoanalytic as well as non-psychoanalytic, who did not accept this formulation (see Silverman, 1975, for a discussion of this controversy and the protagonists on each side). It thus afforded an opportunity to test the efficacy of the new method with respect to its ability to produce data that, rather than being redundant to psychoanalytic clinicians, would bear on an issue about which there was disagreement among them.

The following experiment (Silverman, 1966) was therefore carried out. A group of 30 male patients diagnosed schizophrenic served as participants. The experimental procedure was similar to the one employed in the initial study at the University of Pennsylvania. Since this procedure was used in most of the subsequent experiments, it will now be described in some detail.

The schizophrenic patients were seen individually for two sessions. In the first session, after an introduction to the research, each participant was administered a psychological test that allowed for a "baseline assessment" of psychopathology—specifically, the degree to which, on that particular day, the patient was manifesting "thought disorder," a cardinal pathological manifestation of schizophrenia.[10] There followed for half the participants four tachistoscopic exposures of a stimulus with aggressive content, and for the other half four exposures of a relatively neutral stimulus. These exposures lasted four milliseconds, the same length of exposure as was used in the University of Pennsylvania experiment. Then the pathology was reassessed in what has been referred to as the "critical" test series.

The procedure for the second session was identical except that the stimuli were reversed: Those exposed to the neutral stimulus in the first session were exposed to the aggressive stimulus in the second session; those exposed to the aggressive stimulus in the first session were exposed to the neutral in the second. The aggressive and neutral stimuli were further divided into two types. One group of participants was exposed to human figures: a picture of a man with teeth bared holding a dagger (aggressive) and a picture of a man waving (control). For the other group, animal pictures were used: a picture of a tiger chasing a monkey vs. two bland-looking beagles. As in the previous experiment, the experimenter, the participants, and the psychologist evaluating the test responses for thought disorder were all blind as to which session was experimental and which was control.

As the hypothesis proposed, there was an increase in thought disorder from the baseline to the critical series in the aggressive session that was not in evidence in the control session. Moreover, the intensified pathology in the aggressive session was evidenced both by those who received the human stimuli and those who received the animal stimuli. This was important because, if the overall effect were a function of only one aggressive stimulus, a question could be raised as to whether some other characteristic of the stimulus rather than its aggressive content had produced the effect.[11] Of course, with only two aggressive stimuli being used, this other possibility still had to be considered; it was not until many further experiments were undertaken, reference to which will be made shortly, that the alternative possibility could be ruled out.

As to whether the increased pathological thinking could be ascribed to the *subliminal* registration of aggressive stimuli, here too the data supported the hypothesis. When the participants were administered a discrimination task to test whether partial cues were in awareness (see note 8 for a description of the task), there was no evidence that such cues were present. Thus, the conclusion could be drawn that an aggressive stimulus, presented at a level at which no aspect of it was within the participant's awareness, had the power to affect thought disorder, a major symptom of schizophrenia. This was exciting not only because it had bearing on a point of contention among clinicians treating schizophrenics, but also because of its broader implications for the study of psychopathology.

Before becoming too enthusiastic, however, I had to address the ethical question raised by the results of the initial study at the University of Pennsylvania. It seemed clear that the experimental manipulation had worked well—but had it worked too well? Was the intensifying impact of the subliminal aggressive stimulation on pathological thinking as transient as I believed it would be? To make this determination I examined the *baseline* level of pathological thinking in the first and second sessions, comparing those schizophrenics who received the aggressive stimulation in the first session with those who received it in the second session. If the former group showed an increase in pathological thinking from the first to the second baseline that the latter group did not, it would have to be attributed to the lingering effects of the aggressive stimulation. Happily, that did not turn out to be the case. The intensification of pathology brought about by the aggressive condition had apparently dissipated by the second experimental day. Although this finding did not fully resolve the ethical issue (it was later to be addressed more stringently),[12] it did leave me comfortable enough to proceed with further studies.

THE RESEARCH EXPANDS

During the next several years, before the research turned to oneness fantasies, experiments using subliminal psychodynamic activation addressed themselves to the following questions: (1) How reliable is the finding that schizophrenics show increased psychopathology after subliminal aggressive stimulation? (2) Is it only the stimulation of unconscious aggressive wishes that has this effect or would stimulation of other kinds of unconscious wishes that psychoanalysis has proposed as pathogenic also intensify schizophrenic psychopathology? (3) Would the subliminal psychodynamic activation method reveal a relationship between psychopathology and unconscious conflict-laden wishes in other kinds of clinical populations as well as schizophrenics? (4) Would it prove to be the case, as I had assumed in developing the subliminal psychodynamic activation method, that, in order for a stimulus to activate unconscious conflict and generate symptoms, it must be presented subliminally?

In this phase of the research I was joined in my efforts by a score or so of research assistants and graduate students in doctoral programs in clinical psychology.[13] Their participation was invaluable not only because they could share the work load but also because of the many good ideas they contributed along the way. Rather than detail the 20-odd studies that these coworkers and I carried out, let me simply summarize (with the relevant references for the interested reader) the findings that emerged and the conclusions that were drawn, thus completing the backdrop for the studies on oneness.

(1) Is the finding that schizophrenics show increased psychopathology after subliminal aggressive stimulation a reliable one? Sixteen studies replicated the original findings, while only two failed to replicate.[14] The number of replications (as well as the eight to one ratio of replications to non-replications) was above par for psychological experiments and implied that the finding was reliable. But

this was only the case as far as *group* results were concerned, with there being a number of participants in each replication sample who did not show the anticipated effect. Thus, there was a substantial percentage of schizophrenics for whom the hypothesis cannot be viewed as supported, with it still to be determined what distinguishes this minority from the majority who have shown the hypothesized reaction.[15]

(2) Is it only the stirring of *aggressive* wishes that intensifies psychopathology in schizophrenia? Four studies are relevant (Silverman and S. E. Silverman, 1967; Silverman, Spiro, Weisberg, and Candell, 1969; S. E. Silverman, 1970; Silverman, Bronstein, and Mendelsohn, 1976). In each of these studies at least one additional stimulus condition was introduced that related to a non-aggressive wish that psychoanalysts view as pathogenic. These stimuli contained themes related to incest, exhibitionism, homosexuality, and orality. The central finding here was that while some of these stimuli led to the emergence of certain types of peripheral psychopathology, none of them affected thought disorder, a central aspect of the psychopathology of schizophrenia. Only aggressive stimuli gave evidence of influencing that facet of the schizophrenic condition.

(3) Is the intensification of psychopathology after the stirring of unconscious wishes by subliminal stimuli *limited* to schizophrenics? Eleven experiments were carried out in which the above-described laboratory paradigm was used with different groups of non-schizophrenic participants. In each of these, the subliminal exposure of a particular wish-related stimulus led to an intensification of symptoms that was not in evidence after neutral subliminal stimulation. In three experiments, the homosexual orientation of homosexual men intensified after unconscious incestuous wishes were subliminally stimulated (Silverman, Kwawer,

Wolitzky, and Coron, 1973 [two samples]; Silverman, Bronstein, and Mendelsohn, 1976). In three other experiments, the speech disturbances of stutterers intensified after unconscious anal wishes were stirred (Silverman, Klinger, Lustbader, Farrell, and Martin, 1972 [two samples]; Silverman, Bronstein, and Mendelsohn, 1976). In a seventh study (Hines, 1977), alcoholics showed an intensification of cognitive difficulties after oral wishes were subliminally stimulated. And in the remaining four experiments (Miller, 1973; Rutstein and Goldberger, 1973; Varga, 1973; Silverman, Bronstein, and Mendelsohn, 1976) groups of depressive individuals gave evidence of increased dysphoric feelings after the subliminal stimulation of aggressive wishes.[16]

(4) Is it necessary that the presentation of stimuli be *subliminal* in order to stir up unconscious conflict-laden wishes? In seven experiments (Silverman and Goldweber, 1966; Silverman and Spiro, 1963; Lomangino, 1969; Silverman and Candell, 1970; Rutstein and Goldberger, 1973; Silverman, Klinger et al., 1973; Silverman and Grabowski, 1982), two conditions involving a subliminal wish-related and subliminal neutral (control) stimulus were supplemented by a third condition in which the same wish-related stimulus was exposed for five seconds (rather than four milliseconds) and was thus clearly in the viewer's awareness. In each of these studies, the supraliminal conflictual condition did not affect the level of psychopathology while the subliminal conflictual condition did.

SUBLIMINAL VS. SUPRALIMINAL STIMULI

The results of the experiments cited thus far—particularly the seven referred to in the last paragraph—support the thesis that the subliminal presentation of psychodynamically relevant stimuli provides a "royal road" to the experimental study of the role of unconscious processes in psychopathology.[17] But why does the *supraliminal* presentation of the same stimuli *not* constitute such a road? To answer this, we can first point to the common-sense observation that when a wish-related stimulus is in awareness, a person is in a much better position to use adaptive means to cope with whatever unconscious conflict is stirred up. Thus, the individual can tell him or herself that the disturbing content is "out there" rather than "in my head," thereby muting its impact. Or if the content actually does have an impact, the individual at least stands a much better chance of dealing with that impact non-pathologically—for example, by allowing him or herself either a conscious emotional experience or a conscious fantasy, reactions that seem justified to the extent that there has been an "external provocation." As Kris (1952) pointed out, this is frequently what occurs when people see movies or plays, read fiction, or view art work. Such situations stir up unconscious conflict-laden wishes and simultaneously sanction their emergence into consciousness in the form of images, ideas, and affects, making it possible for the person to avoid a pathological reaction.[18]

We might pose the following question at this point. Since the research data indicate that wish-related stimuli that have entered awareness do *not* affect psychopathology, how can one account for the ebb and flow of symptoms often observed in real life? Depressed people will feel varying degrees of depression at different times; stutterers will often stutter more or less, depending on the situations they are in; schizophrenics will show notable fluctuations in the degree of thought disturbance manifested and so on. Is one to suppose that these variations are the result of a subliminal input from the environment? Or should one assume that these fluctuations are entirely endogenously motivated? Or is some other explanation in order? In an earlier paper (Silverman, 1972) this question was addressed at length; the ground covered will now briefly be reviewed.

An examination of various real-life situations in which psychopathology either intensifies or suddenly appears leads to the conclusion that such reactions regularly occur in response to some environmental event. While in a small percentage of such instances, the event involves a stimulus that is literally subliminal, in the majority of instances, the event registers in full awareness. But a crucial aspect of its *meaning* remains unconscious—"subliminal" in a more figurative sense. Below, we cite examples from the earlier paper of real-life events in which pathological reactions were evoked. These are presented here for three reasons. First, they can be contrasted with the experimental situation in which wish-related stimuli are presented supraliminally, that is to say, in which both the stimulus *and* its meaning are apparent. Second, by linking our laboratory situation with real life, the discussion of the former and its bearing on human behavior will seem less artificial and contrived. And finally, it should be of interest to the reader to learn about the type of circumstances in real life that activate psychodynamic processes.

The first example is of a real-life event in which actual subliminal registration seems to have occurred.

> The patient was a 25-year-old man who had been in psychoanalytic treatment for several years. His wife had recently become pregnant, an event about which both of them were consciously ambivalent; so much so that they were considering abortion. The material emerging in treatment at the time centered on the patient's view of the fetus as an unwanted rival for his

wife's affection and attention, a feeling that related rather clearly to the anger and jealousy that beset him when, at age nine, he learned that his mother was pregnant with his brother, his only sibling. The abortion under contemplation had, as an important unconscious meaning, the venting of death wishes directed most immediately toward his prospective child, but more basically toward his sibling; and the symptom this conflict gave rise to was an anxious obsessive preoccupation with his wife's situation. It was during a period of treatment when the meaning of all this had been interpreted to him, but not yet worked through, that the following event took place. The analysand reported at the beginning of one session something "interesting" that had happened during the day. He was walking in the street feeling at ease when suddenly he became anxiously preoccupied. While so beset, he looked up and noted a sign on a building that he was passing that read "floor scraping." He experienced a sudden insight, and with that the anxiety symptom remitted. The understanding that he reported was that "floor scraping" symbolized the contemplated abortion and thus stirred up in him his angry and guilty feelings toward his surrogate and real sibling [Silverman, 1972, pp. 310-311].

It is impossible to estimate how often in real life subliminal stimuli activate psychodynamic processes, as appeared to have occurred in this case. The "floor scraping" sign had apparently registered subliminally—before the patient looked up and noted it consciously. Yet this subliminal perception had been sufficient to arouse an anxiety reaction. The patient was able to link his anxious preoccupation with the street sign because he possessed unusual sophistication about symbols, subliminal perception, and his own psychodynamic processes. As noted, however, instances of this kind appear to be in the minority of those cases in which there is the appearance or intensification of pathology as a result of an external event. The next two cases provide examples of the more frequent situation—in which a wish-related stimulus impinges on a person well above the threshold of consciousness, but the relevance of the stimulus to the wish is hidden.

> . . . a 30-year-old male analysand . . . regularly reported bodily discomfort, restlessness, and somnolence while watching movies and plays. As might be expected, his analysis revealed . . . intensely strong and much conflicted voyeuristic [wishes] and many derivatives of primal-scene memories. [These wishes] and the related memories were understood as becoming stimulated whenever he found himself in the role of "viewer." The hypothesis that these events required the [wish] relevance of the stimuli to be out of his awareness in order for them to be pathogenic was rather interestingly supported in this case. The analysand reported that the most notable exception to the appearance of these symptoms was when the movie or play had an explicitly sexual theme; at such times, he observed, he was symptom-free [pp. 311-312].

A 24-year-old unmarried woman in analysis, who felt exceedingly frustrated over the fact that she was childless, received a birth announcement from an old friend toward whom she had always felt rivalry. She reacted to the announcement with an intensified longing for a child of her own and jealous feelings toward her rival, although not symptomatically. Some time later, however, while reading a book during a train ride, she suddenly, and at the time inexplicably, felt depersonalized. This was a symptom from which she had suffered in the past but which, at that point in analysis, no longer plagued her. She reported that the symptom came on when she began to read a particular article, but she could see no relationship between the article itself and her conflicts and symptoms. Suddenly, in the session, she remembered with a laugh that the name of the author of the article was "Rothschild," to which she instantly associated the married name—Roth—of the friend who had sent her the birth announcement a few weeks before. She felt convinced that she was unwittingly reminded of "the child of Roth" and that it was the unconscious hostility this "silently" aroused that brought back her symptom. [p. 312].

In both these cases, the patients experienced symptoms in precisely those situations in which the relevance of the stimulus to their wishes was hidden, and were symptom-free in those situations in which its relevance was apparent. In the first case, the patient was symptom-free when sexual themes were apparent, and symptomatic when they were not. In the second case, the patient was symptom-free when she consciously experienced feelings of jealousy and longing in response to the birth announcement, and symptomatic when the relevance of the author's name to her wish was hidden. In all three of the examples we have cited, the patients became symptomatic when circumstances were such that the *direct* expression of their stimulated sexual and aggressive wishes was extremely difficult. Whether it was the inciting external event that was out of awareness or merely its underlying meaning, psychodynamic processes were activated and a pathological outcome ensued.

The above discussion thus points to a link between the activation of psychodynamic processes by events in real life and the activation of these same processes by the subliminal psychodynamic activation method in the laboratory. In both situations, these processes prove to be highly responsive to precisely those environmental stimuli the meanings of which elude the individual's awareness. Not only does this suggest why the *supraliminal* presentation of wish-related stimuli does not arouse symptoms in our participants, it also provides further justification for the claim with which we opened this chapter: that the subliminal psychodynamic activation method can be a useful research tool in the study of those unconscious processes with which psychoanalysis has been so typically concerned.

NOTES

A word about the note sections that we have appended to each of the chapters of this book. As should be apparent from what we have presented thus far, we will touch a number of very different bases in discussing the search for oneness. These will range from the results of laboratory experiments to considerations about psychopathology and the conduct of psychoanalytic treatment to discussions of infant development and adult real-life experiences. Since it is unlikely that most readers will be equally interested in these different domains, we have relegated the more specialized material and many details to the notes.

1. There have been a number of experimental studies carried out within the "psychoanalytic community" the findings of which have been related to psychoanalytic theory. But in contrast to the studies that will be described here—which relate to psychopathology and what has come to be known as the "clinical theory of psychoanalysis"—these other studies have focused on more or less normal ego functioning (i.e., ego functioning in individuals without known psychiatric disturbance and under relatively conflict-free conditions). These studies thus have relevance to the "general theory of psychoanalysis" (see Rapaport, 1960). Included among these works are the investigations of Paul (1959) on memory, Fisher (1960) on subliminal perception, Dement

and Fisher (1960) on dreaming, Schwartz and Rouse (1961) on attention, and Goldberger and Holt (1961) on sensory deprivation.

Another distinction can be made between research involving laboratory experimentation and research involving systematic observation (usually) of children or parent-child interactions. As one of us has pointed out elsewhere (Silverman, 1975), the latter research is relevant to "genetic propositions" in psychoanalysis—that is, propositions bearing on the relationship between early experiences and current behavior—while the former is relevant to "dynamic propositions," with a bearing on current intrapsychic motives for behavior.

2. Unresolved controversial questions among psychoanalytic clinicians today include the following: (1) Is there a relationship between different kinds of psychosomatic symptoms and specific libidinal and aggressive wishes? (See Alexander, French, and Pollock, 1968, Chapter 1.) (2) Is male homosexuality rooted only in conflict over oedipal wishes or are preoedipal wishes also involved? (See Gillespie, 1964.) (3) What are the determinants of so-called narcissistic pathology? (See Kernberg, 1975 vs. Kohut, 1971.) (4) Is insight the only legitimate agent of change in psychoanalytic treatment or are non-insight agents of change (e.g., "identification with the analyst" [Sterba, 1934] or "the holding environment" [Modell, 1976] also legitimate? (See Silverman, 1979.) This last disagreement, as Friedman (1978) demonstrates, is a good example of a controversy that has ebbed and flowed repeatedly since the early days of psychoanalysis.

Relevant to our point here is the following comment by Gill (1979):

> Many . . . aspects of psychoanalytic theory and practice . . . fade in and out of prominence. . . . There are doubtless many reasons for this phenomenon. But not the least, in my opinion, is the almost total absence of systematic and controlled research in the psychoanalytic situation. . . . I believe that only with such . . . research will analytic findings become solid and secure knowledge [p. 286].

3. Criteria have been proposed by some (Schmidl, 1955; Wisdom, 1967; Wallerstein and Sampson, 1971) for confirming or disconfirming the validity of interpretations in the treatment situation. As meritorious as these proposals are, it is evident that none of them allows for tight control over contaminating variables of the sort referred to above, as is possible in laboratory

experiments. This should not be viewed as reflecting deficiencies of the proposals, but rather, as we have argued earlier, as due to the inherent limitations of the treatment situation with respect to validating theoretical propositions.

4. The offering of incorrect interpretations is being characterized as of dubious control value for the following reason. It has been learned from the study of various medical and psychological interventions that the bias or expectations of the interventionist can create the illusion that an intervention is producing an effect due to its specific properties when, in fact, it is not. We are referring here, of course, to the ubiquitous "placebo effect" (see Shapiro, 1978), which can only be ruled out if the interventionist is "blind" as to whether the intervention (e.g., a capsule being administered) contains the (hypothesized) therapeutic ingredient or an inert placebo. Thus, in terms of psychoanalytic treatment, only if the therapist were blind as to whether an interpretation was correct or incorrect, could one rule out the placebo influence. This obviously is not feasible in the clinical situation.

5. We speak of "participants" rather than "subjects"—the more common term—because of both quasi-ethical and pragmatic considerations that are detailed in Silverman (1977). See also the cogent discussion of these considerations by Argyris (1968, 1975).

6. A more operational definition of a "subliminal stimulus" is a stimulus "whose intensity is below that where a differentiated or discriminated verbal report can be obtained" (Eriksen, 1960, p. 281). See note 8 for a description of how this determination is made.

7. "Convincing data" would have consisted of results from a "discrimination task" (to be described below) demonstrating that participants were unable consciously to distinguish the presumably subliminal exposures of one stimulus from those of another.

8. This task, which is typically administered at the end of the experiment, proceeds in the following way. Under the same tachistoscopic conditions that existed during the experiment proper, each subject is asked either to discriminate the exposures of the experimental stimulus from those of the control or to discriminate between the experimental stimulus and a blank stimulus card. (See Silverman, 1966, p. 107, for details.) Only when participants are unable to make such discriminations can the exposure level during the experiment proper be referred to as "subliminal."

9. We follow convention here, referring to a "statistical trend"

where the probability value is between .05 and .10. All results reported in this and subsequent chapters, unless otherwise specified, refer to statistically significant findings—findings for which the probability value is below .05.

10. The test used in this first experiment was the Rorschach, with the thought disorder measure derived from Holt's (1969) "Manual for Scoring of Primary Process Manifestations in Rorschach Responses"—specifically, that part of the manual entitled "Formal Manifestations of Primary Process."

11. For example, I considered it possible that the difference in the impact of experimental and control stimuli was due to the greater ambiguity of the former; previous work had demonstrated that ambiguous stimuli can intensify pathological thinking in schizophrenia. This possibility was directly evaluated in the study under consideration (Silverman, 1966) and was found not to be applicable.

12. In a study by Silverman, Candell, Pettit, and Blum (1971), a critical assessment was made of the participants immediately after the experimental (and control) stimuli were subliminally presented. Thereafter, a second assessment was made after 15 minutes had elapsed. While on the first assessment there was an intensification of pathology from baseline to critical in the experimental session that did not appear in the control session, on the second critical assessment this difference had dissipated. That is, after the 15-minute lapse of time following the pathology-intensifying stimulus, the participants' pathology level had returned to its baseline level. See Silverman (1977) for a detailed discussion of the ethical issues involved in subliminal psychodynamic activation experiments.

13. Maxine Antell, Esther Bucholz, Lewis Cox, Robert De-Martino, Carolyn Ellman, Jacqueline Farrell, Virginia Glover, Elaine Gould, Jeffrey Golland, Jay Kwawer, Eli Leiter, Thomas Litwack, Louis Lomangino, Jill Miller, Thomas Moriarty, Eleanor Rutstein, Stephen Silverman, Robert Spiro, Richard Steinberg, Michael Varga, and Janet Weisberg.

Research assistants who joined the research later, participating in the studies of oneness fantasies, included James Bartow, Abbot Bronstein, Lynn Carlo, Penny Dachinger, Edward Dunne, Susan Frank, Eric Mendelsohn, Gail Rodin, Patricia Thornton, Roseanne Ungaro, and Carol Wolitzky. Graduate students whose doctoral dissertations involved the study of oneness fantasies are cited later.

14. Studies that replicated the original findings were: Silver-

man and S. E. Silverman (1967); Silverman and Spiro (1967, 1968); Spiro and Silverman (1967); Lomangino (1969); Silverman and Candell (1969, 1970); Silverman and Gordon (1969); Silverman, Spiro, Weisberg, and Candell (1969; two samples); S. E. Silverman (1970); Litwack (1972); Leiter (1973); Silverman, Bronstein, and Mendelsohn (1976); Loveland (1977); and Forest-Letourneau (1974).

In these experiments, various kinds of aggressive and neutral stimuli were used. They ranged from pictures of animals (e.g., a lion charging vs. a bird flying) to pictures of humans (e.g., a snarling man holding a dagger vs. a man holding a newspaper) to verbal messages (e.g., CANNIBAL EATS PERSON vs. PEOPLE ARE WALKING). All told, nine different aggressive stimuli have been used and eleven different neutral stimuli, and for each pairing, it was always the aggressive stimulus that produced the increase in "ego pathology."

The two attempts at replication that did not produce positive results were Silverman, Candell, Pettit, and Blum (1971) and Greenberg (1977). An explanation was offered in the former article to account for the discrepancy between the results of that study and the results of the 17 studies reporting positive findings (the original study and the 16 replications). But this explanation would not account for Greenberg's negative results, which thus far remain unexplained.

15. An important start on this determination was recently made by Litwack, Wiedemann, and Yager (1979).

16. In one of these studies (Silverman, Bronstein, and Mendelsohn, 1976), the question was asked whether the above-cited results were simply a consequence of the general negative affective quality of the experimental stimuli rather than their specific content. This question was viewed as important because psychoanalytic theory has posited that different symptoms are related to different unconscious conflicts and that symptoms can be viewed as symbolically expressing aspects of particular underlying conflicts. In the article just cited, groups of schizophrenics, depressives, male homosexuals, and stutterers were studied, each for two experimental conditions in which the following stimuli were subliminally exposed: first, the wish-related stimulus that intensified the pathology of each group in prior studies: aggressive for the schizophrenics and depressives (the verbal caption DESTROY MOTHER accompanying a picture of a person with teeth bared about to stab an elderly woman); incestuous for the male homosexuals (the caption FUCK MOMMY accompanying a picture of a man and a woman in a sexually

suggestive pose); and anal for the stutterers (the caption GO SHIT accompanying a picture of a person defecating); then an "irrelevant" wish-related stimulus, but one that had intensified the symptoms of one of the other groups: incestuous for the schizophrenics and stutterers, aggressive for the homosexuals, and anal for the depressives. The findings for each of these groups were quite consistent. Although further support was obtained for the original psychodynamic relationship studied, in *no* instance did the second wish-related condition influence the symptom under consideration. That is, in each case its effect was indistinguishable from that of a neutral control condition. Thus, the results from this series of experiments support the psychoanalytic proposition that there are specific links between particular unconscious conflicts and particular symptoms. See Silverman (1982a) for a comprehensive review of all subliminal psychodynamic activation experiments completed to date that bear on psychoanalytic theory.

17. This, of course, is intended as a counterpoint to Freud's (1900) reference to the dream as the "royal road" to the *clinical* study of unconscious processes.

There is one other royal road to the experimental study of unconscious processes that should be noted—hypnotic manipulation of unconscious wishes, anxieties, and fantasies (see Reyher [e.g., 1958], who has developed an effective paradigm for the use of this modality). While the use of hypnosis for such study is burdened by certain problems from which the subliminal psychodynamic activation method is free (the inaccessibility to hypnosis of a substantial number of people, the lengthy period of time required to induce a hypnotic trance, and the difficulties in maintaining double blind conditions), it also has its special merits. See Silverman (1976) for a dicussion of these merits and the complementary use of hypnosis and subliminal psychodynamic activation for studying psychoanalytic hypotheses.

18. See Silverman and Frank (1978, pp. 125-126) for experimental evidence that awareness of conflict-laden wish derivatives can not only allow a person to stave off the intensification of pathological manifestations, but can also lead to the diminution of these manifestations.

3

PROLOGUE TO A RESEARCH PROGRAM:
THE SEARCH FOR ONENESS IN
SCHIZOPHRENIA

The first subliminal psychodynamic activation studies with a bearing on the search for oneness involved schizophrenics. These studies took as their touchstone a large body of psychoanalytic writing in which schizophrenia was viewed from the perspective of symbiosis-related issues. In this chapter, we shall review this literature.

The clinical literature that initially stimulated the research to be discussed in Chapters 4-6 pertained primarily to three specific issues: (1) the relationship of schizophrenia to early failures in negotiating the symbiotic and separation-individuation phases of development; (2) the manifest pathology of adult schizophrenics viewed as an expression of symbiotic-like wishes and defenses against these wishes; (3) treatment approaches that either provided schizophrenics with symbiotic-like gratifications or addressed their difficulties in separating and individuating. Before we consider this body of literature, however, we must first review the work of Margaret Mahler and her colleagues—work which has had a profound impact in sensitizing clinicians to the role of symbiosis-related issues in various types of psychopathology. Indeed, Mahler's own research into the "symbiotic" and "separation-individuation" phases of infant development began in the context of her early studies of childhood psychotic disturbances,

disturbances thought to reflect basic developmental failures in these phases. Her pioneering studies thus significantly anticipated more recent attempts to explore the
etiology of adult schizophrenia in terms of symbiosis-related issues. These later clinical writings have, of course,
informed the propositions that we subsequently tested with
the method of subliminal psychodynamic activation; but,
for us, Mahler's work constituted a theoretical point of
departure.

MAHLER'S SYMBIOTIC PHASE OF DEVELOPMENT

Mahler (1968) invoked the term "symbiosis" as a metaphor to describe the relationship of infant and mother in
the developmental phase extending from the end of the
first month to the fourth or fifth month of life. At three
to four weeks, Mahler states, most infants break out of the
condition of "normal autism" into which they are born.
That is to say, the protective stimulus barrier of the newborn infant becomes sufficiently permeable to permit an
increased sensory awareness of the external world. Mahler's recourse to the term "symbiosis" to characterize the
following developmental phase conveys her belief that the
rupturing of the newborn's protective stimulus barrier is
in a significant sense premature—the four-week-old infant
lacks the necessary physiological resources to achieve a
homeostatic equilibrium independently, or, put another
way, to ensure that he or she will not be overwhelmed by
the myriad of incoming stimuli. As a result, the infant's
survival and continued well-being depend on a subsequent
condition of "symbiosis" with the mother. By such a condition, Mahler refers to "that state of undifferentiation, of
fusion with mother, in which the 'I' is not yet differentiated
from the 'not-I,' and in which inside and outside are only

gradually coming to be sensed as different" (1968, p. 9). The mother, in this connection, functions as the infant's "auxiliary ego" (Spitz, 1965). Her ministrations augment the infant's rudimentary faculties through what Mahler terms "the emotional rapport of the mother's nursing care, a kind of social symbiosis" (1968, p. 9). At the same time, the infant arrives at the dim awareness that need satisfaction is not provided independently but comes from something external to him or her. In this way, the infant's symbiotic bond to the mother issues in the gradual recognition that the maternal presence is somehow involved in his or her sense of well-being. From this recognition, the infant "turns libidinally toward that mothering source or agency," so that the need for symbiotic mothering gradually becomes a "wish" for the mother and, ultimately, an object-bound affect of longing for the mother (Mahler, Pine, and Bergman, 1975, p. 46).

From a functional standpoint, the symbiotic bond between infant and mother replaces the infant's inborn stimulus barrier; it becomes the functional means of protecting the infant from stress and trauma. Infant and mother, in the mind of the infant, constitute "an omnipotent symbiotic dual unity" (Mahler, Furer, and Settlage, 1959, p. 822). Correspondingly, the infant tends to project all unpleasurable perceptions—both internal and external—outside the protective symbiotic "membrane."

In the course of normal development during the symbiotic phase, the infant undergoes a dramatic change. Within the secure confines of the symbiotic relationship, and in the course of need gratification by the mother, the infant increasingly comes to recognize an external reality that extends beyond his or her self-boundaries and that is at first represented by the mother. Within the symbiotic matrix, moreover, the infant experiences inner sensations as constituting the core of his or her self (Mahler, 1968, pp. 10-11; Mahler, Pine, and Bergman, 1975, pp. 46-47). At a descriptive level, Kaplan (1978) has summed up this maturational achievement:

> Day by day he becomes more alert and attentive to the actual happenings in his environment. In moments of quiet aloneness, waiting for mother, looking at the faces of strangers, studying his hands, sucking his fingers, fingering his bottle, the baby is commencing to sort out and classify the world into me and not-me, inside and outside, human and nonhuman, mother and not-mother [pp. 94-95].

Although infants at this stage of development become increasingly aware of an external world embodied in the separateness of the mother, they remain unable to experience themselves and others as clearly differentiated entities. In Mahler's language, the mother—the most highly invested part of the external world—necessarily remains a "part object" during this developmental stage (Mahler, Pine, and Bergman, 1975, p. 49).

Mahler and her colleagues hypothesize that the symbiotic phase draws to an end as the infant's maturing capacity for sensory perception stimulates "outward-directed attention" (Mahler, Pine, and Bergman, 1975, p. 53). But the maturational readiness for separation and individuation is also crucially linked to the adequacy of the symbiotic relationship between infant and mother during the first months of infancy. To the extent that the symbiosis was adequate, providing relief from inner tensions, pleasure in the safe anchorage provided by the mother, and a viable sense of self proceeding from the mother's "mirroring function" (i.e., her affirmation of the infant's expressions of self), the infant is ready to differentiate smoothly beyond the symbiotic orbit (Mahler, Pine, and Bergman, 1975, p. 53). Under these circumstances, the five-month-old infant, increasingly cognizant of the external world, is ready to be "hatched" from the symbiotic state of oneness with the mother and to progress through the sequential subphases of separation-individuation. Although Mahler, Pine, and Bergman conceptualize the phase of symbiosis as ending at this time, they caution that the transcendence of symbiosis is not absolute: "Vestiges of this phase remain with us throughout the entire life cycle" (1975, p. 48).

MAHLER'S SEPARATION-INDIVIDUATION PHASE OF DEVELOPMENT

In Chapter 1 we proposed that symbiotic-like oneness fantasies can further adaptation if, simultaneously, a sense of self can be preserved. Consideration of Mahler's separation-individuation phase is thus important to our argument in that it circumscribes the particular developmental issues implicated in the emergence of a viable sense of self.

The separation-individuation phase of development — viewed by Mahler and her coworkers (Mahler, Pine, and Bergman, 1975) as spanning the period from about five months to two-and-a-half years of age—involves two distinct but related phenomena. Psychological "separation" results in the young child's increasing awareness of his or her "separateness," especially from mother; "individuation" leads to the acquisition of distinct personal characteristics. Both developmental achievements hinge on the continuing availability of mothering responsive to the phase-appropriate requirements 'of the maturing infant. Such requirements encompass the infant's need to explore the external environment and his or her concurrent need to receive nurturance in the course of such exploration.

To the extent that mothering activity during the separation-individuation phase strikes a suitable balance between the distance needed to encourage the infant's autonomous behavior and the proximity conducive to continuing nurturance, such mothering activity will be "good enough," i.e., will facilitate the infant's "hatching" from the symbiotic state and equip the young child to complete the process of development successfully.

Mahler identifies four distinct subphases of the separation-individuation process: (1) the "differentiation" subphase (from roughly 5 to 9 months of age); (2) the "practicing" subphase (9 to 14 months); (3) the "rapprochement" subphase (14 to 24 months); and (4) "consolidation of individuality and beginnings of object constancy" (24 months on). Although there is some overlap between these subphases, each can be delineated in terms of a characteristic cluster of behaviors. We will briefly review each of them here.

Differentiation, the first subphase of the separation-individuation process, marks the inception of the infant's tentative attempts to separate him or herself from the mother. Such attempts follow the emergence of partial locomotor functions: Infants acquire the capacity to distance themselves somewhat from the mother's body and to explore her body with their own bodies. Relying on the visual and tactile senses, the differentiating infant repeatedly searches the mother's face and body, pulling and grasping at her nose, ears, hair, and mouth; the youngster strains to push his or her body away from mother in order to have a better look at her, subsequently scanning the immediate environment as if to compare it with her. In such comparative scanning, the infant differentiates the mother's feel, smell, taste, sound, appearance, and other special qualities from those of the "other-than-mother world" (Mahler, Pine, and Bergman, 1975, p. 59).

Following the differentiation subphase, Mahler, Pine, and Bergman posit a two-part practicing subphase: (1) an early practicing period characterized by the infant's beginning ability to move away from the mother by means of crawling, creeping, and climbing; and (2) a practicing period proper characterized by free upright locomotion.

While the expanding capacity for locomotion enlarges the infant's world considerably and exposes him or her to a wide variety of sights, sounds, and new objects, the mother continues to remain at the center of the infant's universe when the practicing subphase begins. Indeed, Mahler and her coworkers argue that one of the purposes of the infant's attempts to distance him or herself from the mother is the desire to perceive and enjoy her from a distance (1975, p. 67). Gradually, using mother as "an anchor, a center to his world" (p. 67), the infant moves out into the external world from the maternal "home base." Nonetheless, at the same time as the youngster increasingly ventures away from the mother, appearing to be wholly absorbed in exploring the expanding environment, he or she periodically returns to her and initiates physical contact. This phenomenon, designated "emotional refueling" (p. 69), points to the infant's continuing need for the mother as a "beacon of orientation," i.e., a stable point from which to explore the world and from which to take pleasure in an increasing mastery of the world.

The two major developmental tasks of the early practicing subphase—becoming familiar with a wider segment of the external world and enjoying the mother from a greater distance—are facilitated by the child's continuing confidence in adequate mothering. To the extent that the mother reliably relieved tensions during the preceding differentiation subphase and still earlier symbiotic phase, and to the extent that the mother can now tolerate increased distance from her developing offspring while maintaining adequate "distance contact" (Mahler, Pine, and Bergman, p. 67), the child's faculties will be turned to pleasurable exploration of the external world and will be sharpened by their own exercise.

The practicing subphase proper is ushered in by the development of upright locomotion. At this point, the infant/toddler enters into a phase-appropriate "love affair with the world" (Greenacre, 1957). This "love affair" is associated with the six- to eight-month-old's great pleasure in the developmental feat of walking, along with the exhilarating mastery of the external environment that this new form of locomotion allows. The toddler not only sees the world from an upright position but acquires a vital new means for expanding his or her universe and testing reality. Mahler and her colleagues underscore the great significance and symbolic meaning of walking for both toddler and mother: "The expectation and confidence that mother exudes when she feels that the child is now able to make it out there seems to be an important trigger for the child's own feeling of safety and perhaps also the initial encouragement for his exchanging some of his magic omnipotence for pleasure in his own autonomy and his developing self-esteem" (1975, p. 74).

With the acquisition of upright locomotion, the young toddler enters the rapprochement subphase. At this time he or she becomes more aware of and makes greater use of the ability to separate physically from mother. This developmental achievement is accompanied by the toddler's maturing ability to perceive the mother as an individual distinct from him or herself. With the onset of the rapprochement subphase, however, the elation of the practicing subphase and the relative unconcern with the mother's presence gradually give way to a rediscovery of the mother, and a concomitant wish for closeness with her.

During this subphase, the toddler's renewed (albeit ambivalent) need for maternal closeness manifests itself in a variety of ways. Two of the characteristic behaviors associated with the new need for closeness are "shadowing" and its opposite, "darting away." The former refers to the toddler's tendency to watch continuously and follow the mother's every move; the latter to his or her proclivity to fly away "with the expectation of being chased and swept into [the mother's] arms" (1975, p. 77). The pattern represented by these two behaviors suggests both the toddler's "wish for reunion with the love object and his fear of reengulfment by it" (p. 77).

Ultimately, the toddler's growing realization of separateness from the mother results in the sense of heightened vulnerability that initiates the "rapprochement crisis." This crisis embodies the ambivalence between the toddler's wish for reunion with the mother and his or her fear of engulfment by her; behaviorally, it manifests itself as a conflict between the toddler's wish to exercise autonomy and the concurrent wish to remain within the protective orbit of the mother. The rapprochement crisis follows from the toddler's ill-fated attempt to mediate between these competing needs, to deny the now reactivated dependency on the mother while restoring the position of omnipotence that characterized the preceding subphase. When toddlers are frustrated by their inability to disavow their dependency on mother, their behavior is often marked by whining, temper tantrums, separation anxiety, and sadness.

Because of the toddler's increased vulnerability during this subphase, the mother's attitude is especially important. Mahler and her associates posit that the mother's "continued emotional availability" is essential for fostering the psychological growth of the child. They point out that the mother must be "quietly available" during rapprochement and must possess the "emotional willingness" to let go of the toddler—"to give him, as the mother bird does, a gentle push, an encouragement toward independence" (1975, p. 79).

Unlike the other three subphases discussed thus far, the final subphase of the separation-individuation process, beginning in the third year of life, is open-ended; it involves "the consolidation of individuality" and "the beginnings of emotional object constancy" (Mahler, Pine, and Bergman, 1975, 109-120). Since it would take us too far afield to discuss this subphase in detail, we would only remark that in this period, parallel to the various achievements mentioned above, the child's mother comes increasingly to be perceived as both a separate entity in the external world and as someone with a very special meaning in the child's internal world.

SCHIZOPHRENIC PATHOLOGY AND SYMBIOTIC FAILURES DURING INFANCY

It fell to Mahler, in her early work, to describe the severe pathology of children who had not experienced an adequate symbiotic relationship with their mothers during infancy. Referring to a syndrome Kanner (1949) had earlier designated "early infantile autism," Mahler (1952) coined the expression "autistic infantile psychosis" to characterize childhood psychotic disorders that involved a profound withdrawal from contact with people, a single-minded desire for the preservation of sameness, and "mutism or the kind of language which does not seem intended to serve the purpose of interpersonal communication" (Kanner, 1949, p. 416). The inability of this type of infant to move beyond the autistic orbit characteristic of the early weeks of extrauterine life is revealed in the fact that mother "never seems to have been perceived emotionally by the infant" (Mahler, 1952, p. 289). Mahler views as typical, comments like the following from the mothers of autistic children:

> "I could never reach my baby."—"He never smiled at me."—"The minute she could walk, she ran away from me."—"It hurt me so when I saw other babies glad to be in their mother's arms; my boy always tried to creep away from my lap as soon as he could."—"He never greeted me when I entered, he never cried, he never even noticed when I left the room."—"She never was a cuddly baby, she never liked caresses, she did not want anybody to embrace or to kiss her."—"She never made any personal appeal for help at any time". . . [quoted by Mahler, 1952, p. 290].

According to Mahler, the absence of an affective awareness of mother (as well as of people generally) is combined with a seeming inability to appreciate the maternal role that mother could serve.

> Whenever Lotta was in great distress, her whole little body shook with tearless sobs, yet she neither sought nor accepted help from anyone, but threw herself flat on the floor and pressed against the solid support of it. Likewise she would cling to the familiar high chair, but not to father or mother [1952, p. 291].

Obviously, this autistic child (whom Mahler views as typical) was unable to utilize what earlier was referred to as the "auxiliary ego functions" of the symbiotic partner, the mother, in order to orient herself in the world.

Mahler also delineated another form of severe childhood disturbance with an etiology different from that of "autistic psychosis." Whereas the latter related to a failure to establish or maintain symbiosis, "symbiotic infantile psychosis" related to a failure to *surmount* the symbiotic stage of development.

In these cases, the initial mother-infant symbiosis was indeed pronounced but no progression took place to the next stage of development wherein mother was perceived as a relatively distinct and separate entity: "The mental representation of the mother remains, or is regressively *fused with* . . . the self. It participates in the delusion of omnipotence of the child. . ." (Mahler, 1952, p. 292). Children of this type, she proposed, are singularly unprepared to function separately from mother, and when faced with the necessity of doing so, become panicky and confused. Consequently, they are unable to keep pace emotionally with the accelerated rate of central nervous system development and physical and cognitive growth of the first three years of life. Their disturbance becomes apparent at a time that has been referred to as the "crossroads of personality development" (Mahler, 1952, p. 242) when the child is otherwise prepared to effect separation from mother and to master an ever-increasing segment of reality independent of her. These children, however, experience the world as hostile and threatening because it has to be encountered as a separate entity. As a result, the anxiety attendant on separation from mother overwhelms their already tenuous personality development. Severe panic reactions are followed by hallucinations and delusions, understood as attempts to restore and perpetuate "the mother-infant fusion of the first year—a period in which the mother was an ever-ready extension of the self" (Mahler, Furer, and Settlage, 1959, p. 826).

DISTURBANCES IN SYMBIOSIS AND ADULT SCHIZOPHRENIA

Mahler's view of childhood psychoses as related to failures either to enter into, or to negotiate successfully, the symbiotic stage of development finds its counterpart in the more recent literature on adult schizophrenics which suggests that these patients encountered similiar problems in infancy. Many of these studies report not only that adult schizophrenics experienced great difficulty during the developmental phases of symbiosis and separation-individuation, but that deficient mothering was responsible for these difficulties. Those who have adopted this focus (in contrast to those who have focused on the contribution of heredity) have emphasized the ascendancy of the mother and the helpless dependency of the infant. Lidz (1968) thus remarks that "the young infant can do nothing about his part in establishing a proper symbiosis with his mother. The creation and development of a mutuality in which the mother is perceptive . . . and responsive to her infant's needs must depend upon the mother. . ." (p. 121). And Winnicott (1965) wryly comments that the "mother brings to the situation a developed capacity, whereas the infant is in this state because this is the way things begin" (p. 15).

In several papers, Winnicott details what he considers to be the fate of the infant who misses "good enough" care in the early period before the infant has separated the "not me from the me" (1962, p. 58). He enumerates the consequences of mothering that is "absent, weak, or patchy" and discusses the relationship between this type of mothering and the onset of various types of schizophrenia later in life. He points to the mother's role in keeping the infant free from "unthinkable anxiety," the presence of which can result in "going to pieces, falling forever, having no relationship to the body [and] having no orientation. . . . [These phenomena] are specifically the stuff of psychotic anxieties . . . and belong, clinically, to schizophrenia" (Winnicott, 1962, p. 59).

As reviewed in the literature, maternal behavior believed

to contribute to the development of schizophrenia in adults takes two forms, the more extreme versions of which we might expect to find associated with Mahler's original categories of autistic infantile psychosis and symbiotic infantile psychosis. On the one hand, behavior is cited that relates to the mother's failure to provide an adequate climate within which the necessary symbiosis can be established and maintained in the early months of the infant's development. On the other hand, we find behavior relating to the mother's failure to permit the appropriate resolution of the symbiosis. Belonging to the first category are references to maternal rejection and deprivation, and to the second category, instances of maternal overprotectiveness and intrusiveness.

With regard to the former, Reichard and Tillman (1950) studied the mothers of 79 adult schizophrenics, and identified one "schizophrenogenic" type as having overtly rejected her children. All the mothers in this group were described as affectively cold, and many as having refused to suckle their babies.

Reichard and Tillman also identified another group of so-called schizophrenogenic mothers who fall under the second heading referred to above, mothers thought to impede the *resolution* of the symbiosis. They were described as "covertly rejecting," harboring unconscious hostility toward their children that was covered over by a reaction formation. Their consequent clinging to the infant was so extreme, according to Reichard and Tillman, that it merited the appellation "smother love" (p. 253).

Clinicians working with patients have also inferred that the mothers of adult schizophrenics prolonged a symbiotic mode of relatedness. Searles (1951) speaks of a type of mother he terms "incorporative," whose anxieties preclude the possibility of treating her child as a separate entity.

Her overprotectiveness is referred to as "the one all-important environmental influence which tends to keep the child from advancing beyond the infantile sense of union with the mother to a mature awareness of the self as a separate individual" (p. 42). Similarly, Burnham, Gladstone, and Gibson (1969) write of the mother who prevents the child "from emerging as a person in his own right" by treating the child "as part of [her] personality or at best as an appendage of her" (p. 44). And Winnicott (1960) discusses the mother who prolongs the symbiosis unnecessarily and robs the infant of developing autonomy by anticipating his or her needs too much: "The creative gesture, the cry, the protest, all the little signs that are supposed to produce what the mother does, all these things are missing, because the mother has already met the need just as if the infant were still merged with her and she with the infant" (p. 51).

From the observations of Lidz, Mahler, Searles, Winnicott, and Reichard and Tillman, it would seem warranted to conclude that the mothers[1] of *some* adult schizophrenics contributed to the failure of their children to resolve adequately issues related to symbiosis and separation-individuation. We say "some" schizophrenics rather than "all," because the clinical literature only warrants the more conservative phrasing. Not only are there reports from clinicians with orientations different from those of the writers we have cited (e.g., Goldfarb, 1943, 1961) maintaining that interviews with mothers of schizophrenics have often *not* revealed psychopathology of the kind described above, but there are even reports from those who *do* emphasize "schizophrenogenic" mothering that not all the mothers studied can be so characterized. And we refer to schizophrenogenic mothering as having "contributed to" rather than "produced" schizophrenic offspring because there is extensive evidence that heredity plays a significant role in the etiology of schizophrenia.[2]

SCHIZOPHRENIC PATHOLOGY AS AN EXPRESSION OF AND DEFENSE AGAINST SYMBIOTIC-LIKE WISHES

There is a substantial consensus among clinicians that schizophrenics are strikingly prone to merge mental representations of themselves (self-representations) with representations of others (object representations). This idea has been expressed in different ways. Burnham, Gladstone, and Gibson (1969) speak of the schizophrenic's disturbed "capacity to distinguish inner from outer events" (p. 19); Bak (1954) writes that "a schizophrenic individual has taken the position where the world and the self fall into one unit" (p. 132); and Blatt and Wild (1976) refer to a disturbance "in the establishment of . . . fundamental boundaries between self and non-self" (p. 18). All of these conceptualizations allow for a linking of the schizophrenic disorder as it appears later in life with the disturbed development of the schizophrenic-prone infant described earlier. The "boundary problem" of the schizophrenic, that is, can reasonably be viewed as a direct outgrowth of the environmentally and/or genetically determined failure during infancy of the child to emerge with a sense of self that is firmly demarcated from a sense of "not self."

A number of writers view all schizophrenic symptoms as reflecting this single issue of boundary deficit. Thus, Freeman, Cameron, and McGhie (1958) write that "once this basic disturbance is appreciated, all other schizophrenic manifestations can be viewed as necessary elaborations of it" (p. 51). Blatt and Wild (1976) have more recently presented a detailed and thoughtful account of this view. They describe not only how certain symptoms

of schizophrenia (e.g., thought disorder and hallucinations) can be viewed as direct expressions of the "inability
to maintain boundary distinctions" (p. 66), but how other
symptoms (e.g., paranoid thinking, assaultiveness and
withdrawal) can be seen as serving to maintain or restore
boundary differentiations and to ward off the feelings of
merging, dissolution, and annihilation that the absence of
boundary distinctions frequently leads to.

But should a schizophrenic's boundary problem be
viewed as *only* a reflection of the failure to have separated
psychologically during infancy? Or does it also serve a psychodynamic function—that is, does it express an unconscious motive? In the minds of some clinicians (Federn,
1952; Freeman, Cameron, and McGhie, 1958; Des Lauriers, 1962), it is viewed in the former way—as what can
be termed an "unmotivated ego defect." But to others (e.g.,
Searles, 1951; Rosen, 1953; Bak, 1954; Burnham, Gladstone, and Gibson, 1969), an important psychodynamic
consideration is involved. While this latter position acknowledges the existence of a boundary deficit resulting
from the early failure to attain a state of sufficient psychological separateness, it is further seen as an expression
of an *unconscious wish to obtain symbiotic-like gratification*. Put
another way, the schizophrenic can be said to capitalize on
his or her ego defect by merging self- and object representations so as to maintain the illusion of a symbiotic relationship. It is in this sense that certain schizophrenic
symptoms—the ones that Blatt and Wild view as reflecting
an inability to maintain boundary distinctions—can be seen
as expressing hidden symbiotic-like wishes. And other
symptoms—those that Blatt and Wild conceive of as maintaining or restoring boundary differentiation—can be seen
as serving defensive needs to ward off these wishes.

While the second group of clinicians referred to above

agree that unconscious symbiotic-like wishes are implicated in schizophrenic symptoms, they differ as to the specific psychological need served by these wishes. Some implicate the need to ward off aggressive, particularly destructive impulses. Among these is Bak (1954), who writes of the schizophrenic's impaired ability to "neutralize" aggressive impulses with the result that he or she falls back on "fusion between the self and the object [in order to insure that] aggression has been eliminated" (p. 132). Searles (1951), in a similar vein, speaks of the schizophrenic as "feeling himself to be at one with the person with whom he is in interaction" (p. 39) in order to defend against hostility directed against the needed "object," typically the mother.

Others view the symbiotic-like wish as stemming from ungratified oral needs. Thus, Rosen (1953) speaks of the schizophrenic wanting to reunite with mother because, during infancy, "he never had enough breast" (p. 141), and Sechehaye (1951) writes of the schizophrenic's "need for receiving maternal food" (p. 50).

Still others suggest that underlying the schizophrenic's wish for a merged state is a need for omnipotent control. Mahler (1968) thus refers to the schizophrenic as being fixated at the "phase of magic hallucinatory omnipotence" (p. 112) wherein mother is felt to be an extension of the self and thus at the disposal of the self.

Finally, it has been suggested that the schizophrenic's wish for oneness with mother serves to reassure him or her that mother will always be present and can be relied on for much-needed structure and support. In the words of Burnham, Gladstone, and Gibson (1969), the schizophrenic's proclivity for symbiotic-like relatedness arises out of an "inordinate need for structure and control. He requires others to provide the organization and regulation which he is unable to provide for himself" (pp. 27-28).

Conditions that Exacerbate and Diminish Schizophrenic Symptoms

It follows from the view of the schizophrenic boundary problem as motivated by unconscious wishes that, under certain external conditions, the problem will be aggravated such that symptoms will either emerge or intensify, while in other conditions, the problem will be alleviated such that symptoms will diminish or disappear. The exacerbating conditions are those in which symbiotic-like wishes are frustrated, or else satisfied in a way that threatens the sense of self. (Allusions here and elsewhere to the sense of self as "threatened" refer to conscious or unconscious experiences of the self as nonexistent, hazy, or fragmented.) With regard to the frustration of such wishes, Searles (1951) reports the onset of an acute schizophrenic episode when the rupture of a "symbiotic relationship"[3] with a parental figure occurred. Likewise, Limentani (1956) refers to several cases in which an acute breakdown was preceded by a disruption of the patient's symbiotic relationship with his or her mother: "Joseph [became psychotic after he] rebelled against his mother when he grew dissatisfied with the restrictions she imposed on him. . . . Mary became ill shortly after her mother's death. James's mother had left for an extended trip abroad just prior to his illness" (p. 233). Lyketsos (1959) makes similar observations in a study of nine cases of symbiotic relationships between mothers and their schizophrenic daughters. He notes that in each of the cases "the daughter's breakdown occurred during an attempt to adjust herself outside the symbiotic bond" (p. 163). This view is consistent with the report of one of Stierlin's (1959) female patients who said, " 'I could have easily lived in the world had it turned out to be as mother represented it to me. But growing up I realized the world was different and I broke' " (p. 146).

As for intensifications resulting from a threat to the sense of self, Blatt and Wild (1976) give a dramatic example of a 28-year-old schizophrenic man who sought treatment complaining of fears of "losing himself" in the family. In describing a schizophrenic married sister who visited their mother every day, he said:

"They can't separate. . . . They lean on each other. . . . People in the family don't know their bounds. No one is himself, sister is mother. . . . I have to prevent myself from being swallowed up."

And in a subsequent session:

"I felt bad last night. It was tense in the house with my mother. I have to get away from her. She's there, lording it over everyone, controlling everyone. I felt my identity leaving me, going into her" [pp. 87-88].

What are the conditions that *alleviate* the boundary problem of the schizophrenic and thus lead to pathology *diminution?* It would follow from the prior discussion that these would be conditions in which symbiotic-like wishes are gratified safely—that is, gratified without threatening the sense of self. A number of clinicians have described the tendency of schizophrenics to establish symbiotic relationships in psychotherapy. Thus, Lidz and Lidz (1952) speak of the schizophrenic repeatedly attempting to establish "a symbiotic bond with [the therapist], to be completely protected by an omnipotent and omniscient figure. . ." (p. 169). Similarly, Arieti (1974) characterizes the schizophrenic patient in treatment as attempting to establish a relationship "reminiscent of the fetus completely taken care of by the mother" (p. 558). And Limentani (1956) states that schizophrenics strive "to place the therapist in an omnipotent role and then regard themselves as being one with him" (p. 233). This striving and its origin in the earlier relationship with the mother was dramatically conveyed by one of Limentani's patients:

"My mother understands me . . . she feels for me. . . . I don't even have to open my mouth [for her] to understand . . . me." [Then, referring to his therapist] "I try to make your feelings and mine one and the same thing. I try because it makes living easier, it makes me feel stronger" [p. 232].

One group of clinicians who write of the schizophrenic's need for a symbiotic relationship in the treatment situation attempt to foster the relationship, and thus provide symbiotic-like gratifications. Mahler (1968), for example, in describing her treatment of schizophrenic children, refers to the therapist providing a "corrective symbiotic experience" (p. 5). The therapist, she says, "offers himself as a symbiotic partner" (p. 183). Similarly, Alpert (1959) refers to the necessity of what she terms "corrective object relations [therapy]" (p. 169) with schizophrenic children. She describes one child who formed a symbiotic relationship with a teacher who was part of the treatment team as first taking a "regressive path down" and then later moving "progressively back up to more age-adequate behavior. . ." (p. 171).

In the treatment of adult schizophrenics as well, a number of clinicians have underscored the importance of fostering a symbiotic relationship. Searles (1959) thus writes that a symbiotic mode of relatedness between patient and therapist "constitutes a necessary phase" in the therapy of schizophrenic patients (p. 308). Analogously, Limentani (1956), in describing observations made in the course of long-term psychotherapy with six schizophrenic patients, concludes that "the establishment by the therapist of a 'symbiotic' relationship . . . is, I believe, essential if the patient is to [make progress]" (p. 235). And Little (1960), using slightly different language, refers to "a state of . . . basic unity [to which schizophrenics] need to regress in order to repair the . . . psychic 'fracture-dislocation'—i.e., to find their psychic roots" (p. 378).

There is another group of clinicians, however, who have adopted a very different psychotherapeutic strategy in treating schizophrenics. Instead of providing symbiotic-like gratifications, they devote their efforts toward encouraging in their patients a sense of psychological separateness. Thus, Lidz (1973) speaks of how he "seeks to differentiate his ideas given back by the patient from the patient's own ideas in order to help the patient establish clear self-boundaries" (p. 106). In a related vein, Knowlton (1954) discusses the importance of the therapist's intrusive behavior as enabling the patient "to gain a sense of himself in relation to another person rather than seeing [the therapist] as an extension of his autistic behavior" (p. 795). And Des Lauriers (1962) advises that "the therapist must emphasize that his own ideas, his own feelings, his own actions are different from those of the patient" (p. 88). He details the types of interchanges that typically occur in the therapy he conducts:

> Jimmy, an extremely regressed youngster of fourteen years of age, staring somewhat vacantly, extends his arms in front of himself, in a feeble and searching gesture, trying to touch the face of the therapist, who comments: "You're touching my face, Jimmy; your hand is touching my face, you feel it in your hand. It's my face, Jimmy, not yours. Here's your face. I'm touching it with my hand. This is your face. And this is my hand. You're there, and I'm here. Do you like to touch my face? You're there and I'm here. You

touch my face with your hand, and you know I'm here. Tell me who I am."

"You're Dr. D."

"That's right! And you're Jimmy, and I touch your face and you feel it, and you touch my face and you know I'm here and you're there" [pp. 73-74].

The treatment strategies of Knowlton, Des Lauriers, and Lidz can be seen as addressing the defects resulting from the schizophrenic's failure during infancy to have successfully negotiated the separation-individuation phase of development. Not only should some corrective to these defects be therapeutic in its own right, but the further strengthening of the sense of self may allow the schizophrenic to feel less threatened by potentially ameliorative symbiotic-like gratifications.

It is possible that each of the two treatment strategies we have described—the one just presented and the earlier one of Limentani, Little, and Searles offering symbiotic-like gratifications—is optimally effective with a different type of schizophrenic patient. It is also possible that for schizophrenic patients generally some kind of alternation of the two approaches would be more effective than the use of each exclusively. At the end of the next chapter we will consider the bearing of our research data on these possibilities.

NOTES

1. The citations in this chapter have all been to the role of the mother in the development of schizophrenia. Lidz (1973) has also implicated the father, as well as the parents' interaction with each other. Since the latter factors have been studied in much less detail by clinicians, we have not included them in our presentation.

2. While the first study demonstrating that a genetic compo-

nent plays a role in the etiology of schizophrenia was carried out almost seven decades ago (Rudin, 1916), it was not until the late 1930's that evidence for this proposition began to accumulate. In the early investigations, most of the evidence came from studies that sought to determine whether the "morbidity risk" (the chance of developing schizophrenia) is (1) higher in families with a schizophrenic member than in the general population, and (2) higher in closer genetic relationships within these families than in more distant relationships.

Kallmann (1938, 1946), an early pioneer in the study of the role of hereditary factors in schizophrenia, reported a good deal of data that support what he called "the genetic theory of schizophrenia." In one study of twins, for example, Kallmann found that, among monozygotic twins, there was a concordance rate (i.e., the percentage of instances in which both twins were schizophrenic) of 85.8 percent, as compared to a concordance rate of only 14.7 percent for dizygotic twins. He also found that the full siblings of schizophrenic patients had a higher expectancy (14.3 percent) of developing schizophrenia than half-siblings (7.0 percent) and that half-siblings had a higher rate than step-siblings (1.8 percent). He concluded that "the predisposition to schizophrenia . . . depends on the presence of a genetic factor" (Kallmann, 1946, p. 321).

The early studies, such as those by Kallmann, were subject to a number of methodological criticisms. Both the criticisms and the work itself stimulated a large number of methodologically sounder investigations that have also produced data supporting the "genetic hypothesis." In one group of these (Erlenmeyer-Kimling, 1968; Wender, Rosenthal, and Kety, 1968; Kidd and Cavalli-Sforza, 1973), it was found that the greater the genetic loading toward schizophrenia, the more likely that an offspring would have the disorder. Thus, while the likelihood of a child of two non-schizophrenic biological parents being schizophrenic is less than 1 percent, it has been estimated that 8 to 16 percent of the children of one schizophrenic parent and 53 to 68 percent of the offspring of two schizophrenic parents will develop the disorder. These data, however, while of some relevance, are hardly decisive: The "environmental contribution" of being raised by one or two schizophrenic parents could alone account for these differing percentages.

More compelling are the studies comparing the concordance rate of schizophrenia in monozygotic and dizygotic twins—studies that are improved versions of Kallmann's 1946 study. Many of these investigations (e.g., Slater, 1953; Kringlen, 1967, 1968;

Gottesman and Shields, 1972) found, as Kallmann did, that the concordance rate was considerably higher for the former group than for the latter. These investigations, however, are again not decisive since they do not hold the "environmental variable" constant: A parent, it can be argued, is apt to respond more similarly to monozygotic than to dizygotic twins.

This then brings us to a third group of studies, studies that have been able to examine the influence of heredity independent of environmental input by studying the offspring of schizophrenics who were raised away from their biological parents. In one classic study of this kind, Heston (1966) compared a group of 47 adults who had been permanently separated from their schizophrenic mothers within three days after birth with a group of 50 control subjects. He found substantial support for the presence of a genetic factor in that a significantly higher proportion of the experimental subjects developed schizophrenia or some other "severe mental disturbance" than did the controls. Similar findings have been reported by Rosenthal (1972). In a related vein, there have been a few studies in which the concordance rate for schizophrenia among monozygotic and dizygotic twins separated from each other soon after birth were compared. In these (reviewed by Gottesman and Shields, 1972; Farber, 1981), monozygotic twins have consistently shown a higher concordance rate than did dizygotic twins.

It is important to note that many of the studies that have provided evidence for a genetic etiological component have also yielded data indicating that an environmental contribution is at work as well. Thus, in each of the twin studies that have been cited, there were cases in which one monozygotic twin was schizophrenic and the other was not, with the differential outcome, at least in some cases, due to different postnatal experiences. Similarly, in the studies of the children of schizophrenics, a consistent finding has been that the percentage of schizophrenia among those raised by their biological parents was higher than it was for those who were not. And, finally, in the Heston (1966) study referred to earlier, it was found that a large percentage of the experimental group (almost half) not only did not develop schizophrenia but were judged to be "notably successful adults," more creative, artistic, and imaginative than the subjects in the control group. This suggests that a genetic disposition to schizophrenia may result in an unusually felicitous outcome if a child is exposed to some particular (so far unspecified) postnatal experience.

While the results just noted do not validate the earlier-cited formulations as to specific schizophrenogenic environmental influences brought to bear by the parents of schizophrenics, they are clearly consistent with these formulations. At the very least, the current evidence can be viewed as congruent with Kidd and Cavalli-Sforza's (1973) conclusion that "both genetics and environment contribute [to schizophrenic development] in an important way" (p. 263), a view that today enjoys a broad consensus. Of course, this still leaves a number of questions that are currently being debated: How large are the respective contributions of heredity and environment to the development of schizophrenia and do these differ for different forms of the disorder? What particular genetic factor or factors are involved? What specific psychological deficit emerges from the genetic defect? Does this deficit adversely affect development in the symbiotic phase, the separation-individuation phase, or both? And how does the environmental contribution interact with the genetic contribution to produce a schizophrenic outcome?

3. We use the term *symbiotic relationship* in this section because this is the term generally employed by the writers we are citing. In keeping with our discussion in Chapter 1, however, the term *symbiotic-like* would be more apt.

4
EXPERIMENTAL STUDIES OF ONENESS FANTASIES IN SCHIZOPHRENIA

In the previous chapter, the views of a number of clinicians were cited that allow for the following formulation: Schizophrenics, because of pathological parenting and/or innate defects, are characterized by powerful symbiotic-like wishes that can threaten the sense of self. Schizophrenic pathology is, in part, a response to these wishes and can consequently wax and wane in reaction to the degree to which these wishes are gratified on the one hand, or experienced as threatening on the other.

Two testable propositions are embedded in this formulation: (1) that schizophrenic pathology will diminish when symbiotic-like wishes are gratified safely—i.e., without threatening the sense of self; and (2) that schizophrenic pathology will intensify when these same wishes are either frustrated or rendered more threatening. In the current chapter we will cite extensive data from experiments employing the subliminal psychodynamic activation method that bear on these propositions.

Why is it necessary to subject these propositions to controlled experimentation? From the standpoint of the clinical literature just considered, one can infer that the present evidence for the propositions consists of clinical observations of two correlative phenomena: (1) the appearance in therapy of diminished pathology concomitant with experiences of symbiotic-like gratification; and (2) the appearance in therapy of heightened pathology concomitant with experiences of symbiosis-related frustrations and conflict intensifications. But the clinical evidence for these two propositions is, by itself, hardly compelling. As our analysis in Chapter 2 suggested (see also Silverman, 1975), such clinical evidence can only be persuasive when a number of specific steps are taken to render the data from the treatment situation viable evidence for theoretical propositions. We noted that such steps would include the collection of verbatim or at least detailed accounts of patient-therapist interchanges in the treatment situation, systematic assessment of the material collected, and careful efforts to minimize the effects of bias in both the collection and evaluation of the data.[1] If under these conditions, the relationships described above were found to occur regularly, the clinical situation could be said to have provided as much evidence as it could for the propositions under consideration.

Unfortunately, the steps outlined above have not been taken. But even if they had been, and even if optimal clinical data were available to support these propositions, they still could be challenged on substantive grounds. We have already pointed out in Chapter 2 the weakness of clinical data with respect to establishing cause-and-effect type relationships; that is, alternative explanations can be offered for the observations that have been cited. For example, consider the situation in which the therapist observes in a particular session evidence both that a schizophrenic patient is experiencing him or her as symbiotically gratifying and that the level of pathology being manifested is lower than usual. While according to proposition 1 above, the symbiotic-like gratification would be seen as having brought about the improved functioning, the sequence may actually have been reversed. The pathology may have remitted for some other reason, allowing the patient to move closer to the therapist with the symbiotic-like gratification a *result* rather than the cause of the clinical improvement.

In light of the above discussion, it should not be surprising that whereas the propositions that have been posited are based on the views of one group of clinicians, there is another group of clinicians whose writings (explicitly or implicitly) contradict these propositions.[2] As we argued earlier, it is in precisely this kind of situation—one in which psychoanalytic clinicians disagree—that experimental data are called for.

In order to subject the controversial theoretical propositions to a decisive experimental test, a laboratory procedure would be needed that could simultaneously satisfy two crucial requirements. First, it should be a procedure in which the experimenter can "manipulate" unconscious mental processes, since the symbiotic-like wishes, gratification or frustration of which has been proposed to affect schizophrenic symptoms, are clinically understood to be unconscious. Second, it should be a procedure capable of being tightly controlled. Ideally, it should be one that (a) allows for a comparison of an experimental condition in which unconscious symbiotic-like wishes are being gratified or frustrated with a "control" intervention that is the same as the experimental intervention in all but one respect—its ability to affect these wishes, and (b) provides for the evaluation of the effects of the experimental and control interventions under double-blind conditions—conditions in which, as in double-blind drug studies, neither the person receiving the intervention nor the person administering it knows whether the experimental intervention or the control has been administered. The subliminal psychodynamic activation method meets both of these requirements. The following section continues the narrative begun in Chapter 2. Since it refers once again to experiments that predate the authors' collaboration, it is written in the first person singular (by L.H. Silverman).

THE RESEARCH ODYSSEY CONTINUES

In the winter of 1967, after a consideration of some of the clinical literature reviewed in the preceding chapter (and also the telling personal communication from Dr. Robert Spiro, described in Chapter 1), I contemplated the possibility of designing a laboratory experiment that could test the hypothesis that the gratification of symbiotic-like wishes reduced pathology in schizophrenics. The knowledge that there was no clinical consensus on the value of these gratifications provided an additional impetus for my efforts to devise an experimental procedure by means of which the posited relationship could be studied in the laboratory.

Although it hardly seemed possible to gratify symbiotic-like wishes *directly* in the laboratory, I thought it might be possible to use the subliminal psychodynamic activation method to stimulate *a fantasy* of these wishes being gratified, just as that method had stimulated other psychodynamic motives in earlier experiments (described in Chapter 2). Thus, the first task was to devise a stimulus that could activate what were later to be conceptualized as "symbiotic-like oneness fantasies."[3] Should a verbal message be used, as it had been in some of the earlier experiments, a picture, as in others, or perhaps a combination of the two? I hedged my bets in the initial experiment and divided the sample of 48 male schizophrenics into two groups, giving each a different "oneness stimulus." For one group, the stimulus consisted of a two-headed sheep; for the other, a picture of a man and a woman merged at the shoulders like Siamese twins, accompanied by the verbal message MOMMY AND I ARE ONE. (I came upon this phrase in a conversation with my wife—a psychologist—who quoted a patient who frequently used these words when referring to her tie to her mother.)

For each of the two groups, experimental and control stimuli were also devised to test further the impact of stimulated aggressive wishes. For the "animal stimulus group," the aggressive stimulus consisted of a picture of a charging lion with teeth bared; the control stimulus depicted two bland-looking beagles. For the "human stimulus group," the aggressive stimulus was a picture of a man about to stab a woman, and was captioned DESTROY MOTHER; the control stimulus showed two expressionless men, and was captioned MEN THINKING.

Both groups of schizophrenics were then seen for three sessions in which they were exposed to oneness, aggressive, and control stimuli in counterbalanced order (i.e., the order of presentation of the three stimuli, was varied, with an equal number of schizophrenics receiving each possible order). In each session, a baseline assessment of psychopathology was made, followed by the administration of four subliminal exposures of one of the three types of stimuli. A critical assessment of psychopathology was then made to determine the impact of the subliminal stimulus on the pathology measures. (In this study and the subsequent studies of schizophrenics to be reported, two dimensions of pathology were assessed—"pathological thinking" and "pathological behavior." "Pathological thinking" is defined as unrealistic, illogical, or loose thinking and is assessed by means of such psychological tests as the Rorschach, a word association test, and a story recall test [see Rapaport, Gill, and Schafer (1945) and Schafer

(1948) for a general discussion of the use of such tests for detecting thought disorder in schizophrenia]. "Pathological behavior" refers to nonverbal behavior manifested during testing that would be viewed as pathological in a clinical situation. It includes behaviors ranging from those typically labeled "psychotic" [e.g., inappropriate laughter, peculiar mannerisms, and severe speech blocking] to those labeled "anxiety equivalents" [e.g., nervous tapping of fingers and leg shaking]. Both pathology variables are scored from manuals obtainable from the New York University Research Center for Mental Health and have demonstrated good reliability [.73 to .98 for pathological thinking and .85 to .96 for pathological behavior]).

As in previous (and subsequent) subliminal psychodynamic activation studies, this experiment was carried out under double-blind conditions: Neither the participants, the experimenter, nor the scorers of the protocols knew which subliminal stimulus was being presented at any point in the study.

For both samples, the aggressive condition produced the expected increase in pathology, this serving as a further replication of the finding described earlier. With regard to the oneness stimuli, however, the results were more complicated. First, the group that was exposed to the two-headed sheep stimulus was left unaffected; it was only the group that received the picture of the people merged at the shoulders, accompanied by the caption MOMMY AND I ARE ONE, that evidenced the hypothesized reduction in pathology. And second, even for this latter group, the pathology reduction seemed to be dependent on the degree to which a particular characteristic was present in the schizophrenics—something I came to refer to as their "level of differentiation from mother." This requires some explanation.

Each participant in the study had, for another purpose, filled out two rating scales, one of which bore on how he perceived himself and the other on how he perceived his mother. It was noted that when the ratings given to self and mother were compared, there was wide variability among the participants in the extent to which the ratings coincided—i.e., the degree to which the schizophrenic experienced himself as similar to (or conversely as differentiated from) his mother.[4] When the relationship between the scores on this differentiation-from-mother measure and the participants' responses after the oneness condition was examined, it was discovered that, whereas for the more differentiated patients, the hypothesized reduction in pathology was solidly in evidence, for the less differentiated patients, this clearly was not the case.[5]

This unexpected finding suggested an interesting possibility. Perhaps the disagreement among the clinicians referred to earlier as to whether symbiotic-like gratifications were ameliorative for schizophrenics could be accounted for by the fact that their clinical experience had been with different types of schizophrenics. In other words, it seemed possible that the conclusion that these gratifications were ameliorative was based on observations of more differentiated schizophrenics whereas the differing judgment was based on observations of less differentiated schizophrenics.[6] Later a rationale will be offered for why more and less differentiated schizophrenics might respond differently to oneness stimuli, but for now, I will continue sequentially and describe the experiments that established the reliability of the relationship that the first experiment suggested.

The next experiment involved a group of schizophrenic men who were pre-selected as "relatively differentiated" on the measure just described. (As has been learned in subsequent studies, anywhere from 50 to 80 percent of hospitalized schizophrenics obtain scores on this measure that allow them to be classified in this way.) The same type of experiment was conducted except that this time only oneness and control conditions were introduced and only the human-picture-plus-verbal-message stimuli were used. In support of the conclusion drawn from the first experiment, this group showed a decrease in pathology after the MOMMY AND I ARE ONE condition (Silverman, Spiro, Weisberg, and Candell, 1969).

Following this initial pair of experiments, ten additional investigations have been conducted in which a similar finding emerged, three in the New York Veterans Administration laboratory (Silverman and Candell, 1970; Silverman, Candell, Pettit, and Blum, 1971; Bronstein, 1976) and seven elsewhere (Leiter, 1973; Kaye, 1975; T. Spiro, 1975; Kaplan, 1976; Fribourg, 1981; Jackson, 1981; Mendelsohn, 1981). In each of these, for a group of relatively differentiated schizophrenics, the oneness condition resulted in a decrease in pathology that was not in evidence after the control condition. (In about half of these studies, the experimental condition consisted of the phrase MOMMY AND I ARE ONE by itself and in the other half the phrase was accompanied by the picture described earlier.)

Moreover, in three of the above investigations (Leiter, 1973; T. Spiro, 1975; Fribourg, 1981), groups of relatively undifferentiated schizophrenics were also put through the identical procedure and in each case failed to show pathology reduction after the oneness condition. Thus, the conclusion tentatively reached earlier, that more and less differentiated schizophrenics differ in their reaction to the fantasied fulfillment of symbiotic-like wishes, could now be viewed with reasonable confidence.[7]

A NON-REPLICATION

In contrast to the 12 experiments in which the subliminal presentation of the MOMMY AND I ARE ONE stimulus produced a reduction in pathology in relatively differentiated schizophrenics, there was one investigation in which this experimental manipulation produced no effect. Since 11 out of 12 replications of a non-trivial finding in psychological experiments is considerably above par, the non-replication could simply be viewed as an anomaly and not further considered. But this would be a mistake in our* view since the negative finding has important implications both for the research that is being discussed and for the formulation under consideration.

The experiment in question was carried out by Loveland (1977). It was mentioned earlier (Chapter 2) as one of those in which a subliminal aggressive condition significantly increased the level of pathology in a group of schizophrenics. But at the same time as the aggressive condition had its expected pathology-intensifying effect, the oneness condition did not, as predicted, diminish pathology. The former positive finding limits somewhat the possible interpretations of the latter negative finding in that, if the aggression condition had also produced no result, one might wonder if either mechanical or procedural anomalies had interfered with subliminal registration.[8] But in the light of Loveland's results for the aggressive condition, it can be assumed that the stimuli were registering and affecting the participants. Thus, one can focus on the narrower question of why the symbiotic-like stimulus did not have the same impact that it did in the other investigations.

* In the mid-1970's, discussions began among the three authors that eventually led to their collaboration on this book. Thus, from this section on, the first person plural is used.

The answer, we believe, resides in the fact that this study was carried out in a psychiatric hospital in Virginia, while all the others were carried out in various hospitals in New York State.[9] The significance of the different locale was suggested when Loveland's findings were discussed in a telephone conversation with the staff psychologist who had supervised her study.[10] She made the following comment about the use of the MOMMY AND I ARE ONE stimulus: "I think you used the wrong word for mother with our Southern schizophrenics. For most of us down here the word 'Mommy' is rather foreign. Southern children typically call their mothers 'Mama.' "

This remark brought to mind another puzzling finding. In the results obtained in the earlier New York studies, both white and black schizophrenic patients had shown the hypothesized effect,[11] while Puerto Rican patients had not. This had been the case not only for Puerto Ricans who were bilingual, but also for those who had spoken only English for many years. We inferred that, for the latter group as well as the former, the word "Mommy" had not been used during childhood, and that this factor had interfered with the impact of the MOMMY AND I ARE ONE message. (As a result of this finding, the selection of research participants for many subliminal psychodynamic activation experiments has been limited to native-born Americans.) Loveland's negative results for Southern schizophrenics could be understood in the same way.

But why should it be necessary to use a word for mother in the symbiotic-like oneness message that was actually used by the schizophrenic during childhood? One could safely assume that both the Puerto Rican and Southern research participants knew the meaning of "Mommy" so that the problem was not one of having used a word beyond the participant's comprehension. Rather, we think it was because "Mommy" for the "non-users" did not have the particular connotation that it has for those who have used the word—that of the *good* mother of early childhood.

What has been implicit in our formulation can now be stated in the following way: In order for a fantasy of oneness with mother to be ameliorative, it must be with a mother viewed as loving and gratifying. This would be particularly true with respect to schizophrenics, who so often experience their mothers as ungratifying or in other ways "bad."[12] Oneness fantasies involving the "bad mother" would be anything but ameliorative. Consequently, only when the word for mother used in a oneness message specifically stimulates "good mother" associates should a positive outcome be expected.

There are two testable implications of this revised formulation: first, that the use of the message MOTHER AND I ARE ONE should not have the same ameliorative effect as the use of MOMMY AND I ARE ONE, since, in most instances, the former does not refer specifically to the *good* mother; and, second, for schizophrenics who use a word other than "Mommy" for the good mother, the use of *that* word in the oneness message should produce the same pathology-reducing effect that MOMMY AND I ARE ONE has produced in the studies other than Loveland's. These implications remain to be examined in the laboratory.

THE INTRODUCTION OF NEW STIMULI

After a number of studies replicated the MOMMY AND I ARE ONE effect on differentiated schizophrenics, several doctoral students in clinical psychology asked themselves the following question in carrying out their dissertation research. What would happen if certain key words in the

MOMMY AND I ARE ONE phrase were changed? Would the outcome be the same? Or would the pathology-reducing effects vanish? This was an important question for two reasons: First, on the basis of the results reported thus far, a critic could justifiably argue that the effects found for the MOMMY AND I ARE ONE stimulus were simply a function of a generally positive fantasy involving "Mommy"—the good mother of infancy—rather than a specific fantasy involving *oneness* with her. And second, even if it could be demonstrated more definitively that a oneness fantasy *was* involved, the question could be asked as to whether the fantasied oneness had to be with "Mommy" in order for it to be ameliorative. In order to address the first question, other words would have to be substituted for "one" in the message, while in order to address the second question, other words would have to be substituted for "Mommy."

How Important Is the Reference to Oneness?

Kaplan (1976) was the first to investigate the question as to whether a reference to oneness was essential to the pathology-reducing message. She carried out her study with the same type of population that had shown pathology reduction in the earlier studies—80 male schizophrenic patients, scored as "relatively differentiated" on the measure described earlier. These patients were randomly assigned to one of four groups, each of which received two stimulus conditions. One condition, for all four groups, involved subliminal exposure to PEOPLE ARE WALKING, the message that had served as a control in many of the earlier studies. The second stimulus condition (and as before, the experimental and control stimuli were presented in reverse order to half the participants) varied. For

one group it was MOMMY AND I ARE ONE, for the second MOMMY FEEDS ME WELL, for the third MOMMY IS ALWAYS WITH ME, and for the fourth I CANNOT HURT MOMMY.

The results of this study were strong and clear-cut. For the first group, the MOMMY AND I ARE ONE stimulus, when contrasted with the control, reduced pathology on both the measures that have been used in the experiments with schizophrenics under review—pathological thinking and pathological behavior. For the other three groups, on the other hand, there was no difference between the experimental and the control conditions on either measure.

What are the implications of this finding? For one thing, it demonstrates that the stimulus must contain more than a reference to "Mommy" in order to be pathology-reducing. For another, that even when "Mommy" messages sound a note of reassurance, as did each of the messages presented to the latter three groups, they are insufficient to produce an ameliorative outcome.

Finally, it should be noted that Kaplan conceived of each of the three non-ameliorative "Mommy" messages as implying a fantasized satisfaction of one of the needs proposed in Chapter 3 as served by a symbiotic-like gratification: the need to allay fears of mother's loss (MOMMY IS ALWAYS WITH ME); the need for oral satisfaction (MOMMY FEEDS ME WELL); and the need to defend against aggressive intent (I CANNOT HURT MOMMY). The failure of these stimuli to affect the schizophrenics in the same way as the MOMMY AND I ARE ONE stimulus most likely means one of two things. Either the oneness stimulus is ameliorative because it satisfies a need not included among the three listed above; or it has its positive effect because of its ability to satisfy more than one need. We will return to these alternate possibilities in Chapter 6.

A second study bearing on the importance of the oneness element in the subliminal message was carried out by Bronstein (1976). His particular interest was in determining whether messages involving other kinds of "internalizations" of "Mommy" would prove ameliorative. Using definitions of internalization proposed by Schafer (1968), Bronstein compared the messages MOMMY IS INSIDE ME (viewed as an "introjection fantasy"), MOMMY AND I ARE THE SAME (a "sameness fantasy"), and MOMMY AND I ARE ALIKE (a "likeness fantasy"), in addition to MOMMY AND I ARE ONE (a "oneness fantasy"). Each of four groups of relatively differentiated male schizophrenic patients was given one of the four internalization messages in addition to the PEOPLE ARE WALKING control stimulus. And in parallel with Kaplan's findings, only the oneness stimulus reduced pathology. These two studies, particularly when considered together, speak strongly for the proposition that the oneness element in the message is responsible for its ameliorative effect on schizophrenics.

It must be noted, however, that two of the most recent studies demonstrating reduced pathology in differentiated schizophrenics following the MOMMY AND I ARE ONE stimulus also demonstrated an ameliorative effect for an additional experimental stimulus. Fribourg (1981) produced such an effect with the verbal message MOMMY GIVES ME EVERYTHING, accompanied by a picture of a mother cradling an infant in her arms. Significantly, this effect obtained only for pathological nonverbal behavior, a much less specific measure of schizophrenic psychopathology than is pathological thinking. The latter measure, which refers directly to the schizophrenic's thought disorder, was unaffected by MOMMY GIVES ME EVERYTHING, but was reduced after the MOMMY AND I ARE ONE stimulus.

Mendelsohn (1981), on the other hand, did elicit pathology reduction for the more important pathological-thinking measure after the subliminal message MOMMY AND I ARE TWO, accompanied by a picture of a man and a woman standing side by side. On first consideration, this finding appears to militate against the assumption that the oneness element in the MOMMY AND I ARE ONE message is responsible for the pathology reduction. But Mendelsohn offered an alternative explanation. There was evidence, he noted, that the phrase MOMMY AND I ARE TWO, together with the pictorial component, did in fact activate symbiotic-like oneness fantasies, even though the word "one" was not contained in the message. The evidence he referred to were associations to the stimuli (i.e., both the messages and the accompanying pictures) that he had obtained from a number of the research participants after the experiment was completed. He found that many of the associations to MOMMY AND I ARE TWO had much in common with those to MOMMY AND I ARE ONE. That is, rather than eliciting associations of alienation and separation (his initial expectation), the "two" stimulus elicited references to a close bond and even a kind of oneness in spirit. Dauber (1979, 1980), whose work with depressed women will be discussed in the following chapter, provided further evidence for Mendelsohn's interpretation. He, too, demonstrated an ameliorative effect for the stimulus MOMMY AND I ARE TWO and the accompanying picture, and found this overall finding to have been produced specifically by those in his study population who had subsequently produced associations linking the "twoness" stimulus with symbiotic-like fantasies.

Clearly, further experiments are in order to clarify the findings of Mendelsohn and Dauber. On the basis of the work completed to date, however, it is reasonable to conclude that oneness fantasies involving a maternal representation can be activated by subliminal stimuli the *manifest content* of which do not include an explicit reference to "oneness." The MOMMY AND I ARE TWO message, and its pictorial accompaniment, seems to be such a stimulus.[13]

Does the Fantasied Oneness Have to Be with "Mommy?"

Two studies have been carried out that have focused on a second key word in the oneness stimulus, "Mommy." Kaye (1975) asked the question whether a oneness fantasy involving some important figure in the schizophrenic's life other than mother would prove ameliorative. Again working with relatively differentiated male schizophrenic patients, he divided them into three groups, each receiving a control stimulus (PEOPLE ARE WALKING) and a oneness stimulus. The latter consisted of, alternatively, MOMMY AND I ARE ONE, DADDY AND I ARE ONE, and MY GIRL AND I ARE ONE.

In keeping with the findings of Kaplan and Bronstein, Kaye found that MOMMY AND I ARE ONE decreased pathology, whereas DADDY AND I ARE ONE did not, again suggesting the special properties of the former stimulus. But the third oneness stimulus *did* produce an ameliorative effect. MY GIRL AND I ARE ONE lowered pathology, and to Kaye's surprise, to a degree that was greater than that produced by the MOMMY AND I ARE ONE stimulus.[14]

Kaye interpreted his results in the following way. The fantasy of oneness, in order to be pathology-reducing for male schizophrenics, cannot involve just *any* significant figure in a schizophrenic's life (the DADDY stimulus had no effect), but must involve a *maternal* representation. That the MY GIRL AND I ARE ONE stimulus was *more* effective

than the MOMMY AND I ARE ONE stimulus was taken
to mean that the words "my girl" refer to a more positive
good-mother image than the word "Mommy." Apparently,
"Mommy," which we suggested earlier is the usual referent
for the *good* mother of early childhood for most people in
this country, can have somewhat threatening connotations
for schizophrenics, connotations that "my girl"—which
makes no reference to the *actual* mother of childhood—does
not have. As Kaye suggests, perhaps oneness with "Mommy"
can stimulate shame over infantile dependence or guilt
over incestuous wishes that oneness with "my girl" does
not.

There is another possible interpretation of Kaye's findings. We have earlier noted that symbiotic-like fantasies
involving mother constitute but one category of oneness
fantasies. We need not assume, then, that the words "my
girl" necessarily activated a maternal representation. Perhaps the subliminal message MY GIRL AND I ARE ONE
acivated a different type of oneness fantasy, one that involved a non-maternal sexual partner but one that still had
its own ameliorative properties. But even if the "my girl"
image evoked by the stimulus *was* fused with a maternal
representation, there is no reason to assume that it necessarily represented the same "symbiotic mother" evoked
by the message MOMMY AND I ARE ONE. It is possible
that the fused "my girl-mommy" image involved a post-
symbiotic maternal representation, perhaps the "oedipal
mother" of later development. Here, too, further clarifying experiments are necessary.

A Study of Female Schizophrenics

All of the investigations cited thus far in this chapter
have involved male schizophrenics. This is due to the fact

that the initial studies were carried out in Veterans Administration hospitals where the populations are almost exclusively male. The later investigations, such as those of Kaplan, Bronstein, and Kaye, sought to replicate the early findings (as well as study the effects of the new messages) so that they, too, examined a male schizophrenic population. In 1977, Cohen decided to rectify this one-sided situation by carrying out the same type of experiment with female schizophrenics. She was particularly interested in determining whether Kaye's findings, as described above, could be replicated with females. She thus employed messages parallel to his.

Cohen's findings came as a surprise. In sharp contrast to Kaye, she found that the MOMMY AND I ARE ONE stimulus did *not* reduce pathology, whereas the DADDY AND I ARE ONE stimulus *did*. It thus seemed as if male and female schizophrenics responded adaptively to different kinds of oneness fantasies. But this conclusion needed confirmation in a single study with schizophrenics of both sexes, in which both MOMMY AND I ARE ONE and DADDY AND I ARE ONE were used. Such a study was recently conducted by Jackson (1981). Male differentiated schizophrenics responded with decreased pathology after MOMMY AND I ARE ONE, but not after DADDY AND I ARE ONE, whereas female differentiated schizophrenics responded in precisely the reverse way. Thus, the sex difference between schizophrenic men and women regarding the type of oneness fantasies that are ameliorative is now a replicated finding.

How are the results for schizophrenic women to be interpreted? Cohen and Jackson both offer an explanation based on the writings of Lidz (1973) who has studied the families of schizophrenics extensively. Lidz reports that it is specifically in the families of female schizophrenics that fathers often assume a symbiotic-like role with their daughters. Thus, Cohen and Jackson suggest that the ameliorative effect of the DADDY AND I ARE ONE stimulus for schizophrenic women derives from the same symbiotic-like fantasy that is activated in schizophrenic men by the MOMMY AND I ARE ONE stimulus. But another possibility is that the DADDY AND I ARE ONE stimulus is not symbiotic-like at all and that it activates instead a type of post-symbiotic (perhaps oedipal) oneness fantasy similar to that we considered in relation to Kaye's findings for MY GIRL AND I ARE ONE. Before deciding between these explanations, research is called for that could shed light on what the representations "Daddy" and "my girl" convey to schizophrenics.

PATHOLOGY INTENSIFICATION IN RESPONSE TO FRUSTRATED OR THREATENING SYMBIOTIC-LIKE WISHES

The research propositions derived from our literature review in Chapter 3 posit not only that schizophrenic pathology will diminish when symbiotic-like wishes are safely gratified, but that this same pathology will intensify when such wishes are either subject to external frustration or threaten the sense of self. This second proposition, dealing with the intensification of schizophrenic pathology, has generated substantially less research than the first proposition, but a few relevant experiments have been carried out and will be considered here.

What kind of stimulus creates an inner state analogous to a real-life circumstance that frustrates symbiotic-like wishes? Litwack, Wiedemann, and Yager (1979) conducted a subliminal psychodynamic activation experiment using a stimulus that could activate such a state—the verbal message I AM LOSING MOMMY. If the schizophrenic seeks symbiotic-like gratification from "Mommy," the fantasy of her loss can be viewed as antithetical to that wish. Consistent with this view, there was an *increase* in psychopathology after the I AM LOSING MOMMY stimulus was subliminally introduced.

Two experiments bore on the fate of symbiotic-like oneness wishes that threaten the sense of self. In Leiter's study (1973), referred to earlier as one of those in which MOMMY AND I ARE ONE reduced pathology in relatively differentiated schizophrenic patients, it was found that a group of relatively undifferentiated schizophrenic patients not only did not respond in the same way, but experienced significantly *increased* pathology. How is this finding to be interpreted? In Chapter 3, we reviewed literature suggesting that gratifications of symbiotic-like wishes could intensify schizophrenic pathology when they threatened the patient's sense of self. We would now point out that it is precisely relatively *undifferentiated* schizophrenics for whom this threat is most apt to arise. Less differentiated schizophrenics are those whose self- and mother representations are more closely bound together; the resulting lack of psychological separateness would make them particularly vulnerable to loss of the sense of self. Thus, the subliminal activation of the MOMMY AND I ARE ONE fantasy can be seen as having threatened the sense of self, resulting in an intensification of pathology.

A second experiment carried out at the New York Veterans Administration laboratory can be interpreted along similar lines. In this case, a new subliminal stimulus—the phrase I AM MOMMY—was used with the same type of differentiated schizophrenic population for which so many studies had shown MOMMY AND I ARE ONE to reduce pathology. Rather than reducing pathological manifestations in a comparable way, however, the stimulus I AM MOMMY increased pathology. This finding was attributed (Silverman, 1970) to the fact that the new phrase conveyed a degree of merging of self- and object representations that posed a threat even to these more differentiated schizophrenics. This interpretation presumes the existence of a threshold for the merging of self- and object representations below which oneness fantasies will be perceived as safe. This threshold was presumably not exceeded in the earlier experiments, where the phrase MOMMY AND I ARE ONE suggested the existence of a "Mommy" and an "I" who were separate persons in some respects, while "one" in others. The phrase I AM MOMMY, on the other hand, implies an act of total merging antithetical to the very notion of a secure sense of self, apparently going beyond the threshold of a safe oneness fantasy even for differentiated schizophrenics. The result was a threatened loss of the sense of self and a consequent intensification of pathology.[15]

OPTIMAL CONDITIONS FAVORING PATHOLOGY REDUCTION IN SCHIZOPHRENIA

The last two studies cited bear on a circumstance that leads to pathology intensification in schizophrenics—one in which there is a further loss of separateness. By implication, these investigations also suggest that a circumstance which strengthens separateness should result in pathology *reduction*. Such an expectation would be consistent with the clinical reports of Knowlton (1954), Des Lauriers (1962), and Lidz (1973) whose therapies, as we noted in Chapter 3, are aimed at such strengthening and can be seen as addressing the schizophrenic's failure to have negotiated the separation-individuation phase.

Two experiments relevant to this expectation have been carried out in our laboratory. In the first of these (Spiro and Silverman, 1967), separateness was strengthened by means of a very different kind of experimental intervention than those that have been described thus far—one not involving subliminal stimulation. The intervention, which has been termed "self-focusing," is based on Des Laurier's (1962) treatment approach referred to in Chapter 3, wherein the therapist, in the course of interacting with the schizophrenic patient, continually highlights differences between him or herself and the patient. In the study cited, a group of 36 schizophrenic patients were administered, in one session, the following self-focusing instructions:

> In front of you is a mirror and alongside it is a picture of another person. As you probably know, each person is unique and there are no two individuals exactly alike. Part of my work deals with differences between people, and in a moment I'll be showing you how different two people really are. I'm going to ask you to look in the mirror at yourself and then to look at the other person, and I'll be asking you to observe carefully certain parts of your face, and then to observe carefully certain parts of the other person's face. Each time you do this I want you to tell me whatever differences you can notice. Look at your hair, and now look at the other person's hair [eyes, ears, nose, and whole face, respectively]; what differences do you see? [During this part of the task, if the schizophrenic failed to verbalize a difference, the experimenter did so for him.]
>
> These are just some of the ways in which people differ; let us look at some others. This person is from Providence, R.I.,; where are you from? He is 5 ft. 2

in. tall; how tall are you? He weighs 130 lbs.; how much do you weigh?

Now that many of your unique characteristics have been brought to your attention, I am going to ask you to make a series of very simple movements which will enable you to experience other feelings which are unique for every individual. Put your hands around your face and say, "I can feel my face." Clasp your hands and say, "I can feel my hands." Put your hands on your legs, squeeze them, and say, "I can feel my legs." Move your feet and toes and say, "I can feel my feet and toes."

In another session a control intervention was administered (again, both interventions were given in counterbalanced order). This consisted of a vocabulary test, which, like the self-focusing task, involved the interaction of the researcher with the schizophrenic and lasted for the same amount of time—approximately 15 minutes. Measures of psychopathology were obtained before and after both interventions, with a comparison of the two indicating that the self-focusing condition resulted in greater pathology reduction.

In the second study (Silverman, Levinson, Mendelsohn, and Ungaro, 1975), there was an opportunity to evaluate the effect of *both* conditions that have been shown in this chapter to be ameliorative for schizophrenics: strengthening separateness by the use of self-focusing, and activation of unconscious oneness fantasies by means of subliminal stimulation. Four conditions were compared: (1) a subliminal oneness stimulus accompanied by self-focusing; (2) a subliminal neutral stimulus accompanied by self-focusing; (3) a subliminal oneness stimulus accompanied by a control intervention for self-focusing; (4) a

subliminal neutral stimulus accompanied by the same control as used in Condition 3.[16]

The major findings from this investigation were that
both Condition 2 and Condition 3 produced better functioning than Condition 4 (the control condition), thus demonstrating the value of each treatment intervention, and
that Condition 1 resulted in the most adaptive functioning
of all, indicating that the combined use of the two interventions was more effective than the use of either one
singly. More specifically, the group that received only the
oneness stimulus (Condition 3) compared to the control
group (Condition 4) responded with a more positive self-
concept, a reduction in pathological ward behavior (as
evaluated from nurses' ratings), a reduced number of re-
hospitalizations, and, on an overall measure derived from
a number of variables, reduced psychopathology. The
group that received only self-focusing (Condition 2), on
the other hand, showed a more differentiated sense of self
than did the control group (Condition 4).[17] The group that
received both the oneness stimulus and the self-focusing
interventions demonstrated both types of improvement.[18]

TREATMENT IMPLICATIONS

The research we have reviewed allows us to draw a number of conclusions with implications for the treatment of
schizophrenics. First, the data from 12 laboratory experiments support the proposition that providing relatively
differentiated schizophrenics with symbiotic-like gratifications has ameliorative consequences. For relatively *undifferentiated* schizophrenics, however, four studies indicate
that these same gratifications are not ameliorative (and
may even be pathology inducing), presumably because
they threaten the sense of self.

Second, data from two experiments support the view that taking steps to reinforce a schizophrenic patient's psychological separateness also leads to pathology reduction. And the results from one of these investigations suggest that the most favorable condition for the amelioration of schizophrenic pathology may be one in which there is both reinforcement of separateness *and* gratification of symbiotic-like wishes.

Third, the results from three studies imply that treatment interventions that provide a schizophrenic with related gratifications *without* symbiotic-like characteristics—e.g., oral satisfaction, reassurance against object loss, a sense of "likeness" or "sameness"—will not have the same therapeutic efficacy. The fact that schizophrenic behavior often seems to reflect strivings for these other gratifications may simply mean that a wish for oneness can emerge in a disguised or distorted way as a striving for oral satisfaction, sameness, etc.

Finally, the fact that schizophrenic pathology diminished in response to the subliminal exposure of "oneness stimuli" allows for a new perspective on the question of what is needed to gratify a symbiotic-like wish. The clinical literature cited in Chapter 3 conceptualizes such gratifications as outgrowths of "symbiotic relationships" created in the treatment situation. But what took place in the laboratory experiments hardly qualifies as a "symbiotic relationship." The research participant's encounter with the experimenter was very brief, and even more important, was no longer in duration in the experimental session than it was in the control session. And whatever the unconscious significance of the experimenter to the participant, it was the same in the control session as it was in the experimental session. The pathology-reducing effects of the subliminally presented phrase MOMMY AND I ARE ONE (and its variants) can thus better be ascribed to its having activated unconscious fantasies of oneness than to the creation of a symbiotic relationship in the laboratory situation. And in choosing between these alternative explanations for pathology reduction in treatment, parsimony requires that we assume that here, as well, all that is needed to gratify symbiotic-like wishes is the activation of this same type of oneness fantasy.

NOTES

1. See Luborsky (1967); Dahl (1972), and Sampson, Weiss, Mlodnosky, and Hause (1972) for exemplary attempts to institute the types of controls to which we have referred.

2. We would include in this latter group Knowlton (1954), Freeman, Cameron, and McGhie (1958), Des Lauriers (1962), and Lidz (1973).

3. Until the writing of this book, the term "symbiotic" rather than "symbiotic-like" was used to refer to the fantasies activated by the MOMMY AND I ARE ONE stimulus. See Chapter 1 for the reason for the change in terminology.

4. This measure is obtained in the following way. The participant first rates himself on a 5-point scale for 20 descriptive adjectives (e.g., happy, nervous, sociable, depressed, etc.). Then he is asked to make the same ratings either for his own mother (in some studies) or for a picture of a woman intended as a mother figure (in other studies). The sum of the differences between the ratings of self and the ratings of either actual mother or mother figure comprises the "self-mother differentiation score." (For data on the relationship between ratings of the actual mother and mother figure, see Silverman, Levinson, Mendelsohn, and Ungaro. [1975] and Fribourg [1981].)

5. The subjects were separated into more and less differentiated groups by dividing them at the median for their self-mother differentiation scores. This median score (24) was used in all subsequent studies for selecting "differentiated schizophrenics."

6. We leave open the question of whether the designations "more differentiated" and "less differentiated" refer to a trait variable or a state variable. Or stated otherwise, how stable over

time are the scores from the adjective-rating-scale procedure? Fribourg (1981) obtained some relevant data and concluded that for about half of the schizophrenic sample she studied, the designation is a stable one (at least over a six-month period of time), while for the other half, the designation is notably unstable.

7. The consistent finding of pathology reduction after the MOMMY AND I ARE ONE stimulus does not of course mean that all the differentiated schizophenics responded in this way. In fact, in each of the studies cited, although there was a significant group effect, there was a substantial number of participants who did *not* respond with pathology reduction. The search for individual characteristics that correlate with a positive response to the oneness stimulus among the more differentiated schizophrenics is in its initial stages. See Mendelsohn (1979) and Jackson (1981), both of whom address this issue.

8. For a discussion of one such anomaly shown to interfere with subliminal registration, see Silverman, Ross, Adler, and Lustig (1978).

9. These hospitals varied considerably in the types of patients they served. They included Veterans Administration neuropsychiatric and general hospitals, state hospitals, and private institutions.

10. We are most grateful to Elizabeth Y. Williams, who discussed Loveland's findings with us.

11. This was most convincingly demonstrated by T. Spiro (1975), who selected an equal number of black and white subjects and found that for both groups there was an experimental effect of about the same magnitude.

12. Note that the reference to bad mothering is stated in terms of the schizophrenic's experience rather than the actual mothering. This is because, in light of the considerations discussed in Chapter 3, it is certainly possible that experiencing mother as "bad" can result not only from the quality of the actual mothering, but also from genetic defects that interfere with the experience of mother as "good."

13. Fribourg (1981) also considers the possibility that the stimulus MOMMY GIVES ME EVERYTHING with the pictorial accompaniment of a mother cradling an infant in her arms produced ameliorative effects because the picture activated symbiotic-like fantasies.

14. Bronstein's (1976) study, referred to earlier, also utilized the MY GIRL AND I ARE ONE stimulus, but did not obtain a pathology-reducing effect. He attributed the difference between

his results and Kaye's (for this particular stimulus—their findings as to the MOMMY AND I ARE ONE stimulus were parallel) to Kaye's having inadvertently "primed" subjects to think about girlfriends before the experiment began—that is, by conducting an interview in which he questioned them about their heterosexual relationships. As has been detailed elsewhere (Silverman, 1972, pp. 322-323), subliminal stimulation will sometimes not affect subjects if the thought content with which the stimulus is meant to resonate is not sufficiently active in the subject's mind. From this we can conclude the converse: that priming affects the degree of activation. Whether this explanation accounts for the difference between Kaye's and Bronstein's results should be tested in a single study in which half of the schizophrenic participants receive the MY GIRL AND I ARE ONE stimulus with priming and half without.

15. The increase in pathology that followed the experimental intervention in this experiment and the previous one may have been a more complex reaction than it seems on first consideration. It is possible that the threat to the sense of self led the schizophrenics to fend off not only the oneness fantasies activated by the subliminal stimulus but others that they had harbored beforehand. Thus, a more severe than usual state of "deprivation" may have been brought about. If experimental data were to support this formulation, it would imply that both conditions that have been found to exacerbate schizophrenic pathology—the frustration of symbiotic-like wishes and threats to the sense of self—lead to the same state of deprivation. The deprivation of symbiotic-like gratifications would then be the proximal cause of pathology intensification in schizophrenia, at least with respect to pathology apparently unrelated to conflict over aggression (see Chapter 2; Silverman, 1970).

16. This study was different from the others discussed in this chapter in two ways. First, instead of there being one group of subjects who received different conditions, there were four groups, each of which received one of the conditions listed above. Second, instead of each condition being given only once in a single session, it was given three times a week over a six-week period. Our intention was to determine if the experimental interventions, rather than producing only a "laboratory effect" as they had in the previous studies, could produce a more substantive therapeutic effect. In Chapter 5, we discuss "treatment adjunct" studies in detail.

17. This finding emerged from an analysis of the data conducted after the study was reported in the literature.

18. One of us (Milich, 1975) also conducted a "treatment adjunct" study but with a more chronic schizophrenic population. In this study, the effects of the MOMMY AND I ARE ONE stimulus, although less strong than those found in the Silverman, Levinson, Mendelsohn, and Ungaro (1975) study, lent further support to the thesis that the activation of a oneness fantasy can enhance the effectiveness of hospitalization procedures in the treatment of schizophrenics.

5

EXPERIMENTAL STUDIES OF ONENESS FANTASIES IN NON-PSYCHOTIC POPULATIONS

A 30-year-old woman who was a participant in one of our studies came to see one of the investigators three months after the study ended. The investigation was one in which we were interested in determining if the MOMMY AND I ARE ONE subliminal message could aid obese women in reducing their food intake so that they could lose more weight. Thirty overweight women had been given weekly counseling sessions for 12 weeks on how to better control their eating behavior. Each session began and ended with the women looking into the tachistoscope and receiving two exposures of a subliminal message. The women had been divided into two equal groups, with one receiving the oneness stimulus and the other, a control group, the stimulus PEOPLE ARE WALKING. Their weight was checked each week during the 12 weeks of counseling and at two follow-up times, one and three months after the counseling terminated. The woman in question had come for her second follow-up.

To the investigator's amazement, she weighed 20 pounds less than she did two months earlier at the first follow-up. His surprise was not due to the great amount of weight lost per se, since there had been two other women who had shown as much of a loss in a comparable time period. But the earlier participants had received the oneness stimulus while this woman had been in the control group, and no previous "control" had shown anything like a 20-pound loss over this period of time. The woman smiled and then offered the following explanation. "The last time I was here," she recalled, "you explained about the study," making reference to the "debriefing" that had taken place at the one month follow-up. "You told me about the MOMMY AND I ARE ONE message that you were studying and then informed me that I had been in the control group. I must say I was at first disappointed but it then occurred to me that I could capitalize on the information that you conveyed. I had learned self-hypnosis in college and what I have been doing during the past several weeks is nightly putting myself into a light trance. I then repeat over and over MOMMY AND I ARE ONE. The pounds have been melting away."

There are two morals to this story. The first is that the activation of a oneness fantasy can improve adaptation in persons who are not schizophrenic as well as in those who are. And second, this activation may not be dependent on the use of a tachistoscope or even on subliminal registration.

LABORATORY STUDIES

In the early 1970's, after several studies by various investigators had demonstrated that the MOMMY AND I ARE ONE stimulus had a pathology-reducing effect in populations of relatively differentiated schizophrenics, we turned our attention to the possibility that a person might not have to be suffering from schizophrenia—or for that matter from any severe (i.e., psychotic) mental condition—to benefit from the activation of oneness fantasies. Our rationale for expanding the research in this direction related to the universal importance that Mahler and other psychoanalytic writers had accorded the symbiotic phase of development. Both the clinical literature (to be discussed in Chapter 7) and our own clinical experience suggested not only that symbiotic-like wishes persisted throughout adulthood, but that these wishes were often potent motivators of behavior. We thus reasoned that if the maladaptive behaviors of non-psychotics also involved the frustration of, or conflict over, symbiotic-like wishes, then these persons might also respond positively to the subliminal activation of oneness fantasies. (We have since expanded our rationale as to why these fantasies can be ameliorative for non-psychotics. See Chapter 6.)

A number of investigations were thus conducted in which it was hypothesized that various non-psychotic populations would respond to the oneness stimulation with improved adaptation. In a few of these studies, the usual laboratory experiment was conducted in which each participant was given subliminal presentations of the oneness stimulus in one session and a control stimulus in another. Their effects on behavior were then compared.

An experiment of this kind was carried out with homosexual men (Silverman, Kwawer, Wolitzky, and Coron, 1973). Two groups of homosexuals (volunteers, answering a newspaper ad and screened for the absence of psychosis) were given a Rorschach test under the oneness and control conditions. For both groups, there were fewer anxiety manifestations after the former condition. Nissenfeld (1979) conducted a similar study on a group of women who had been diagnosed as "neurotically depressed" at the New York University Medical School Mental Hygiene Clinic. Various measures of depression were obtained from 48 such women after four psychodynamically related stimuli were subliminally exposed. Only the oneness stimulus produced results that were different from a control stimulus; there were fewer depressive indicators after MOMMY AND I ARE ONE. Thus, the symptom of depression as well as anxiety gave evidence of being responsive to the activation of oneness fantasies.

Dauber (1979, 1980) also employed subliminal psychodynamic stimuli with a population of depressed college women and obtained findings divergent from Nissenfeld's. He found that the MOMMY AND I ARE ONE stimulus failed to reduce depression. This finding, in conjunction with Cohen's (1977) and Jackson's (1981) results that this same stimulus generated no pathology reduction in populations of female schizophrenics, suggests that the pathology-diminishing potential of MOMMY AND I ARE ONE may indeed differ by sex; the message has demonstrated a pathology-reducing effect much more reliably in studies using male participants than in studies using females. (More evidence for this will be presented shortly.)

It should also be noted that just as Cohen and Jackson had each found that, while MOMMY AND I ARE ONE had no effect on their schizophrenic women, DADDY AND I ARE ONE had an ameliorative effect, Dauber also obtained positive findings with another stimulus. The same MOMMY AND I ARE TWO stimulus that Mendelsohn (1981) had used successfully with schizophrenic men reduced depression in Dauber's college women. And just as Cohen and Jackson suggested that DADDY AND I ARE ONE activated variants of a symbiotic-like fantasy, Dauber suggested the same for his MOMMY AND I ARE TWO stimulus. He based this supposition on the associations that he obtained from his participants when he showed them this verbal message and the accompanying picture after the subliminal part of the experiment was completed. As we noted earlier, a number of them gave symbiotic-like associations and it was precisely these research participants who "carried" the depression-reducing effect for the overall group. But whether or not these other stimuli worked because they activated symbiotic-like elements (and more data are clearly needed on this question), we simply want to note the following for now. Activating unconscious fantasies that are related to yet different from MOMMY AND I ARE ONE may be more reliably adaptation enhancing for women. We will return to this point later when we discuss sex differences in non-clinical populations.

TREATMENT STUDIES

In Chapters 8 and 9 we will propose that certain psychoanalytic and psychotherapeutic interventions inadvertently activate oneness fantasies and that these fantasies, under certain conditions, will aid the treatment process. In this section we will cite data supporting the second half of this proposition: that the activation of oneness fantasies can help the treatment process.

The first study with a bearing on treatment was carried out by Silverman and C. Wolitzky in 1970. Ten research volunteers—medical patients and hospital employees—were seen for a MOMMY AND I ARE ONE and control session in which they were asked to "make up stories" to the Thematic Apperception Test (TAT). The idea was to see whether, in telling these stories, the activation of unconscious oneness fantasies would reduce defensiveness. The stories were scored for two variables that were thought to bear on defensiveness: openness of expression and acceptance of responsibility for ideas and feelings expressed. The oneness condition did not affect the former measure, but on the latter there was more acceptance of responsibility after the experimental than the control condition.

From this suggestive finding, we proceeded to a series of investigations intended to test the hypothesis that if an actual therapeutic procedure is accompanied by subliminal oneness stimulation, it will be more effective. The rationale for this hypothesis was, that if we were correct in inferring that treatment is ordinarily enhanced by the inadvertent activation of oneness fantasies, a treatment modality will become even more effective if oneness fantasies are deliberately activated via subliminal stimulation.

To test this hypothesis, we used an experimental design different from those that have been described thus far: Instead of administering one experimental and one control session to each participant, we decided it would be preferable to present each participant with *either* the experimental or control stimulus and to repeat this stimulation in a number of sessions over an extended period of time. By comparing the two groups of experimental and control participants at the end of the treatment period, it would be possible to evaluate the cumulative effectiveness of repeatedly activating oneness fantasies.

In the first attempt at using this design (Silverman, Frank, and Dachinger, 1974), a group of 20 women volunteered for treatment of insect phobias. The women were offered four sessions of a variant of systematic desensitization,[1] the most frequently used behaviorist technique for treating phobias. Subliminal stimulation was embedded in the treatment procedure in the following way. As in the usual desensitization procedure, the participants were asked to visualize scenes in which they came into contact with the phobia-related insects. The scenes were ordered hierarchically from the least to the most frightening. After each image was formed, the participant rated herself on a 100-point scale for the degree of discomfort experienced. When the rating was 20 or higher, instead of going on to the next step in the hierarchy, she was asked to look into the tachistoscope and was given two subliminal exposures of a stimulus, ten seconds apart. Half of the women received MOMMY AND I ARE ONE, while the other half received the control stimulus PEOPLE WALKING. Then the women were asked to re-visualize the scene with the insects and again rate the degree of discomfort. If the rating was under 20, the experimenter then went on to the next most frightening image, but if not, the same visualization accompanied by subliminal stimulation was repeated until the discomfort level dropped below 20.

After four desensitization sessions of this sort, the participants were re-assessed for the extent of insect phobia. On two of three measures of change, (the women's ability to make contact with the insects and an observer's ratings of anxiety during these attempts at contact), there was more improvement for the experimental than for the control group.

In a second study of this type, the method was extended to obese women being treated by behavior modification techniques (Martin, 1975). Participants were seen individually for weekly sessions over an eight-week period. In each session, behavior modification techniques were introduced—the kind that Weight Watchers and other groups that teach weight control frequently employ. These included calorie counting, pointers on how to resist high calorie foods, the savoring of food by slow chewing so that the person will be satisfied with less, etc. At the beginning and the end of each treatment session, the woman was asked to look into the tachistoscope and to visualize a situation in which she was tempted to eat but felt that she should not. When this image was vividly in mind, she received two subliminal exposures of a stimulus. For one group of 15 women, the stimulus was MOMMY AND I

ARE ONE while for another equally sized group, it was PEOPLE WALKING. At the end of the eight-week period, the difference in the amount of weight loss between the two groups was in the direction expected (8 lbs. for the experimental group and 5 lbs. for the control) though to a degree that only approached statistical significance. But when the participants returned four weeks later for a follow-up weigh-in, this difference had become larger (11 lbs. to 4 lbs., respectively) and was now statistically significant. What happened during this follow-up period was that the group that had received the oneness stimulus continued to lose weight while the control group started to gain the weight back.

If the experimental activation of oneness fantasies can help overweight individuals eat less, why not attempt the same technique with alcoholics, a group that can also be characterized as "orally addicted." So reasoned Schurtman (1978) who conducted a study at Veritas Villa, a rehabilitation center for alcoholics in upstate New York. The participants in this study were civil servants (90 percent males) who had been referred to the Villa by the counseling services of their various municipal departments. The treatment at the center consisted primarily of AA-type counseling though it also included "rest, outdoor activities, and good diet." Over a two-week period in the rehabilitation program, it was arranged for each participant to meet with the "interventionist" every other day or for a total of six sessions, each lasting approximately 20 minutes. During each of these sessions, the alcoholic was asked to imagine himself in a situation in which he felt tempted to drink and to try to feel the tension of "wanting to drink but knowing that you shouldn't, of wanting to remain sober, but feeling the need for a drink." Four subliminal exposures were given in each of these sessions, with 36 participants receiving the MOMMY AND I ARE ONE stimulus and 36 controls the stimulus PEOPLE ARE WALKING. The main hypothesis tested was that the participants stimulated with the oneness message would show an increase in involvement in the alcoholism treatment program as determined by counselor ratings made both before and after the two weeks of subliminal stimulation. The hypothesis was borne out. Moreover, when the alcoholics were contacted by phone one month after they were discharged from Veritas Villa and asked about their alcohol consumption, those who had been in the experimental group reported a greater reduction in drinking than those who had been in the control group.

The Palmatier and Bornstein (1980) study with cigarette smokers described in Chapter 1 offered further evidence that the activation of oneness fantasies can make treatment techniques used with addictive populations more effective. And as in the Martin (1975) and Schurtman (1978) studies, the effects of this activation were in evidence one month after the subliminal exposures of the oneness stimulus ended: 67 percent of the experimental group and only 12 ½ percent of the controls were abstainers at that time.

From the comparative one-month abstinence rates in the Palmatier and Bornstein study, it would be warranted to maintain that the differential impact of the experimental and control stimuli was not only statistically significant but substantial. The same can be said of the results of a study by Bryant-Tuckett (1980) who investigated the effect of subliminal oneness stimulation on the reading ability of adolescents with severe behavior disorders. Adolescents being treated in a residential center were randomly assigned to experimental and control groups with both receiving subliminal stimulation five times a week over a six-week period. Each administration of subliminal stimuli was accompanied by a five-minute session with the school psychologist, who provided the children with food rewards for their participation. The main dependent variable in the study was the developmental reading level of the children as measured by the California Achievement Test. At the end of the six weeks, the control group had, on the average, increased their reading scores by six months over scores obtained a year earlier on the same California Achievement Test. (This was the usual amount of progress that these severely impaired adolescents made during a one-year period at the residential center.) The experimental group, on the other hand, showed, on the average, a gain of over two years.

STUDIES WITH NON-CLINICAL POPULATIONS

In 1977 Parker (1977, 1982) introduced a new paradigm for the study of the effects of activating oneness fantasies. Before his study, all investigations in which the repeated subliminal exposure over time of MOMMY AND I ARE ONE had been with clinical populations. Parker, in contrast, was interested in determining whether this same intervention could enhance the learning ability of college students (unscreened for psychopathology). He found an opportunity to pursue this interest while teaching a course in business law to undergraduates at Queens College over a six-week summer-session term. His class met five days a week and on four of these days the students received tachistoscopic subliminal stimulation at the beginning of class. They were instructed to imagine a difficult or anxiety-arousing school situation and, when they had that image firmly in mind, were given two exposures of a subliminal stimulus. There were 20 students in each of three groups, the groups matched for grade-point average prior to the summer-session term. For one group the stimulus was MOMMY AND I ARE ONE and for a second, the control group, PEOPLE ARE WALKING. The third group was given a new stimulus, MY PROF AND I ARE ONE, in an attempt to see if a fantasy of oneness with someone other than the "good mother" would have an adaptation-enhancing effect.

The students were given three exams, blindly marked, the first after two weeks, the second after four weeks, and the third at the end of the six-week summer-session term. On the first exam, there were no differences among the groups. On the second test, the MOMMY AND I ARE ONE group obtained higher grades than the controls. And on the final exam, this difference increased so that it was not only statistically significant but substantial as well, with the former group having an average grade of 90.4 and the latter 82.7. The students who received MY PROF AND I ARE ONE had as their average a grade that fell between the other two.(88.4). This average grade was significantly above that of the control group but not significantly different from that of the MOMMY AND I ARE ONE group (Parker, 1977, 1982).

Ariam (1979) followed up Parker's study by translating the messages Parker used into Hebrew and presenting them to Israeli high school students. As in the earlier study, the students were given subliminal stimulation prior to a class (this time in mathematics rather than business law) four times a week over a six-week period and were given tests after two, four, and six weeks. The students were divided into four groups of 18, each group being given a different subliminal message. Two of the groups were given Hebrew translations of MOMMY AND I ARE ONE, in one instance a more literal and the other a more idiomatic translation. The third and fourth groups received

Hebrew translations of PEOPLE ARE WALKING and MY TEACHER AND I ARE ONE (the word "teacher" being substituted for "prof" since in Israeli high schools only the former word is used). Ariam found no difference among the groups at either the two- or four-week testing, but at six weeks, the average grades of both MOMMY groups were significantly and substantially higher than that of the control group (83.4 for the idiomatic MOMMY translation, 80.0 for the literal MOMMY translation, and 65.0 for the control message translation). Whereas these results closely paralleled Parker's, the average grade for the MY TEACHER AND I ARE ONE condition were no better than that of the control group. Ariam attributed this negative result to the difference in connotation of the word "teacher" for Israeli students and "prof" for American students, maintaining that the latter was much more positively toned than the former.

Ariam's findings for the MOMMY conditions were important to us for a number of reasons. They constituted an independent replication of a provocative finding with the research participants of another nationality, in a different age group, and receiving the oneness stimulation for a different school subject. But most crucial of all, the results held up when translated into a different language—the MOMMY stimulus worked with two Hebrew translations. This answered a question about our findings that had been raised from time to time: whether the effects of the MOMMY AND I ARE ONE message may have been due to something other than its meaning. More specifically, it had been suggested that perhaps there was something special about the structure or the configuration of the letters which, when registered subliminally, produced an adaptation-enhancing effect. While there are other data that also contradict this possibility,[2] Ariam's findings offer the best refutation of this alternative explanation.

FURTHER DATA ON SEX DIFFERENCES

Another series of recent experiments with student populations sheds further light on sex-related differences in reactions to the MOMMY AND I ARE ONE stimulus. In the opening section of this chapter, we reviewed findings indicating that this stimulus had no effect on female schizophrenics (Cohen, 1977; Jackson, 1981) and female depressives (Dauber, 1979, 1980). We noted, however, that each of these studies employed a subliminal stimulus that did have an ameliorative effect on the women: DADDY AND I ARE ONE for the female schizophrenics and MOMMY AND I ARE TWO for the female depressives. Three studies with unscreened college students strengthen the conclusion that MOMMY AND I ARE ONE is *not* the optimal oneness stimulus for females.

Florek (1978) reported a study at St. John's University in which a oneness stimulus MY LOVER AND I ARE ONE reduced anxiety as measured by the Spielberger Anxiety Scale. A subsequent review of Florek's data revealed that this result had been carried by his female participants and a replication of Florek's study in our own laboratory confirmed this finding. That is, female college students at New York University showed anxiety reduction following this new oneness stimulus. A subsequent study in our laboratory in which *both* the MOMMY AND I ARE ONE and MY LOVER AND I ARE ONE stimuli were used revealed that only the former stimulus reduced anxiety in college men whereas only the latter had this effect on college women (Silverman and Grabowski, 1982). The failure of the MY LOVER AND I ARE ONE stimulus to produce an ameliorative effect in men was ascribed to the possible homosexual connotations that the phrase "my lover" can have for men, whereas the lack of effect with the MOMMY stimulus for the women is consistent with the results that have already been reported on the unreliability of the MOMMY stimulus for females.

Zuckerman's (1980) recent use of subliminal stimulation with high school underachievers lends further support to the finding of sex-related differences for the MOMMY AND I ARE ONE stimulus. She administered subliminal stimulation to three groups of underachieving students four times a week over a six-week period. One group received MOMMY AND I ARE ONE, a second (control group) received PEOPLE ARE WALKING, and a third group was exposed to a new message intended to have positive effects, unrelated to the concept of oneness: MY SUCCESS IS OK. The MOMMY stimulus improved school performance only for the males, while the female students achieved better grades only after receiving the SUCCESS message.

Taken together, these studies of high school and college students, along with the findings of Cohen, Dauber, and Jackson with clinical populations, point to the conclusion that MOMMY AND I ARE ONE is not the reliably adaptation-enhancing stimulus for women that it is for men.[3] To be sure, the stimulus *has* been effective with some groups of women, but, for other groups, it has produced no such positive results.

Why should it be the case that women do not react as reliably to MOMMY AND I ARE ONE as men do, but, conversely, show gains following such closely related stimuli as DADDY AND I ARE ONE, MY LOVER AND I ARE ONE, and MOMMY AND I ARE TWO? As far as their less reliable positive response to MOMMY AND I ARE ONE is concerned, we suspect this is related to the difference between men and women in the degree to which they are differentiated from their mothers. Bernstein (1980), after considering both the clinical literature and case material of her own, concludes that women tend to be less differentiated from their mothers than men. Her conclusion seems particularly warranted given the following considerations. First, as Maccoby and Jacklin (1974) have noted, many kinds of observations support the proposition that females are notably less aggressive than males, and it has been posited by such psychoanalytic writers as Jacobson (1964) that aggression aids infants in differentiating from their mothers. Moreover, because daughters are the same gender as their mothers, they have less of a basis for differentiating themselves from their mothers than do sons.

Given the above, it is reasonable to suppose that a MOMMY AND I ARE ONE fantasy is more apt to pose a threat to the sense of self for females than it is for males and may thus be less reliably adaptation-fostering for them. And it also makes understandable why oneness-type fantasies will be more consistenly positive for females if they involve a figure other than Mommy (DADDY AND I ARE ONE, MY LOVER AND I ARE ONE) or, alternatively, involve a more differentiated type of oneness-with-Mommy (MOMMY AND I ARE TWO). This explanation is surely not the only way of accounting for the pattern of results that have been reported for women, but it does suggest an interpretive perspective that could guide further research. The relevant concept once more (see Chapter 4) is that of a threshold beyond which oneness is not ameliorative. We shall see that the concept of a threshold separating safe from threatening oneness fantasies also provides a useful perspective from which to evaluate the paradoxical findings reported in the next section.

PARADOXICAL RESULTS

In contrast to the many studies in which improved adaptation followed subliminal stimulation of symbiotic-like content, there were two investigations in which the resulting behavior was characterized as *less* adaptive. One of these paradoxical findings was reported by Podall (1978). She carried out a study with college women fulfilling an introductory psychology course requirement, asking them to participate in what has been termed the Prisoner's Dilemma Game. Developed by Wilson and Bixenstine (1962), this "game" has been used to evaluate a person's willingness to eschew competition and act cooperatively with a partner in order to achieve a common end.

In each of two sessions, scheduled one week apart, the participants received subliminal exposures both before the Prisoner's Dilemma Game began and midway through. For half of the participants, the stimulus presented was MOMMY AND I ARE ONE while, for the other half, it was PEOPLE ARE WALKING. By the end of the two weeks, the behavior of the groups diverged as had been hypothesized, but the *way* they diverged was not expected. Those who had received the oneness stimulus became *less* cooperative than did the controls.

The other paradoxical result was reported by Frank, McLaughlin, and Crusco (1981) who carried out an experiment in which both male and female college students were evaluated for their ability to be empathic after subliminal stimulation in a single session. The participants were given the Test of Implied Meanings (Sundberg, 1966) in which they listened to taped verbal statements for which they had to infer what the speaker "really meant." The students were randomly assigned to two groups, one of which received exposures of MOMMY AND I ARE ONE and the other PEOPLE ARE WALKING. For the male participants there was no evidence that the oneness stimulus affected their empathy, but for the females, in contrast to what Frank et al. had hypothesized, there was *diminished* empathy.

How can one understand the paradoxical findings from these two studies and the results of the many others in which exposure to oneness stimuli led to behavior characterized as "more adaptive?" Frank et al. offered the following explanation. They reasoned that only in their experiment and in Podall's did the task presented to the experimental students possess intrinsic qualities conducive to symbiotic-like oneness fantasies. Frank et al. reasoned that the oneness fantasies activated by the attempt to be either empathic or cooperative, in *combination with* the fantasies stimulated by the oneness message, proved too threatening to the participants. In our terms, the symbiotic-like stimulation provided by the experimental tasks, combined with the oneness stimulus, can be said to have pushed these women beyond the threshold of a safe oneness experience and thereby interfered with the secure sense of self that is a necessary accompaniment of ameliorative oneness fantasies. Consequently, they fled from oneness fantasies and behaved *less* empathically and *less* cooperatively than their control counterparts. Frank et al. also offered an interpretation that is consistent with our consideration of sex-related differences in reactions to oneness stimuli; they submitted that the danger of "too much oneness" was intensified in these studies by the fact that the participants who showed the paradoxical effect were college females, a group for whom symbiotic-like ties pose a particular problem.

Whether or not further studies bear out this explanation, another difference should be noted between the Podall and Frank et al. investigations and those in which exposure to the MOMMY AND I ARE ONE stimulus led to more adaptive behavior. In both of the former studies, the predicted response may not have been "more adaptive" in the minds of the participants. That is, in the other studies, the behavior change that was predicted to be a consequence of the oneness stimulus was a change that the participants were interested in making. The phobics, for example, turned to treatment because they wanted to overcome their phobias; the obese women wished to lose weight; the alcoholics went voluntarily to the Veritas Villa rehabilitation center; the smokers wanted to give up smoking; and the students (we can reasonably assume) desired higher grades. In the Podall and Frank et al. studies there was no equivalent incentive—in fact, the behavior change sought by the experimenters need not at all have been perceived by the participants as being in their interest.

THE IMPORTANCE OF "DOSAGE"

Although there have been a few studies of non-psychotic populations in which the activation of oneness fantasies has produced no effects,[4] none of these has involved "high dosage." Eight studies in which subliminal stimulation was given in three or more weekly sessions all produced positive results and, in most of them, the difference between the experimental and control groups can be characterized as substantial as well as statistically significant (Schurtman, 1978; Ariam, 1979; Palmatier and Bornstein, 1980; Bryant-Tuckett, 1980; Zuckerman, 1980; Parker, 1982; Hobbs, in preparation; Packer, in preparation).

One of these studies investigated the effects of dosage directly. Packer (in preparation) provided behavior assertiveness training accompanied by subliminal stimulation to volunteers who characterized themselves as inhibited in their interactions with others. All experimental and control participants were seen for four sessions a week for three weeks. All the controls received subliminal neutral stimulation in each of the four sessions, but those receiving

MOMMY AND I ARE ONE were divided into two subgroups. One of these received the oneness stimulus for two of the weekly sessions and the neutral control stimulus for the other two; the other subgroup received the oneness stimulus for all four sessions. The latter subgroup showed stronger experimental effects than the former—i.e., they showed a greater increase in their assertive behavior. Considering this finding in conjunction with the results cited above, it would seem reasonable to conclude that the more often and more closely spaced the sessions in which the subliminal oneness stimulus is administered, the more likely it will produce reliable and noteworthy adaptation-enhancing effects.

A Different Way of Stimulating Oneness Fantasies

In the prologue to this chapter, we stated that it might be possible to activate the MOMMY AND I ARE ONE fantasy experimentally without tachistoscopic stimulation. In the vignette presented, the woman claimed that she had done just that by means of self-hypnosis, though whether or not this was indeed the case is open to question. A controlled study would be necessary before one could confidently conclude that this intervention had effectively activated oneness fantasies. While such a study might well be useful, we would give priority to exploring another, very different possibility: symbiotic-like fantasies can be activated by the sound of the human heart. Our expectation here is based on the interesting work of Lee Salk on the positive reaction of infants to the sound of the heartbeat.

Salk described the background of his research in a 1973 article in the *Scientific American:*

Some years ago I was stimulated by a series of random observations on poetry and anatomy to pursue what may seem to be an unlikely project for someone who works in the behavioral sciences. As a psychologist I had learned that the hypothalamus, a small region at the base of the brain, plays an important role in the expression of emotions. Yet in my leisure reading I was repeatedly impressed by the fact that, in referring to the wellspring of deep emotions such as love, poets and lyricists from all periods in history and from all parts of the world consistently chose another part of the anatomy: the heart. References to the heart in connection with the expression of love are of course found not only in poetry, literature and song but also in everyday language: "I love you from the bottom of my heart," "My heart longs for you" and "I am heartbroken". . . .

One day in New York's Central Park Zoo, I reflected that a mother rhesus monkey was holding her new-born infant not close to her hypothalamus but close to her heart. Moreover, in 42 subsequent observations of the same monkey and infant, I found that she had held the newborn on her left side 40 times and on her right side only twice. Could it be, I wondered, that "Close to a mother's heart" is more than just an expression? Could the phrase have a basis in behavior and represent a psychobiological process? A survey of the scientific literature revealed no studies concerned with the problem. I therefore undertook an investigation designed to answer the following question: What does a human mother do when she is presented with her newborn infant?

Of 255 right-handed mothers whom I observed during the first four days after they had given birth,

83 percent held their baby on the left side of their chest or on their left shoulder and 17 percent held the baby on the right side. I also observed 32 left-handed mothers: 78 percent held the baby on the left side and 22 percent on the right. . . .

When the left-handed mothers were asked why they held their baby on the left side, they thought for a moment and replied: "I'm left-handed and can hold my baby better this way." When right-handed mothers were asked why they held their baby on the left side, they replied: "I'm right-handed, and when I hold my baby on the left side it frees my right hand to do other things." It seems unlikely that the right- and left-handed mothers were doing the same thing for different reasons. I felt they were giving me a rationalization for an automatic response that was not related to handedness [p. 24].

Salk accounted for the left-arm preference by reasoning that mothers intuit that in this position the baby can more clearly hear the mother's heartbeat, an experience that apparently has a soothing effect on the infant. A series of additional observations seemed to be consistent with this hypothesis. First, in the great majority of artistic representations (paintings and sculptures) of mothers holding babies, the infant was depicted in the mother's left arm. Here, it was supposed, the artist too sensed the importance of the baby being held in this position.

Second, women carrying things other than babies, both in real life and when artistically represented, were found *not* to favor the use of their left hands. The specificity of the relationship between the left-arm preference and holding babies was viewed by Salk as strengthening the plausibility of his hypothesis.

Third, the left-arm preference for holding babies was

not shown by mothers who were briefly separated from their infants right after birth (as a result of the baby being premature, for example). This was understood as implying that even a brief rift in the mother-infant bond sometimes caused the mother to be less sensitive to the needs of her newly arrived offspring.

Finally, Salk sought a direct test of the hypothesis that the sound of the heartbeat had adaptation-enhancing effects. Two studies were carried out (Salk, 1962), one in a nursery for newborns and the other in a foundling home for older infants (16 to 37 months of age) in which recordings of a heartbeat were played and its effects assessed on indicators of well-being—i.e., the amount of crying, weight gain, and time needed to fall asleep. In both studies there was enhanced well-being (less crying and greater weight gain for the newborns, and less time falling asleep for the older infants) after the heartbeat condition.

A study by Rapaport (1963) offers further support for Salk's thesis. Working as a pediatric resident on a ward of childhood schizophrenics in Bellevue Hospital, Rapaport took measurements of pulse rate, blood pressure, and respiration rate for a group of 14 of these patients, both when they were exposed to the heartbeat sound and when they were not. She reported that on all three measures their physiological functioning was closer to normal under the heartbeat condition.

Salk attributed the ameliorative effect of the heartbeat sound to the "imprinting" of the sound during the prenatal period. But another possibility is that the sound stimulates tactile, olfactory, and other sensations associated with the *postnatal* experience of being held against the mother's body, which in turn activates oneness fantasies. Whether or not Salk's explanation, ours, or both turn out to be valid, it seems safe to say that the ameliorative effect of the heartbeat sound for infants and children can be attributed to the activation of sensations that are related to the imagery stimulated in adults by the subliminal registration of MOMMY AND I ARE ONE.

THE HEARTBEAT, BAROQUE MUSIC, AND SUPERLEARNING

Is there any evidence to indicate that the heartbeat sound has the same adaptation-enhancing effect on *adults* that the MOMMY AND I ARE ONE stimulus has been found to have? We believe there is. It has been suggested that in music, or at least in certain forms of music, approximations of a heartbeat sound are hidden or, if you will, subliminally embedded. That the enjoyment of music is rooted in part in unconscious associations to the heartbeat has been suggested by Salk (1973):

> Consider the rhythm of music in societies throughout the world. From the most primitive tribal drumbeats to the symphonies of Mozart and Beethoven, there is a startling similarity to the rhythm of the human heart. The more primitive the culture, the more closely the musical form approximates the actual sound of the heart. In short, the maternal heartbeat . . . occupies a place of primacy and constancy, and may be associated with a feeling of well-being. This . . . may have a place in explaining, from a psychobiological point of view, the universal appeal of music [pp. 28-29].

What Salk posited for music generally, others have suggested is specifically the case for Baroque music. Many years ago, one of us noted that "a group [of people in the music field], mostly teachers, critics, a few isolated performers, and even some laymen [have maintained] that the beat of all Baroque music is that of the human pulse" (Lachmann, 1950, p. 40). Thus, it is of interest to note that the playing of Baroque background music is a key element in an educational method developed by Georgi Lozanov of Bulgaria. Widely used both in that country and elsewhere in Europe, the method is designed to bring about what its adherents in the United States have referred to as "Superlearning" (Ostrander, Schroeder, and Ostrander, 1979). According to a series of research reports published both here and abroad, the method strikingly increases learning ability.

We think it not far-fetched to suppose that at least one mediator of this enhanced learning is the inadvertent activation of oneness fantasies. A number of components of the Superlearning approach can be viewed as activators of these fantasies, including the recommended accompanying music. (Teacher and student recite material in unison and the teacher assumes an all-accepting, uncritical stance—displaying, that is, characteristics of the "good symbiotic mother.") In describing the music Ostrander, Schroeder, and Ostrander write:

> In the slow movements, we find again that familiar, and it seems, potent rhythm—60 beats a minute. This Baroque music often has a very slow bass, beating like a slow human pulse [1979, p. 74].

Linking such music to the heartbeat thus allows for the supposition that the activation of oneness fantasies is also involved in Superlearning, and that this activation is the common denominator bridging Lozanov's method and another learning aid, the subliminal activation of oneness fantasies used by Parker, Ariam, Zuckerman, and Bryant-Tuckett in the studies described earlier.

It is also of interest to note that whereas for most of the Superlearning session it is recommended that the Baroque music be slow (could the recommended 60 beats per minute—rather than the more typical 72 beats of the human heart—be that of the relaxed and blissfully spent mother holding her infant after nursing?), it is advised that at the end of a learning session there be a flourish of faster (allegro) movements. While for the Superlearning advocates this simply "allows one to come out of the reverie state in a pleasant way" (p. 75), it seems possible from our perspective that the faster music stimulates that sense of self without which oneness fantasies cannot enhance adaptation.

NOTES

1. In this variant, the relaxation procedure that is typically part of the systematic desensitization method was omitted and the tachistoscopic procedure, as described above, was substituted for it.

2. The most compelling additional data comes from the studies of Bronstein (1976) and Kaye (1975) cited in Chapter 3. When these researchers used messages that were structurally very similar to MOMMY AND I ARE ONE (e.g., DADDY AND I ARE ONE and MOMMY AND I ARE ALIKE), there were no experimental effects. Moreover, anyone arguing for this alternative explanation would be hard pressed to explain why the structure or configuration of the MOMMY AND I ARE ONE message would have an ameliorative effect on differentiated schizophrenics but not undifferentiated schizophrenics or, for that matter, why these non-content aspects should lead to adaptation-enhancing effects at all.

3. In almost 30 studies involving male participants completed to date, all but four (Loveland, 1977; Silverman, Ross, Adler, and Lustig, 1978; Silverstein, 1978; Frank, McLaughlin, and Crusco, 1981) reported adaptive behavior after the MOMMY AND I ARE ONE condition. Moreover, for each of the exceptions there were mitigating circumstances. Loveland's (1977) study was discussed in Chapter 4 where it was noted that there

was reason to believe that the word "Mommy" in the stimulus message was not appropriate for the particular population—Southerners. In the study by Frank et al. (1981) (see pp. 114-116, where it is discussed in another context), there is reason to believe that the participants may not have been motivated to change their behavior in the way the experimenters anticipated. (See Silverman [1982a] for a discussion of the relevance of motivation in subliminal psychodynamic activation experiments.) In the other two studies, the MOMMY AND I ARE ONE stimulus and other stimuli were given to college men in dart-throwing contests that were part of research undertaken to test as a major hypothesis the proposition that competitive behavior would be responsive to stimuli designed to activate oedipal fantasies. The oedipal-related stimuli affected dart-throwing performance—e.g., messages intended to sanction oedipal wishes, DEFEATING DAD IS OKAY and WINNING MOM IS OKAY, improved performance—while the MOMMY AND I ARE ONE stimulus had no effect. These results suggest that different types of behavior are responsive to different adaptation-enhancing unconscious fantasies and that oedipal-sanction fantasies are more relevant to competitive situations than symbiotic-like fantasies.

4. See Silverman (1982b, c) for a discussion of these studies. For a comprehensive report of investigations of all kinds using the subliminal psychodynamic activation method (not just those activating oneness fantasies), see Silverman (1982a). There it will be seen that in laboratories independent of those in which the method was developed the ratio of studies supporting vs. those not supporting the phenomenon of subliminal psychodynamic activation has been better than three to one.

6

Unresolved Issues, Current Concerns, and Future Directions

Our major experimental finding—that the activation of unconscious oneness fantasies can have adaptation-enhancing effects—has, over the years, prompted the following thoughtful questions from colleagues: (1) What gives oneness fantasies their adaptation-enhancing power? (2) Doesn't our experimental finding contradict the traditional view that psychological separateness is a developmental achievement necessary for healthy adult functioning? (3) Aren't there instances in which oneness fantasies interfere with, rather than enhance, adaptation? (4) What kinds of people are most likely to benefit from the activation of these fantasies? (5) What drawbacks, if any, accompany the positive effects of activated oneness fantasies? (6) How do oneness fantasies arise?

Although we have touched on most of these questions in the preceding chapters, we shall now treat each of them more systematically by way of restating and supplementing the principal conclusions of our research. Such consideration will further permit us to note certain issues that remain unresolved and to point the way to future research that could address these issues in a fruitful way.

What gives oneness fantasies their adaptation-enhancing power? Or as this question was once more concretely asked, What psychological needs are satisfied by these fantasies? From reports in the psychoanalytic literature and our own clinical observations, the following need satisfactions can be considered. (Some of these have already been noted in our discussion of schizophrenia in Chapter 3.) (1) Fulfillment of wishes for oral gratification and nurturance. Based on the model of the fetus in utero (see Savitt, 1963), a fantasy of oneness may imply a constant flow of supplies that are independent of mother's whims and desires. (2) External dangers can be fended off. A fantasy of oneness may imply protective envelopment and imperviousness to threats from the environment. (3) Object loss need not be feared. In a fantasy of oneness with the "good mother," even temporary separations may be "avoided." (4) Narcissistic equilibrium can be restored. In a fantasy of oneness, self-representations that are defective, hazy, unstable, or negatively toned may be remedied (see Kohut, 1971; Stolorow and Lachmann, 1980). (5) Impairments in thinking, impulse control, judgment, and other ego functions may be rectified. That is, a oneness fantasy may allow for a "borrowing" of strength to remedy these impairments (see Jacobson, 1967; Burnham, Gladstone, and Gibson, 1969). (6) Destructive impulses toward mother may be warded off (see Searles, 1951). The satisfactions that mother is "providing" in such a fantasy may undercut the motivation to hurt or destroy her. (7) Guilt in relation to mother for previous real and imagined hurts inflicted upon her may be dissipated. It is interesting to note that the derivation of the word *atonement* is "at one with" (Thass-Thienemann, 1967, p. 29). Implied here is the idea that if you feel at one with someone you can thereby atone for your aggressive acts and fantasies toward that person. (8) On a higher developmental level the fantasy may either secretly express oedipal wishes or defend against them (see Angel, 1967; the later discussion in this chapter, pp. 132-133, and Chapters 7 and 8).

A further question to be asked is whether the adaptation-enhancing effects of oneness fantasies are due to one particular need that these fantasies satisfy—a satisfaction that is universally crucial for a state of well-being. Or is the ameliorative impact of these fantasies due to their ability to serve different needs for different persons? Or is it that for any given person they serve a confluence of needs?

In Chapter 4 we described a study by Kaplan (1976) who tested the relevance of three of the needs listed above for pathology reduction in a group of schizophrenic patients. She found that the messages MOMMY FEEDS ME WELL ("providing" oral gratification), MOMMY IS ALWAYS WITH ME (which discounts the possibility of her loss), and I CANNOT HURT MOMMY (which discounts impulses to hurt or destroy her) did not have the pathology-reducing impact that MOMMY AND I ARE ONE had. As Kaplan concluded, this could mean either that oneness fantasies are ameliorative for schizophrenic patients because they satisfy some need that was not included among those she tested or because they are able to satisfy more than one need.

In order to test the first possibility, future subliminal psychodynamic activation experiments should be carried out in which messages related to the other need satisfactions are presented to schizophrenic patients. (The same kind of experiments should be conducted with other groups as well, since it is quite possible that there will be different answers to the question under consideration for different groups.) If the introduction of these specific need-related stimuli continues to yield negative results while the MOMMY AND I ARE ONE stimulus continues to elicit positive findings, the second and third possibilities—that oneness fantasies serve different needs for different people or a confluence of needs for any one person—should be addressed. For now, we can only say that current research data do not allow us to choose among the possible answers to the question "From what do oneness fantasies derive their ameliorative power?"

Doesn't the idea that the activation of oneness fantasies furthers adaptation contradict the generally accepted view that the experience of psychological separateness is a developmental achievement necessary for healthy adult functioning? In a word, no! We say this for two reasons. First, one can view the attainment of separateness as a goal to be reached, and yet see the attainment of symbiotic-like oneness as a means to that goal. In the words of Rose (1972) whom we cited in Chapter 1, "To merge in order to re-emerge may be part of the fundamental process of psychological growth" (p. 185). This maxim, it will be remembered, parallels the formulation of Mahler, Pine, and Bergman (1975) that, during infancy, optimal symbiotic experiences are necessary if the child is ultimately to attain a state of separateness.

A second reason for our unequivocal "no" is that the question assumes that oneness gratifications and psychological separateness are mutually exclusive. We believe that both can be sought simultaneously, or at least consecutively, and that the measure of psychological development is the degree to which the individual can tolerate the conflict between the two needs, or, put another way, the degree to which the individual can experience oneness gratifications without experiencing a threat to his or her sense of self. It would follow from this view that the more secure the individual's sense of self, the more he or she can safely experience oneness gratifications. Thus, our formulation is consistent with the generally accepted notion that psychological separateness is necessary for healthy adult functioning, at the same time as it acknowledges the fundamental relationship between oneness and separateness that Rose suggests above. In effect, we are saying that for the *ideally* healthy adult there is *no* contradiction between wanting oneness and wanting separateness; so secure is his or her sense of psychological separateness that oneness gratifications not only cannot threaten the sense of self but, in a process largely unknown to us, actually deepen it. Contrast this situation with that of the schizophrenic children Bettelheim (1972) refers to below. In describing their frequent fantasies about kangaroos, Bettelheim states:

> What they feel they missed out on was . . . the total protection and indulgence after birth that they think the marsupial baby enjoys in the mother's pouch. . . . This is even more attractive because it combines a measure of independence with the always available security of the pouch. The psychotic child wants to venture about in his leisure but is too fearful unless he knows that the protective walls of his defenses will not be closed to him because of it [p. 189].

Giovacchini (1972) describes an analogous dilemma in a description of an adult schizophrenic:

> He was ambivalent; he wanted to feel autonomous and yet separated from me but such independence was frightening. In many fantasies he questioned whether he could survive without my onmipotent support. [But] symbiotic fusion also meant annihilation of his psychic existence as an individual entity and he experienced this as terror. Consequently, he was faced with the unbearable conflict over independent identity in the context of magical fusion [p. 144].

But as the following quote from Ekstein and Caruth (1972) suggests, this dilemma exists more generally. In discussing children's ambivalence about keeping secrets, they write:

> For we are describing here the [paradox] of the human condition, which is to seek constantly for the object with and through which one regresses and restores oneself, while also seeking . . . independence from the object apart from whom one can and must progress and fulfill oneself [p. 201].

Implicit in these passages is the issue that the next question addresses.

Aren't there instances in which oneness fantasies interfere with rather than enhance adaptation? From both our clinical experience and the research data, our answer would be that whereas such instances occur infrequently, they do occur. And as we proposed earlier, this is most apt to happen when the fantasy of oneness threatens the individual with the loss of the sense of self.

A second type of circumstance that can make a oneness fantasy threatening is one in which the fantasy has some forbidden connotation, as in the following two instances.

In one of the studies of the effects of subliminal oneness stimulation on weight loss, a woman in the group that had received the MOMMY AND I ARE ONE stimulus gained weight during the treatment period rather than lost weight (in contrast to the great majority of women in her group). As a result of examining some projective test material that she had produced at the beginning of the study, and material that had emerged from a debriefing interview at the study's completion, the following understanding emerged to account for her paradoxical reaction. The woman's entry into the study had occurred at a time in her life when a longstanding conflict had been revived. A few years earlier, her younger brother had died in a swimming accident and just at the time she had entered the study a negligence suit against the owners of the pool at which the accident had occurred was about to come to trial. From the material she produced, it could be inferred that intense guilt over hidden hostile wishes toward her brother had been activated first at his death and then at the time of the impending trial. It was as if she had felt that it would be out of the question for her to harbor a symbiotic-like oneness fantasy at that time, with its implication of exclusive possession of the mother. In her mind, she would be capitalizing on her brother's death, feeling that her hostile wishes had borne fruit, that he was out of the way, and that mother was exclusively hers. Thus, we inferred that she had warded off oneness fantasies, with weight gain rather than weight loss apparently the consequence.

Our second example involves a young man who was in the MOMMY AND I ARE ONE group in one of the classroom studies we have described. He was the only student in this group whose marks got progressively worse rather than better as the term progressed. When he was debriefed at the end of the experiment, and told what message he had been receiving, he responded in a way that nobody else did. "God," he exclaimed, "that's the last thing in the world I need—my problem has always been that she has been too much involved with me." He then went on to describe his mother's seductiveness, which he said had become intolerable when his parents had divorced and he had lived alone with her. "She treated me more like a lover than a son and I've been trying to get out of her clutches ever since." From this, it seemed possible that MOMMY AND I ARE ONE had incestuous meaning for this student, evoked guilt, and led to a rejection of the fantasy, with consequent maladaptive effects on his school performance.

What kinds of people are most apt to benefit when oneness fantasies are activated? It is not enough here to state the converse of our previous response: that those people benefit for whom oneness fantasies do *not* threaten the sense of self and for whom these fantasies do *not* have forbidden connotations. In each of the research studies cited in which there were significant group effects, there were some participants (anywhere from 10 percent to 60 percent) who seemed to have been unaffected by subliminal oneness stimulation and yet did not belong, at least according to our evidence, to either of the two categories just referred to. Thus, for them it seemed more likely that, rather than being threatened by these fantasies, the fantasies simply had little or no unconscious significance.

Thus, the question needs to be asked: For which people are these fantasies significant? As Chapters 4 and 5 have revealed, subliminal oneness stimulation has had adaptation-enhancing effects with a very wide range of groups—from schizophrenics to non-psychotic clinical groups to non-clinical groups of college students. It thus seems likely that these fantasies can be significant to people at very different developmental levels. But just who, at each level, is responsive to this stimulation is still by and large to be determined.

In future investigations of this question, we think it would be useful to explore different psychological relationships for persons on higher and lower developmental levels. For those more developmentally advanced, it would be fruitful to investigate whether positive reactions to the oneness stimulation correlate with degree of active oedipal conflict. In-depth clinical interviews and projective tests could be used to assess the extent to which conflict over oedipal wishes is in evidence, and, in addition, might allow for inferences as to what the relationship is between such conflict and oneness fantasies. Possibilities to consider would include: (1) that oneness fantasies ward off oedipal wishes; (2) that oneness fantasies create a sense of safety and protection so that modulated oedipal gratifications can be sought with diminished guilt and anxiety; and (3) that oneness fantasies themselves serve as a disguised fulfillment of oedipal wishes.

For those less developmentally advanced, we think it would be promising to assess the degree to which adaptation-enhancing responses to subliminal oneness stimulation correlate with the seeking of gratification for the first seven needs listed under the initial question discussed above (need for nurturance, to avoid object loss, to restore narcissistic equilibrium, etc.). Clinical interviews and psychological tests would also allow for these kinds of assessments.

What drawbacks accompany the alleviation of psychopathology or any other enhancement of adaptation that results from the activation of oneness fantasies? This question can be broken into the following subordinate questions: (1) Will the positive changes occur "at a price"—that is, be accompanied by the emergence of new pathology substituting for the old? (2) Will the positive changes be fragile—short-lived and easily vulnerable to reversal?

In answering these questions, one should resist the temptation to draw conclusions based on theoretical inference and turn instead to the relevant observational data. In the experimental studies that have been carried out with the MOMMY AND I ARE ONE stimulus, all the data obtained bearing on these two questions argue for a "no" answer to both. But we hasten to add that the amount of relevant data is modest so that the largest part of the task in addressing these questions empirically lies ahead of us.

With regard to the first question, the following data are

relevant. In four of the subliminal psychodynamic activation studies in which the subjects who received the oneness stimulus showed greater improvement on the targeted behavior, other behaviors also were assessed. Thus these studies have a bearing on whether the positive effects of activating oneness fantasies are balanced by negative changes. Parker (1977), in his study of college students, and Silverman, Martin, Ungaro, and Mendelsohn (1978), investigating weight loss in obese women, assessed their subjects for the emergence of new symptoms through the administration of an extensive symptom checklist. Both found that the positive changes brought about by the oneness stimulation were *not* accompanied by new symptoms. Schurtman (1978), in his investigation of alcoholics, and Bryant-Tuckett (1980), in her study of adolescent behavior disorders at a residential treatment center, found that the improvements they obtained for the oneness condition (in Schurtman's study, increased involvement in AA-type counseling and in Bryant-Tuckett's, marked improvement in reading scores) were accompanied by other positive changes in other variables assessed. Thus Schurtman found that at the same time as the alcoholics who had received the oneness stimulus became more involved in their counseling, they also showed enhanced self-esteem. And Bryant-Tuckett's adolescents who received the oneness stimulus manifested a number of positive changes in addition to improved reading, including an enhanced ability to work more independently in the classroom. We make a point of singling out Bryant-Tuckett's finding because it addresses a specific question that is sometimes asked as part of the more general question under discussion. If oneness fantasies are activated, won't the person respond to the symbiotic-like gratification by regressing to a state of symbiotic-like dependence? The Bryant-Tuckett finding suggests, to the contrary, that the activation of unconscious fantasies of having attained a state of oneness allowed her adolescents to give up to some degree their symbiotic-like inclinations and behave in a more independent manner.

Let us turn now to the second subordinate question: Will changes brought about by activating oneness fantasies be short-lived? Here, too, the available data suggest a negative response. In six studies (Martin, 1975; Silverman, Levinson, Mendelsohn, and Ungaro, 1975; Schurtman, 1978; Silverman, Martin, Ungaro, and Mendelsohn, 1978; Palmatier and Bornstein, 1980; Parker, 1982) follow-up data were available, and in all instances the positive effects of the subliminal oneness stimulation could be observed at least as well at the follow-up evaluation as it had been observed immediately after the study ended. It should be noted, though, that the longest follow-up in any of these studies was six months so that one cannot speak at this time of long-range positive effects.

Thus, there are some data currently available that argue against pathology substitution and the fragility of positive changes, but more data are badly needed. To return to the first question, the data sought should bear not only on the emergence of new symptoms, but on character change as well. This point deserves underscoring. Researchers who have sought to determine whether positive changes brought about by a therapy occur at a price, typically have only looked for new symptoms. An evaluation of character change must be viewed as equally relevant, and only if no evidence can be found for the emergence of maladaptive character change, would one feel comfortable concluding that no price has been paid for the amelioration. And for both new symptoms and character change, evaluations should be made at various follow-up points as well as immediately after the study has ended.

For both subordinate questions that have been asked, the data to be collected should come from patients with diverse symptoms who vary in degree of pathology and level of development. The large number of needs that have been proposed as being served by oneness fantasies suggests that the answers to these questions may well be different for different kinds of people.

How do oneness fantasies arise? One possible answer is that these fantasies are rooted in memory traces from the symbiotic phase of development. But since the symbiotic phase is postulated as occurring between one and six months of age, can a verbal stimulus "contact" experiences from these preverbal times? Schur (1966) has suggested a link between preverbal memories and later language development. After citing an early speculation of Freud in the Wolf Man case, the writings of some academic psychologists, and a compelling personal observation, Schur concluded: "Any registered and stored [sensory] impression can at any time combine partly or wholly with [later learned verbal] impressions" (p. 478). It would be consistent with this conclusion to infer that the MOMMY AND I ARE ONE stimulus evoked oneness fantasies that were originally nonverbal.

A second and related possibility is that the oneness stimulus makes contact with symbiosis-related memory traces that come from a later time during infancy, after language has been acquired. As we noted in Chapter 3, although symbiotic-like oneness experiences are believed to originate during the symbiotic phase, they are understood as present during later phases as well. (As development proceeds, of course, these experiences are understood as occurring less and less frequently and are accompanied more and more by a sense of psychological separateness.)

A third possibility is related to the point made in Chapters 4 and 5 that oneness fantasies may involve either the post-symbiotic (perhaps oedipal) mother or some other figure ("Daddy," "my girl," "my lover," "my prof") who is not unconsciously linked with the symbiotic mother. Thus, the oneness stimulation may have stirred memory traces unrelated to symbiotic-like gratifications.

Finally, it is possible that oneness fantasies are not rooted in memory traces at all. Rather, they may be purely psychological constructions serving wish-fulfilling or defensive needs (just as activated memory traces may serve wish-fulfilling or defensive needs).

It would not be easy to decide among these alternatives, even for a particular clinical or non-clinical group. (It is possible that the answer to the question will not be the same for different groups or even for different members of the same group.) Eliciting associations from research participants to the object of the oneness fantasy that the stimulus is attempting to activate ("Mommy," "Daddy," "my girl," etc.) may shed some light on the developmental period in which either the memory traces or the fantasy constructions are rooted.

We are also considering another approach that might yield data on whether memory traces are involved. Beebe and Stern (1977) have conducted a series of studies in which they videotaped mother-infant interactions. Among their interesting observations was that infants, at different ages, manifest characteristic body movements and facial expressions when their mothers are "in tune" with them. In discussing this finding with one of the authors (Beebe, personal communication), it seemed feasible to us to investigate whether remnants of any of these early patterns could be observed in adults exposed to subliminal oneness stimuli. The study under consideration would call for the videotaping of behavior segments of an experimental and control group after prolonged exposure to MOMMY AND

I ARE ONE and a neutral message. This material would then be scrutinized and evaluated by a trained observer. Without knowledge of group membership, the observer would make judgments as to whether any such remnants can be identified, and if so, would then estimate the age period during infancy with which the facial expressions and/or body movements are likely to be associated. Whereas negative findings in a study such as this would hardly rule out the possibility that activated oneness fantasies make contact with early memories, positive findings would compellingly argue for such an inference and would further allow for a judgment of the period during infancy that is reawakened when the MOMMY AND I ARE ONE stimulus is subliminally exposed.

SOME UNREASONED REACTIONS

Both at professional meetings and on informal occasions we have had many opportunities to present to colleagues our search for oneness thesis and the supporting experimental and clinical evidence. What has been the response? From some there has been an immediate, seemingly intuitive resonance with the thesis and the offering of associations that the colleague believed were in keeping with it. (See Chapter 1.) From a larger group, there has been interest mixed with skepticism, but a willingness to listen carefully to the details, followed by searching questions such as those that we have just addressed, alerting us to conceptual ambiguities and unresolved empirical issues. But from still others there have been unreasoned responses that we have found troubling, coming as they did from persons whose professional commitment to openness and objectivity should be unquestioned.

If the unreasoned responses simply represented momentary emotional reactions from which the critics then took distance, so as to be able to evaluate the supporting data objectively, they would not be of concern. In fact, such an affective reaction to subliminal phenomena of any kind is both widespread and understandable. When a person is told that someone's behavior has been influenced by what appear to be mere flickers of light, a sense of disbelief is bound to arise. And if it is difficult to accept conventional subliminal effects—in which aspects or derivatives of a stimulus of which a person is unaware emerge in associations or images (see Dixon [1971] for a comprehensive and scholarly review of "conventional subliminal effects")—how much more difficult it is to accept the idea that, under certain circumstances, the stimulus can affect adaptive functioning. An image of a "1984" society can easily be conjured up. Indeed, recent reports of commercial and crass uses of subliminal messages (soon to be detailed) can make such images seem like more than idle fantasy.

But in the instances to which we have just referred, considerably more than a momentary affective reaction of disbelief was involved. Rather, both data and thesis were dismissed out of hand, often with irritation.

How can one understand such reactions? For some, the well-known discomfort with the role of unconscious motivation may be decisive. Data from subliminal psychodynamic activation experiments contradict the view that unconscious motivation was the invention (rather than the discovery) of Freud. For others, discomfort with the specific thesis may be involved. As we noted earlier (Chapter 3), the thesis that oneness fantasies can be ameliorative, while consistent with the views of some clinicians, is contrary to the views of others. As Arthur Shapiro has concluded (personal communication) from his study of physicians' attitudes toward double-blind studies in medicine, it is not easy for clinicians to give credence to research findings, no matter how well-controlled the study, if they run counter to assumptions that have governed their clinical work. In clinical psychology, psychiatry, and psychoanalysis, this is even more true than in medicine, since in the former there has been no tradition of viewing experimental laboratory data as potentially helpful in addressing problems with which the clinician is confronted.

OTHER CONCERNS

Commercial exploitation of subliminal stimulation in general and subliminal oneness stimulation in particular can pose a significant problem for future research. There have been two books written recently (Key, 1973, 1976) about the use of subliminal stimulation in television and magazine advertising. Articles have appeared in periodicals about auditory subliminal messages being used to deter theft in department stores, increase the productivity of salesmen, and influence voters.[1] Whether or not these reports are exaggerated (as some have claimed) and apart from whether subliminal stimulation can be effectively used for these purposes (which can be questioned),[2] there can be no doubt but that many people are becoming justifiably uneasy. (The American Civil Liberties Union has recently added its voice to the protest against these practices.)[3] All of this concern is, of course, understandable, given that people are being exposed to subliminal stimuli without their consent, without knowledge of the nature of the stimuli, and without the opportunity to reverse possible side effects and paradoxical reactions, to say nothing of the inherent unethicality of at least some of the uses to which subliminal stimulation is being put. And as far as subliminal *oneness* stimulation is concerned, it does not require much imagination to envision commercial "clinics" offering, without the necessary safeguards, treatments for obesity, alcoholism, or cigarette addiction involving the techniques described in this book or in earlier journal articles.

All of this can pose dangers not only to the public, but also to those who wish to pursue the scientific study of subliminal oneness stimulation in particular and subliminal psychodynamic activation more generally. Grant-giving agencies can become uneasy funding such work and overzealous legisators may feel impelled to pass omnibus laws that throw out the baby with the bath water.

Even within university and hospital settings, the use of subliminal oneness stimulation, particularly when it is used as a treatment and educational aid, raises ethical and quasi-ethical questions which, if not addressed, can turn many against the procedure. These questions relate to matters of informed consent and the manipulation of behavior. They have been discussed at length elsewhere (Silverman, 1977), but for now we should only like to point out the following. We have been able to proceed in good conscience, meet the requirements of human-subjects committees, and meet the needs of the research participants themselves by instituting the following safeguards: (1) Participants are informed beforehand that they will be receiving subliminal stimulation, and briefed on the purpose which this is intended to serve; (2) they are debriefed after their participation as to the stimulus received and the rationale for its use; (3) the investigator is alert to indications of paradoxical reactions or side effects (which perhaps have occurred one percent of the time) and is prepared to take remedial measures when they are in evidence.

In the future, it might even be possible to inform the

participants beforehand of the stimuli they will be receiving when subliminal oneness stimulation is used as a therapeutic or educational aid. That is, whereas we know that when the stimuli are presented supraliminally, they do not have adaptation-enhancing effects (Silverman and Candell, 1970; Silverman and Grabowski, 1982), it may be that subliminal presentation either preceded or followed by information about the stimulus would not mute the potency of the oneness stimulus. (We are reminded here of Freud's [1915] comment about "the possibility that an idea may exist simultaneously in two places in the mental apparatus" [p. 175]). If this turns out to be the case (and studies testing this are being planned), it would not only permit complete disclosure of all aspects of the procedure before the person participates, but open up the possibility that the effectiveness of activating unconscious oneness fantasies would be enhanced by conscious mental processes. That is, as the person notes the adaptation-enhancing effects that the subliminal oneness stimulus is having, he or she will have the opportunity to reflect on why this is happening —particularly if the interventionist explains the rationale for the stimulus as well as revealing its content—and thus be able to broaden the scope of his or her self-knowledge.

FURTHER STUDIES OF SUBLIMINAL ONENESS STIMULATION AS A THERAPEUTIC AND EDUCATIONAL AID

It would seem eminently worthwhile to pursue further the potential of subliminal psychodynamic activation for fostering adaptive behavior. Obvious possibilities would be to investigate the effects of oneness stimulation on other treatment and educational modalities and to explore the effects on these modalities of activating other (non-oneness) unconscious fantasies which there is reason to believe may be adaptation-enhancing.

Another possibility would be to seek to strengthen and make more durable the effects of the subliminal oneness stimulation. It might be fruitful to investigate the impact of this stimulation in conjunction with either the heartbeat sound or Baroque music with its heartbeat-like cadence (see Chapter 5). Whereas the adaptation-enhancing effects of the two kinds of interventions may not be additive (and conceivably might even interfere with each other), we think it more likely that they will prove to be mutually enhancing. We base this expectation on the assumptions (thus far untested) that therapeutic interventions will be more effective if they are "received" by two sense modalities rather than one and if they result in both the left and right hemispheres of the brain being stimulated. Since the MOMMY AND I ARE ONE verbal message can be assumed to be processed predominantly in the left hemisphere and the heartbeat sound in the right, the combined use of both interventions would seem to fulfill this second assumption.

Another possibility would be to increase dosage. As was discussed in Chapter 5, there is now good reason to believe that the greater the number of weekly sessions, the more effective will be the subliminal activation of oneness fantasies. Since four or five sessions have produced stronger and more reliable effects than one or two, would six or seven sessions be even more effective? And what if the amount of subliminal stimulation at any one session was increased? Would this increase effectiveness or would it have the opposite effect? Could it induce too much merging of self- and object representations and thus violate the proviso that activations of oneness fantasies should not threaten the sense of self if they are to have positive consequences? Perhaps combining heavy doses of subliminal

oneness stimulation with another intervention that rein-
forces sense of self, as proved successful in the treatment
study of schizophrenics reported earlier (Chapter 4, pp.
91-92), would produce the best results.

Another fruitful avenue to explore with respect to increasing the effectiveness of subliminal oneness stimulation would be one in which we took individual differences
into account in the choice of adaptation-enhancing stimuli.
In the research completed to date, little effort has been
made to identify personality characteristics that have a
bearing on whether a person will be positively affected by
MOMMY AND I ARE ONE, or to find other stimuli that
can enhance adaptation in those for whom the standard
stimulus is not effective.[4] Recent writings by Blatt and Wild
(1976) and Pine (1979) call attention to personality dimensions related to symbiosis-related needs that may well
be useful in pursuing such an inquiry. The next section
considers this possible approach in some detail.

UNUSUAL REACTIONS TO CONTROL STIMULI: RESEARCH IMPLICATIONS

Just as in some instances the oneness stimulus appears
to have produced unanticipated effects, in others the control stimuli seemed to trigger unexpected reactions. This
is understandable given the fact that people can have idiosyncratic associations to any stimulus. In contrast to drug
studies, in which the placebo substance will be biochemi-
cally inert for all who ingest it, there are no words or
pictures that can be assumed to be without significant psychological impact for everyone. Consider the following
three examples, the first amusing, the second and third
not so.

A woman in the control group in one of the weight loss

studies came in for a session with a look of pleasure on her face. "I don't know what message you've been showing me," she announced, "but whatever it is, it certainly has raised my activity level. I was never interested in walking before, but since I started getting those flashes, it becomes, at times, an uncontrollable urge. Just this morning I decided to walk from my home [in Queens] to the hospital [in Manhattan]." Of course, one cannot be certain, but it seems more likely than not that her newly found interest was related to the "neutral" message that she was receiving: PEOPLE ARE WALKING.

The more sobering examples involve study participants whose personal histories caused reactions to a control stimulus that were anything but neutral. In one of these, a woman in the control group of another weight loss study received the message PEOPLE ARE WALKING. This woman came for three sessions and then precipitously withdrew from the study. When contacted and asked about her withdrawal, she replied that for some reason, unknown to her, the initial sessions had been upsetting. As is our general practice when a research participant withdraws, she was "debriefed," and informed of the message that she had received. Shortly afterward, she wrote a letter in which she attributed her withdrawal to the stimulus she had been exposed to:

> [The information you conveyed about the] subliminal message I received, PEOPLE ARE WALKING . . . is of great interest to me because of my childhood history of forced walks in the snow. . . . I am enclosing a story written around those episodes in my childhood entitled . . . *Autobiography of a Nine Year Old.*

The story she sent was a touching account of a little girl's struggle to survive psychologically in a home with a hateful and sadistic father. It was he who had often sent her walking in the snow as a punishment. The woman's linking of her anxiety-laden flight from the study with these childhood occurrences was particularly convincing given one other point that she made in her letter. She noted that the idea to withdraw occurred to her just before her fourth session when it had snowed and she had contemplated walking from her home to New York University where her appointment was.

The second episode is more complex than the first and is reported at greater length.[5] Although it did not occur in an experiment in which oneness fantasies were being investigated, it has clear implications for such experiments.

A 19-year-old man—a nursing assistant at a hospital—was serving as a research volunteer in a subliminal psychodynamic activation study of the effects of activating aggressive fantasies in a non-clinical population. He was exposed to subliminal stimuli on four different occasions (a different one for each occasion) and then asked to respond to inkblots in an abbreviated Rorschach Test.

After the fourth set of subliminal exposures, the man's Rorschach responses changed dramatically. On each of the cards he was shown he responded with unmistakable expressions of depressive feelings. On two cards he saw "the faces of sad men," on another "a man crying," on a fourth "a drowning person going down," and to a fifth he said, "This gives me the feeling of sadness; I don't know why but that's the feeling I get." On none of the other three Rorschach series did he respond in this way, nor did any other participant in either this experiment or in others that were carried out with the same inkblots react in this fashion. Something unique was experienced by this man right after the fourth picture was put into the tachistoscope for subliminal presentation.

What was the stimulus that triggered this unusual reaction? It was the control stimulus—a photograph of a man with his arm over his head. Why should the four-millisecond exposure of this picture be followed by a flood of depressive images, as it was for this young man? Two pieces of information helped us arrive at an answer to this question.

The first emerged when at the end of the experiment each of the pictures that he had been exposed to subliminally was shown to him at longer and longer exposures until he could accurately describe it. In his response to the picture in question, this participant's reaction was different from all the other participants in the experiment in two respects. First, he misperceived the man in the picture as a woman. And second, he described the person as "waving farewell or goodby," while all the other participants interpreted the arm waving as someone "gesturing hello," "dancing," or "leading a band."

The importance of this for understanding his depressive responses during the subliminal part of the experiment can only be appreciated in the context of the second piece of information that emerged. This he offered after the experiment was over when he approached the experimenter and mistakenly assumed that he was one of the hospital treatment personnel. "Doc," he said, "I have a problem that you might be able to help me with." He then proceeded to describe how he had no control over the muscles in and around his left eye. He said that he could not close this eye while the other eye was open and that someone had commented to him that when the rest of his face was showing emotion, this area was immobile. In his own words, "part of my face is dead." He stated that he had developed this condition three years earlier and was told by a physician that it would disappear within six months. Why, he wanted to know, was it still present?

Then he made the following revealing comment. "It all began shortly after my mother died. You know, it was a funny thing. At her funeral I couldn't cry. In fact, I have never been able to cry over her death and it's been three years now." He went on to explain that what had made his reaction particularly strange was that he had always felt close to his mother, and what's more, he had always been someone who cried a great deal. Further discussion revealed that the young man was psychologically unsophisticated, and had not considered any possible substantive relationship between his inability to mourn for his mother and his symptom. The description of the two as related was simply, in his mind, a report of contiguous events. To someone more sophisticated, however, a psychological connection strongly suggested itself. His somatic symptom most likely reflected both the blocking of an urge to cry and an identification with his mother, in that part of his face was "dead," just as she was.

With the additional information, it was not difficult to reconstruct what occurred when he gave the string of depressive responses in the fourth Rorschach series. The subliminal registration of the picture of someone waving set off a stream of unconscious associations that ended in thoughts of his mother's "departure." His response to this "recollection" was to attribute representations of his mourning reaction to the inkblots—a reaction which, for reasons that we do not know, he could not express directly in real life.

These two striking episodes of personal reactions to control stimuli highlight the potential usefulness of obtaining biographical information about research participants in studies employing subliminal psychodynamic activation. The studies conducted to date have obtained very little, if any, information about the participants beyond their group membership, i.e., their status as schizophrenics, phobics, smokers trying to give up smoking, students trying to raise their grades, etc. The failure to obtain relevant biographical material derives entirely from practical considerations: It is necessarily difficult and time-consuming to obtain biographical information of sufficient depth to throw light on the idiosyncratic aspects of a given study participant's response to subliminal stimuli.

But the preceding examples suggest that it may be important to obtain such data nevertheless. There is no question in our minds but that biographical material can illuminate the idiosyncratic aspects of a participant's response to subliminal psychodynamic activation. (In the early laboratory investigations employing stimuli that were *designed* to intensify underlying conflict, for example, there was rarely a reaction as striking as that of the young man described above, who unconsciously attributed an intensely personal meaning to the control stimulus he was administered.) Moreover, the relationship of personal history to experimental reaction suggests that biographical material and personal associations obtained in a clinical interview preceding an investigation might suggest variants of the oneness stimulus that could heighten its ameliorative impact in the therapeutic and educational aid studies.

We offer these proposals, like the others in this chapter, in the hope that they will stimulate further exploration. While we believe that the ameliorative potential of activated oneness fantasies has been demonstrated beyond any reasonable doubt, this thesis, like those of science generally, requires further study and refinement.

NOTES

1. See *Time*, Sept. 10, 1979, and the Montreal *Gazette*, Oct. 11, 1978.

2. Of the many experiments that have been carried out demonstrating subliminal effects of various kinds (see Dixon's 1971 review), there has been only one to our knowledge (Zuckerman, 1960) that has demonstrated with adequate controls that subliminal messages can influence volitional behavior such as is involved in the buying of products.

3. A spokesman for the American Civil Liberties Union expressed his concern on one of Art Athen's "Reports," WCBS radio, July 10-15, 1978.

4. Studies in which there has been some success in identifying "responders" and "non-responders" to the MOMMY AND I ARE ONE stimulus are those of Leiter (1973), Zuckerman (1980), Jackson (1981), and Mendelsohn (1979). Those that have found new adaptation-enhancing oneness stimuli are Kaye (1975), Cohen (1977), Florek (1978), Mendelsohn (1981), and Parker (1982).

5. This episode was originally reported in Silverman (1965, pp. 453-454).

7

The Search for Oneness in Masochism, Homosexuality, and Narcissism

In the following chapters we shall suggest that the concept of unconscious oneness fantasies has relevance for the understanding of (1) certain forms of non-psychotic behavior; (2) the therapeutic action of both psychoanalysis and psychotherapy; (3) the motivation underlying a variety of activities to which an increasing number of people have been turning in contemporary society to counter anxiety, depression, and other disturbances in their sense of well-being.

To a degree, certain recent developments in psychoanalytic theory dovetail with the concept of symbiotic-like oneness fantasies.[1] As we hope to demonstrate, the concept is consonant with some present-day psychoanalytic views on the role of preoedipal dynamics in general and symbiotic dynamics in particular. In our opinion, the oneness concept also resonates with the recent writings of some psychoanalytic clinicians on the importance of the "therapeutic alliance" and the "holding environment" in psychoanalytic treatment. And it has a bearing, we believe, on various proposals that have been made during the past decade regarding the psychoanalytic treatment of disorders that have been termed "narcissistic disturbances" and "developmental arrests."

We do not claim to offer here a definitive or complete

151

understanding of unconscious oneness fantasies; it is for future laboratory and clinical research to provide data that will allow for more precise and comprehensive formulations about their origin, significance, and function. For the present, however, we believe that with our conceptualization of oneness fantasies we have isolated a clinical category that can enhance psychoanalytic theorizing about psychopathology, treatment, and certain phenomena outside the clinical situation.

THE PLACE OF THE MOTHER-CHILD RELATIONSHIP IN FREUD'S THEORIZING

In certain important ways, Freud was a child of his time. Although he clearly transcended the limitations of his culture when he discovered the significance of childhood sexuality in general and the Oedipus complex in particular, he espoused other ideas that were very much a part of the contemporary view of child-rearing. First, he viewed the very young infant as totally self-centered, self-absorbed, and unattached, a view embodied in his concept of "primary narcissism." Attachment to mother was hard won in the sense that the child's narcissism was converted into "object love" only after the child experienced the frustration of needs essential to his or her survival.

Second, in considering the role of the parents in the development of the older infant, Freud's writings, in keeping with the patriarchal tenor of his time, were heavily skewed toward the father-child, rather than the mother-child, relationship. This is nowhere clearer than in Freud's case histories—Dora (1905), Little Hans (1909a) the Rat Man (1909b), Schreber (1911), and the Wolf Man (1918), all of which reflect the almost singular emphasis Freud placed on the father-child relationship. In this regard,

Zetzel (1966) has offered support for the view that Freud's inattention to the mother-child relationship was not the result of observational scotoma—Freud being the acute observer that he was—but rather his neglect of his own observations in formulating his theory. In reconsidering Freud's treatment of the young nobleman referred to as the Rat Man, she points out that whereas Freud referred to the patient's mother only six times in his published paper (in contrast to over 50 references to the father), in his original notes, made after each consultation with the patient and published separately in 1955, he alludes 40 times to the patient's mother and even describes a complicated relationship between the patient and his mother. (For some interesting psychobiographical inferences and speculations on Freud's neglect of the mother-child relationship in his writings, see Stolorow and Atwood [1979].)

In light of Freud's view of the young infant as unattached and the comparatively little weight he gave to the impact of the mother on the older infant, it is not surprising that the role of symbiotic dynamics in neurotic behavior went unrecognized. In fact, Freud had little to say about the role of what are today referred to as "preoedipal dynamics" of any kind. It is true that he wrote about the role of preoedipal oral and anal impulses and the defenses against them, but he mainly envisioned such factors as secondary rather than primary psychological motivators of neurosis. To Freud, neurotic symptoms by and large stemmed from oedipal conflict; oral and anal dynamics typically entered the picture only when there was regression from genital to anal or oral psychosexuality.

CURRENT STATUS OF THE ROLE OF PREOEDIPAL DYNAMICS IN THE PSYCHONEUROSES

Just as there are important differences among psychoanalytic clinicians in their understanding of schizophrenia (see Chapter 3), there are notable differences among them in their understanding of the neuroses. For one group (e.g., A. Freud, 1969; Brenner, 1976), preoedipal development typically plays only a secondary role in the development of neurosis. It may determine the point to which a person regresses (Freud's view); it may determine the type of defense the person will come to rely upon, and thus, in a somewhat different manner, shape the particular form that his or her oedipally based neurosis will take; or it may make a person less able to cope with oedipal conflict and thus more vulnerable to developing an oedipally based neurosis. What this group of analysts largely rejects, however, is the view that preoedipal dynamics can contribute a major share to neurotic symptoms—that symptoms can express unconscious preoedipal wishes, anxieties, defenses, and fantasies that are important in their own right rather than merely for the fact that they have been mobilized in response to oedipal conflict.

For a second notable group (e.g., Fairbairn, 1952; Guntrip, 1969) the situation is reversed. Non-psychotic disturbances (as well as psychotic disturbances) are understood as preoedipally rooted, with the oedipal dynamics viewed at most as a top layering or cover beneath which lurk the crucial preoedipal dynamics.

Finally, a third group—and this probably comprises the majority of psychoanalytic clinicians—believes that many non-psychotic patients are grappling with oedipal conflicts, many others with preoedipal conflicts, and another sizable segment with conflicts of both kinds.

We identify with this third position, having seen in our clinical practices each of the three types of patients just described. In addition there is some strong supporting evidence for the third position from the research that has used the method of subliminal psychodynamic activation:

(1) In a study of a group of male homoesexuals, there was an intensification of their homosexual orientation after a subliminal message with oedipal content was introduced, but *not* after a subliminal message with preoedipal content was presented (Silverman, Bronstein, and Mendelsohn, 1976); (2) conversely, in an investigation of male hospital employees, what were described as "clinical reactions" emerged after preoedipal conflict was stimulated, but *not* after oedipal conflict was stirred up (Silverman and Goldweber, 1966); (3) in an experiment involving stutterers (from an outpatient speech clinic), their speech disorder intensified after a preoedipal conflict-related stimulus was presented, but *not* after an oedipal conflict-related stimulus was subliminally introduced. But, interestingly, for the same group, other types of psychopathology were in evidence after the latter stimulus condition, but *not* the former (Silverman, Bronstein, and Mendelsohn, 1976). Thus, for this last group, it could be argued that both oedipal *and* preoedipal conflicts were present, but that they were pathogenic for different types of behavior. These research results lend objective support to the position that some nonpsychotic patients grapple with oedipal conflicts, others with preoedipal conflicts, and still others with conflicts of both kinds.

THE ROLE OF SYMBIOTIC DYNAMICS IN NON-PSYCHOTIC BEHAVIOR

Let us now turn our attention to the specific role of *symbiotic* dynamics within the framework of preoedipal considerations. We believe that the symptoms of certain neurotic patients, like the symptoms of schizophrenics, express in disguised form conflicts over the wish for oneness. Bychowski, in 1950, had already alluded to this view in an early discussion of neurotic obesity. He said of one such patient: "Introjection of the maternal breast had led to the retention of food in [the] form of fat deposits . . . . obese patients want to incorporate their love objects, in part, in order to retain and preserve them indefinitely" (p. 304). Translating this into our terminology, we would say that neurotic obesity may secretly express a oneness fantasy.[2] Similarly, in considering a neurotic patient who suffered from depersonalization, Beskind (1972) described her as being intensely conflicted over symbiotic-like wishes. At one point in treatment, the patient herself could say: "How can I live my own life and still love my mother? . . . My feeling unreal is always in connection with my mother. . . . I see myself bound to her forever. . . . I am trying to get away. . . . She is not holding onto me but I feel [that] if I am my own person, I won't feel real anymore" (p. 54).

Thus, in both these case reports, we find support for the view that a motivational determinant of the symptoms was the need to maintain a fantasy of symbiotic-like oneness with mother. We shall now examine in detail three behaviors that we believe often involve such fantasies—masochism, homosexuality and the so-called narcissistic disorders. We will draw on case material of three sorts: (1) early clinical reports that antedate formal psychoanalytic consideration of symbiotic dynamics; (2) recent reports by clinicians who expressly consider the role of symbiotic dynamics in their patients' behavior; (3) clinical reports from the psychoanalytic practice of one of us (F. M. Lachmann).

MASOCHISM

Just what prompts people to seek or remain in unpleasant or even painful circumstances has been a challenge to many students of human behavior. Freud (1919b) initially tried to explain masochism as the sadistic component of sexuality, split off and then turned against the self. Later he reversed himself and posited a primary "death instinct" from which masochism was derived (1924). (In this later paper, sadism was viewed as a deflection outward of this death instinct.) Freud imaginatively attempted to combine three, until then, disparate clinical phenomena under the masochism label: sexual perversions in which pain is experienced as pleasurable, the seeking or unnecessary acceptance of psychological pain (termed "moral masochism"), and aspects of women's behavior that he viewed as "normal feminine masochism." Our clinical examples will be drawn only from the first two categories. (For a recent discussion of masochism and femininity, see Lachmann [1982].)

In a paper written in 1925, Fenichel described a young man who, immediately upon indulging in some slight pleasure, would experience an inner command to be wretched, exhausted, and ill. The patient's father was a clergyman of a sect that professed a strict moral code and narrow-minded bigotry. His mother belonged to the same sect and was described as hysterical, fanatical, and temperamental. She overwhelmed her children with excessive demonstrations of affection, though she also beat them for trivial misdeeds. The patient had been exposed to the primal scene on numerous occasions and as a child had suffered from pavor nocturnus.

According to Fenichel, the father's harshness, in conjunction with the mother's overwhelming and excessive affectional expressions, overstimulated the boy's Oedipus complex. This, in turn, forced the young man into a defensive identification with his mother resulting in both feminine-homosexual inclinations and noteworthy sadistic urges (his mother, it will be recalled, had beaten her children for misdeeds). Thus Fenichel understood his "moral masochism" as: (1) a punishment for his oedipal wishes; (2) a distorted and desexualized expression of sexuality that had taken on a feminine-homosexual cast; and (3) an expression of sadistic impulses turned against the self.

Interestingly, there were aspects of the material that Fenichel presented that permit a formulation along the lines of symbiotic dynamics. First, when the patient suffered his night terrors as a young child, he would cry for his mother, would be unwilling to allow her to leave, and would suddenly anxiously imagine that she knew all his thoughts without his having to tell them to her. The last can be viewed as an expression of a oneness fantasy.

Also relevant were two "attacks" that the patient recalled, one at age 12 and the other at age 16. Both left him in a dysfunctional state, unable to move or walk. The first followed his reading some books that his mother had prohibited; the second occurred after a certain young man had entered his school whom the mother had warned him not to befriend because she did not approve of his conduct with girls. Could it be that when he engaged in behavior that went contrary to his mother's express prohibitions, behavior that might have furthered his own separation and individuation, he needed to re-establish his symbiotic-like tie to her by creating the illusion that he was a small infant, unable to walk? Support for this formulation can be found in the fact that, in the second incident just described, the patient believed that his mother knew of his fondness for the young man without having to be told about it. This can also be seen as expressing a symbiotic-like fantasy.

Wilhelm Reich (1933) described a young male patient who, from the age of 16, had been unable to work and was sexually withdrawn. His sexual life was consumed by masturbation accompanied by fantasies in which he was being beaten. The patient was described as having often slept in the same bed as his mother in childhood and even into puberty. While in bed with her, she would encourage him to embrace and stroke her. She also showed a keen interest in his excretory functions long after the age at which this would have been appropriate.

Reich discussed the patient's psychopathology from the standpoint of the Oedipus complex. Thus, as with Fenichel's patient, the mother's behavior—in this case clearly seductive and sexually stimulating—was seen as intensifying the boy's Oedipus complex, which led to a distorted expression of sexuality. The beating fantasies, then, were viewed by Reich as reflecting both a punishment for his incestuous sexual wishes and feminine proclivities rooted in a defensively motivated identification with his mother. When the patient described his fear of a "melting sensation" during orgasm, Reich explained it as follows:

> As a result of the fear of punishment, the "melting" sensation of warmth, which occurs with the increase of excitation before the acme, is experienced as the advent of the anticipated penis catastrophe; thus it inhibits the normal course of the sexual excitation and produces, on purely physiological grounds, unpleasure which may increase the pain. This process takes place in three phases: 1) "I strive for pleasure"; 2) "I begin to 'melt'—this is the punishment I feared"; 3) "I must kill the [pleasure] if I want to save my penis" [p. 240].

Here, too, we can formulate some of the clinical data in terms of symbiotic dynamics. The patient's inappropriate physical involvement with his mother can be seen as reflecting a symbiotic-like as well as an incestuous tie, the strength of which becomes apparent when the patient says at one point, "To be left alone means death"—the end of my life" (pp. 227-228). We would assume that aloneness is dreaded to this extent only when other people are experienced as merged with oneself, so that not to have another is to feel destroyed. Moreover, the "melting sensation" during masturbation can be viewed as reflecting an unconscious oneness fantasy—serving to gratify the patient's symbiotic-like wishes. The conscious beating fantasies in this context may have served to reinforce the patient's sense of his own body, so that the symbiotic-like gratification he allowed himself in the melting experience would not threaten his sense of self. Thus, the masochism of both Fenichel's and Reich's patients, we are suggesting, may have served a dual function, related to symbiotic as well as oedipal dynamics.

In contrast to the papers by Fenichel and Reich antedating the contributions of those who introduced the concept of symbiosis into psychoanalytic thinking, a paper by Bychowski (1959) explicitly made use of these contributions. Bychowski described a woman whose masochistic involvements were ascribed to her "symbiotic dependence on her mother" (p. 270). The patient's father had died when she was two years old, a loss compounded by her mother's then having to go to work. This was understood by Bychowski as intensifying the patient's already inordinately strong symbiotic need for her mother. As an adult, the patient in her marriage, her friendships, and her analysis had "tried rather hard to push [these] relationships to the brink of disaster" (p. 251). These attempts, which were an important part of her masochistic pattern, were viewed by Bychowski as attempts to reaffirm the bond with mother. It was as if the patient were saying, "If I end my relationships with other people, then there will be mommy and me."

Other behaviors that were seen by Bychowski as further

expressions of symbiotic dynamics were anxieties over separation, excessive eating, smoking, and clothes buying, all of which "revealed the fantasy that the patient carried her mother around in her stomach" (p. 252). Similarly, bodily pain and conversion symptoms were viewed as gratifying the wish to be bound to her unhappy mother by a common suffering.

It is of further interest that a motive Bychowski ascribed to his patient's symbiotic-like fantasy is one that has not been implicated by those who have discussed the role of these fantasies in schizophrenics (see Chapter 3). Describing his patient as unconsciously guilty over the enormous hostility she felt toward her mother, he viewed her symbiotic-like fantasy as serving to diminish the guilt. In the patient's words:

> "My margin of unhappiness serves as a protection against [mother]. By being unhappy, I weaken the quality of her anger. When I take over her anger, then there is less anger left in her. The more destructive I am, the more I feel her badness. It is her badness that I am acting out" [p. 253].

From this, Bychowski formulated that his patient's symbiotic-like fantasy served to effect an "exchange" in which the "badness" of the mother was diminished by the patient's remaining weak, miserable, and humiliated. With the mother then perceived as a better person, the patient no longer had to harbor hostile wishes toward her, and her guilt was thereby alleviated. Considering this motivation for a oneness fantasy in contradistinction to the motivations cited earlier by clinicians treating schizophrenics, it would seem that, although the same fantasy can be present in both non-psychotics and psychotics, the *motivation* for the fantasy may be different.

The following material from a recently treated patient (described in detail elsewhere [Lachmann, 1982]) further illustrates the role of oneness fantasies in masochism.

Judith, a 30-year-old woman, sought analytic therapy after having suffered through two marriages and two divorces and a number of similarly patterned relationships. Her attachments to men were clearly masochistic. She was consistently submissive, self-sacrificing, and self-deprecatory, and on occasion took part in slave-master sexual games in which she played the role of the slave.

Judith's father had been killed in an automobile accident when she was two years old, at which point her mother had quickly moved back to her own parents' home. She remembered her mother as a generally uncaring, frequently absent woman who spent her nights at bars. Judith recalled sleeping in a crib until she was seven years old and then sharing a bed with her mother until her graduation from high school. This only made her yearn even more for the closeness with mother that she had never had, and the care and mothering she had never received. Judith vividly remembered awakening each morning and feeling revulsion at finding her mother's lipstick-smeared face on the pillow next to hers. Her grandparents, as she recalled them, hardly offered compensation for her mother's deficiencies. There were numerous memories of her grandparents and mother verbally abusing her and physically beating her. On several occasions they threatened to abandon her to an orphanage as a punishment for seemingly mild self-assertion.

Resulting fears of abandonment, as well as outright discouragement of self-assertion, interfered with Judith's psychological separation from her mother. She retained into adulthood a profound longing for the care and mothering she had never received. This frustrated longing was expressed in unconscious oneness fantasies which, for Judith, posed a danger at the same time as they promised comfort. Judith had had a recurring dream since childhood: While sleeping in her crib, she would dream of "a small dot becoming larger and larger and turning into a witch. The witch swallowed me up and I would wake with the feeling that something was stuck in my throat." This dream, which remained with her until her analysis, clearly expressed, at one and the same time, Judith's fantasy of oneness with her mother and the threatening quality of that very fantasy.

It is interesting, then, that once Judith established a superficial independence from her mother, she displaced her wishes for oneness with her onto her relationships with men. Indeed, all her relationships with men were remarkably alike. She nurtured them and cared for them devotedly. Unconscious fantasies of oneness with them then allowed her to experience vicarious gratification of her own needs for nurturance and care. In effect, Judith *became* her own idealized "good mother" of infancy, the "good mother" she still vainly hoped to find in her actual mother. But just as the dream of oneness with mother had threatened her sense of self, so too did the fantasy of oneness with her lovers. And so, Judith took part in the slave-master games that allowed her, in two ways, to reinforce her sense of self. First, in these games she dramatically emphasized the difference between herself and the men in her life. And, second, by being the slave in these games, she reiterated the relationship of victim and victimizer that had dominated her childhood and that now served as the basis for her sense of self. To the question, "Why did Judith seek out psychological pain?" we answer simply: Because it served to confirm her sense of self. The unconscious wish for oneness had become so powerful and yet so threatening to her sense of self that Judith sought out experiences of psychological pain in order to counter this threat. Confirmation for our view that Judith's masochism with men was unconsciously linked to the threat of the fantasy of oneness with her mother can be found in the very nature of her relationships with men. Where her mother had been derogatory of men and unable to form long-term attachments with them, Judith maintained her relationships by being extremely submissive and self-sacrificing. And where her mother had never allowed herself to be put upon by men, Judith was their slave. That is, Judith was warding off her wish to be one with her mother by being dramatically unlike her.

Judith's masochism, then, like that of Reich's patient as we earlier reconstructed it, expressed both oneness fantasies and attempts to affirm her threatened sense of self. These cases can be contrasted with those presented by Fenichel and Bychowski in which oneness fantasies seemed to be reacted to without ambivalence. These contrasting pairs of patients reflect two types of masochistic patterns that we have seen in our clinical work. In some masochistic patients, the accent is on the expression of unconscious oneness fantasies, while in others it is on affirming the sense of self. While in the latter instances this affirmation is designed to allow for the ultimate expression of oneness fantasies, most immediately, the emphasis is on preventing engulfment and self-dissolution.

HOMOSEXUALITY

Explanations as to why a person should prefer homosexual to heterosexual relationships have been plentiful in the psychoanalytic literature. (Throughout this section we refer only to the psychodynamics underlying homosexuality. The much-debated question of whether homosexuality should be viewed as pathological is beyond the pale of our discussion.) With regard to homosexuality in males, Wiedeman's (1962) survey of the literature reveals that there was, for many years, a near consensus among classical psychoanalytic writers that oedipal dynamics were chiefly at work. More specifically, the common denominators motivating male homosexuals were thought to be strong incestuous impulses toward their mothers and the consequent arousal of intense castration anxiety, leading both to defensive flight from sexual involvement with women (unconsciously equated with the mother) and a turning toward males, representing, in part, a denial of the possibility of castration (the partner's penis confirming, in effect, that there is no such thing as castration).

Other related oedipal dynamics were often implicated in specific types of homosexual preference. Thus, the homosexual man's desire to perform fellatio was most often understood as reflecting the secret wish to devour his partner's penis, the partner having been unconsciously equated with the father so that, simultaneously, the oedipal rival is castrated and his phallic strength incorporated. In fantasy this makes the "devourer" more desirable to his mother.

For female homosexuality, there was less of a consensus, but here too oedipal dynamics were the point of focus (Freud, 1920; Jones, 1927; Deutsch, 1932).

In our view, the relevance of oedipal dynamics for understanding homosexuality, at least in males, has well stood the test of time. But are these unconscious motivations *sufficient* for a dynamic understanding? To this question, Anna Freud has answered with a firm "yes," Charles Socarides with an equally firm "no."

In the most explicit statement of her position, Freud

(1969) stated that for all behavior she terms psychoneu-
rotic—and she includes homosexuality—oedipal conflict
is central. Still, in a talk reported by Waldhorn (1951),
Freud experienced some difficulty in conceptualizing male
homosexuality *exclusively* in oedipal terms. She concluded
that the "fear of the father in the Oedipus complex could
not alone explain the homosexual's rejection of his own
masculinity. . . . The passivity . . . of such patients was
shown in the analyses by [their] occasionally falling asleep
on the couch and . . . [by their expressing] the wish for
the most infantile irresponsibility in mother's care" (pp.
357-358). Nevertheless, she ascribed this passivity to
regression, and asserted that these patients "had had relatively healthy development up to the phallic phase, where
their abnormality began with the failure to identify with
the father. . ." (p. 338).

Miss Freud thus accounted for the passivity of some
homosexual men by ascribing it to the same oedipal dynamics that had led to his object choice in the first place.
She acknowledged, however, that even after interpretations relating to oedipal conflict had led to heterosexual
potency, "the persistence of fantasies stemming from submissive and passive desires hindered restoration of [the]
full ability to possess and love a woman . . . [and included
a] fantasy of dissolving into nothing at the height of male
potency" (p. 38). Could this be a sign, according to psychoanalytic treatment criteria, that something has remained unanalyzed? Should not the oedipal interpretations
have also resulted in the disappearance of the regression-
induced submissiveness and passivity?

We would suggest that for the homosexuals Anna Freud
is describing "the wish to be irresponsible in mother's care"
and the general unremitting passivity reflect an unconscious wish to merge "at the height of male potency"—that

is, during orgasm. The fantasy of "dissolving into nothing" then accords with the fear of the loss of self that sometimes accompanies symbiotic-like oneness fantasies as we have described them.

In contrast to Anna Freud's singular conceptual focus on oedipal dynamics in explaining homosexuality, Charles Socarides (1969, 1978) views this form of sexual behavior as oedipally based in certain instances, preoedipally based in others, and in still others as rooted in *both* kinds of psychodynamics. To exemplify the third category, Socarides (1969) makes reference to a man that he treated psychoanalytically:

> My patient was exclusively homosexual until entry into psychoanalytic therapy at the age of twenty-seven. His homosexual activity consisted of picking up partners in public toilets and sometimes having intercourse with fellow students at the graduate school he attended, where he was regarded as a gifted pupil and promising scientific practitioner. In the initial interview he stated that he had been living an active homosexual life since the age of eighteen although homosexual contacts had started around fourteen. He was attractive, vivacious, articulate, and generally personable. He complained that his only friends were homosexuals and that these involvements did not lead anywhere. Further, he had become increasingly fearful of exposure which could well interfere with his future career and end in disaster. He was extremely unhappy and suffered intensely because of his inability to desist from homosexual practices [p. 176].

To us, the most striking aspect of the case material that followed is how clearly and directly the patient connected his homosexuality with his early experiences with his mother. Not only did she disrobe in front of him until the age of 13, she often slept in the same bed with him, at times folding his arms around her as they slept. At the same time she was also intrusive and aggressive. The patient recalled that as an infant he had difficulty eating, and at age three or four his mother had force-fed him when he did not finish the food on his plate. When this caused him to vomit, she would insist that he eat the vomit. She criticized his friends, especially his girlfriends, by deeming them unworthy of him, and she made fun of his penis, suggesting that he would never be able to function like a man with a woman. Socarides goes on:

> He was teased, provoked, and ridiculed by his mother. She would scratch him with her fingernails; he would hit her hands violently and strike her on the arms and enjoy seeing her cry. At times she so enraged and goaded him that he would attempt to choke her. On many such occasions she would mockingly offer her throat and invite him to choke her to death [p. 178].

An important consequence in adulthood of his mother's early sadistic and humiliating behavior was the presence of warded-off rage toward her. Relatively early in treatment the patient came to understand frequent murderous feelings he experienced toward his homosexual lovers as revived expressions of this rage. This, in turn, led the patient to understand the degree to which his homosexual partners "were" his mother.

> "When I have sex with a man, I am having sex with my mother. . . . it has to do with the fact that I want her, to be a part of her, and she wants me" [p. 178].

The suggestion of a symbiotic-like fantasy in the fragment "I want . . . to be a part of her" is strikingly confirmed in the following dream and associations:

> "It's only a short dream. It's of my mother bleeding right down the middle and I'm rolling over on top of her. . . . In the dream I'm loving her all over and she is holding me even though she is bleeding and it's mostly her holding me and my clinging and all those things make me feel ashamed. . . . I see now that in loving her, I'm killing her and destroying her. . . . She deserved to die but I was almost choking in the dream myself, like almost it was my death, like Siamese twins together, the blood. I got almost vicious in the dream, pushing away and yet not pushing away, holding tight on her, the way I hold tight to homosexuals. . . . Every time I feel I've hurt my mother I then begin to have homosexual desires. I find I look at certain guys depending on what I feel I'm missing or need at the time. If I feel loneliness I need a gentle guy. If I need strength, I get a fierce looking . . . kind of man" [pp. 182-183].

Not only can we see in these associations the successive expression of incestuous longings and rage toward the mother (functioning most likely both as vengeance for her sadistic and humiliating behavior and to ward off her intrusiveness), but also the even more prominent expression of symbiotic-like yearnings, apparently motivated by guilt over his murderous rage toward his mother and displaced onto his homosexual partners. Thus there is the vivid image of the patient and his mother as Siamese twins (foreshadowed, perhaps, by the bloody wound "down the middle" of his mother), immediately followed by the reference to "pushing away and yet not pushing away" with its suggestion of simultaneous wishes for separation and merger. The patient is then "holding tight on her," the tightness of his grasp suggestive not only of the merger theme but also of the violence and rage with which it is tinged. Indeed, the patient experiences his violence toward his mother as violence toward himself: He is "almost choking in the dream," as though *he* were the victim of his own childhood attempts to choke his mother. It was almost *"my* death," he says. But the most powerful support for our formulation is contained in the final series of associations: the suggestion that, when the patient has hurt his mother, he has lost her, so that *he* is missing something which *he* seeks in other men, just as he had originally sought it in merger with her.

To exemplify further the role of symbiotic dynamics in homosexuality, two clinical vignettes of patients treated by one of us (F.M. Lachmann) will now be offered.

Rick sought psychoanalytic treatment because of mounting anxiety attacks and depression that had reached suicidal proportions. At age 34, his career as a singer had come to a standstill. He was subjectively most distressed by his increasing involvement in homosexuality.

Rick was the middle child in his family. Just prior to his birth, his parents had lost a baby daughter. Rick learned, at a young age, that his mother had been devastated by the death of her child and had wished that the next child would be a girl to replace the daughter who had died. His birth was therefore a disappointment, while the arrival of his younger sister a year later fulfilled his mother's hopes.

Thus, during Rick's first year, his mother was in mourning. From the second year on, she was absorbed with the preferred daughter. As treatment progressed, it became apparent that Rick's later pathology could be understood as showing the stamp of these early interferences in his progress through the symbiotic phase of development—at the very least, that experiences of gratification during this phase were to some extent denied him.

The earliest evidence in Rick's treatment of the importance of symbiotic-like wishes was noted in the extent to which Rick imagined—in fact insisted upon—similarities between himself and his analyst. He at first thought that his analyst, like himself, was a homosexual and, later, when his sexual interests changed (in response to interpretations of his oedipal conflicts), that his analyst, like himself, was a "cured homosexual." A related insistence was that his analyst was experiencing the same painful feelings that he had experienced—alternately, pervasive anxiety, intolerable rage, and hopeless depression.

The analytic work at this time consisted of elucidating the affective states the patient experienced, the similar states he imagined his analyst felt, and the importance to him that he and his analyst "share" the same feelings. Recognition on Rick's part of this latter subjective need then led to distress when differences between him and his analyst became apparent and again when he viewed the treatment as disappointing. These "disappointments" covered a wide gamut ranging from the temperature of the analyst's office, to the termination of sessions at the end of hours in which his yearning for shared affects was fully expressed, to his sensing a slight loss of interest on the analyst's part in what he was saying.

The distress that Rick experienced in response to the differences between himself and the analyst and the disappointments he experienced as "inflicted" on him by the analyst took the form of an intensification of the painful affects referred to above. This would be followed by a period in which he made himself inaccessible to the analyst, behavior serving both as an expression of anger over the analyst's failure to satisfy his symbiotic-like wishes and as a further distorted *fulfillment* of these same wishes. That is to say, by being as unresponsive as he felt the analyst was, Rick could maintain his unconscious fantasy of oneness with him.

When this was interpreted to Rick, his response lent support to the validity of the formulation. First, he gradually recognized the sense of comfort he felt, concomitant with his rage, when he imagined that his unresponsive feelings were shared by the analyst. Eventually, he was able to express verbally rather than symbolically his belief that the analyst was "too detached" and "removed." He no longer needed to *become* inaccessible. The genetic roots of these perceptions then started to emerge. Initially, his view of the analyst had seemed to reflect a transference from his early inaccessible father. But later, an even more important maternal transference emerged. The enduring conscious impression that Rick had had of his mother was that she was a "fury," but in time he came to understand that this perception served an important defensive function as well. That is, it was preferable to view her this way than as "depressed" and "otherwise preoccupied." It was this view of her that was the most important root of his perception of the analyst. A recurring dream image that appeared at this time was of a darkened empty room which apparently suggested an apartment in which he and his family had lived when he was a baby and at the same time expressed metaphorically his early dread of abandonment by his unavailable mother.

Simultaneously, Rick began to understand the extent to which his homosexual relationships replicated his relationship with his mother. Rick described the men with whom he had had sexual relationships as "removed" and "detached." Early in treatment, when the focus was on his oedipal conflicts, this choice could be seen as based upon his sexual attachment to his father, an attachment that was partly rooted in his defensively motivated flight from his incestuous feelings for mother. It later became apparent, however, that the special qualities of his homosexual partners were also unconsciously linked to the image of his mother as too preoccupied with the loss of her first daughter and the birth of her second to be anything but removed and detached from him.

The enduring quality of Rick's homosexuality was further linked to his latency years. He recalled that during this time he developed a tendency to be constipated, which led to what he came to refer to in the analysis as "the enemas." Both parents would accompany him to the bathroom where his mother would administer the enemas while his father tried to comfort him by rubbing his stomach. These incidents not only reinforced his sexual attachment to males (it was his father who rubbed his belly) but stimulated an image of his mother as angry and sadistic (which also played a role in the image that he had of her as a "fury"). All of this was re-enacted in a distorted way in his homosexuality. He was the active partner in anal intercourse and experienced conscious pleasure in what he viewed as the sadistic humiliation of his partner.

Here we find similarities between Rick and the patient described by Socarides. Both expressed feelings of rage toward their homosexual lovers, feelings that not only reflected their vengeful fantasies toward their mothers (who had intruded upon and humiliated them), but also warded off their symbiotic-like attachments to them. For Socarides' patient, insight into the connection between his aggressive behavior toward his homosexual lovers and his anger toward his mother brought to the surface the deeper motivation reflected in the dream of the "Siamese twin" attachment, with its implication that oneness fantasies toward the mother were operative. For Rick, the same insight led to an equally revealing series of associations. He began by describing his financial arrangements with his current lover. On Rick's insistence, they pooled their money. Rick's lover earned more than Rick but also spent more on his analysis, so that Rick's actual contribution to the pool was greater. But by ignoring this fact and focusing on his lover's higher income, he could maintain the illusion that he was being supported and taken care of by his lover. When this was interpreted, he reported in the following session, "Saturday night I was extremely depressed so I worked up a fantasy about being a baby, all curled up and nursing with my mother. She seemed fat and young and it seemed like we were melting together." (Note how often allusions to melting appear as manifest expressions of unconscious oneness fantasies.)

Summarizing at this point, Rick's homosexuality—like that of Socarides' patient—was rooted in both oedipal and symbiotic dynamics. This is nowhere clearer than in his unconscious perception of the enema experiences. On the one hand, his mother's contact with his nude body was unconsciously perceived as a sexual assault which simultaneously served as both a gratification and a punishment for his incestuous wishes toward her. On the other hand, her unempathic and rough manner was an unconscious reminder of her early failures to satisfy his symbiotic needs. Thus, in his homosexual practices, he attempted to experience both this incestuous pleasure and the longed-for symbiotic-like gratification. At the same time, the homosexual interaction allowed him to revenge himself on his mother both for her physical intrusiveness and for her failure as his symbiotic partner during infancy. Finally, the reversal of roles in anal intercourse allowed him to master the painful humiliation that had been inflicted upon him during the enemas. As Rick's case reveals, and as has been elaborated elsewhere (Lachmann, 1975), homosexuality is a complex configuration in which sexual, aggressive, and symbiotic-like wishes, anxieties, defenses, and fantasies are simultaneously expressed.

We turn now to another patient in whom symbiotic dynamics contributed to homosexual object choice to an even greater extent than in Rick's case. Lorna, a school teacher, came for treatment because she was unable to concentrate sufficiently to read and study for an advanced degree. She was also somewhat distressed by her exlusively homosexual orientation, and suffered from blackouts during which she appeared, to the observer, to be dozing off.

It was the blackouts that became the first focus of the analytic work, these occurring in a variety of situations both in the company of friends and when alone. The frequency with which they occurred while she was bathing were of particular concern to her.

As an only child, Lorna had been inseparable from her mother, who was deserted by her husband before Lorna's birth. But when she was four years old, her father had returned. As the memories of her father's return became more and more accessible in the course of treatment, the blackout spells occurred with increasing frequency. While talking to the analyst, she would gradually "fade away" and, though apparently asleep, speak in a high-pitched childlike voice that was different from her normal speaking voice. For several months, her words were not clear and what she said could not be discerned. Then she would "awaken" and continue the thread of the previous narrative. These narratives often revolved around the theme of her rage that her father should have literally displaced her from her mother's bed. (She had slept in the same bed as her mother until she was four.) She also recalled standing outside the parental bedroom in the mornings, waiting for her father to go into the bathroom, which then freed her to join her mother.

As these memories were explored, Lorna was able to recall sexual scenes which she had observed between her parents and which had become the subject of her doll play as a young child. She then remembered from the same period wanting to look like her father. This desire had been intense enough to stimulate her to dress in her father's clothes whenever her parents left her alone. She recalled masturbating during adolescence while dressed in her father's clothes and linked this to her behavior as a young adult, donning men's clothes and frequenting homosexual bars to meet women.

Lorna was able to trace the onset of her blackouts to her adolescence and, later, more specifically, to a bath she had taken on one occasion after having masturbated. She came to understand the masturbation/bath sequence as a distorted re-enactment of her father's entering the bathroom after spending the night in bed with her mother. It then became clear that her courting of women represented an identification with her father and a search for replacements for her mother. In her sexual relationships with these women, she was most immediately trying to recreate what she had imagined and observed of her father and mother's sexual interaction. On a deeper level, however, she was attempting to rediscover the symbiotic-like bond that she had once experienced with her mother and which she had lost upon her father's return.

But what was the unconscious meaning of the blackout spells? And what were the incomprehensible sounds spoken by Lorna in a high-pitched voice when she had these spells during her sessions? The answer to the latter question became apparent first. As treatment continued, the sounds during her spells became more and more distinct. They turned out to be sounds such as "umm," "ooh," and "aah" that she had uttered in childhood to express particularly pleasurable sensations. From her associations, it could be inferred that at the moment she uttered these sounds a oneness fantasy had been activated in which she unconsciously imagined herself being held, soothed, and caressed by her mother, either in bed or sitting in her mother's lap. A further exploration indicated that this image referred to the time prior to her father's return when she had had her mother all to herself. From this it was inferred that her blackouts served to obliterate the return of the father and restore the period of closeness to mother. The specific symbiotic character of this closeness was reflected in Lorna's description of a merging sensation she experienced as her spells would begin, which eventually she elaborated as pleasurable feelings of "losing herself" in her mother's lap.

The insights gained from the analysis of Lorna's blackouts also helped make her reading-studying inhibition and her homosexuality understandable. With regard to the former, the distracted state she experienced when she tried to apply herself to school work appeared to be a subclinical blackout, or at least served the same function as did the blackouts. The interpretation that when she was in this state she was struggling to experience a sense of oneness with her mother as she remembered her from the time prior to her father's return, markedly increased her ability to read, attend to, and concentrate upon academic work.

In contrast to both Socarides' patient and Rick, in whom oedipal and symbiotic-like dynamics codetermined homosexual behavior, symbiotic-like dynamics played a nearly exclusive role in Lorna's case. They expressed the wish to displace the father and, more importantly, reunite with the mother and thus undo the abrupt separation imposed on her after her excessively prolonged symbiotic phase. Interestingly, in her actual homosexual relationships, she sought younger women whom she described as "unformed" and whom she could support and mother. She and her analyst came to understand this preference as a reversal of her underlying yearning to be the baby in her mother's lap.

Narcissistic Disorders

In his biography of Freud (1959) Ernest Jones called narcissism a "disturbing concept." To Jones, the term had been applied too broadly. Not only had it been used to describe people who were in "love with themselves"—or, less literally, people wrapped up in themselves at the expense of their relationships with other people—but also to that state of the young infant which Freud had labeled "primary narcissism"; the psychotic condition (since psychotics were viewed as having lost interest in the world); the state of sleep (in which the person is minimally responsive to the environment); and homosexuality (since the homosexual love object is, in one important respect, more like the self than the heterosexual love object). What led to the grouping of these diverse phenomena under the "narcissism" heading was the assumption that all of them were more or less characterized by a pronounced self-concern and a relative lack of concern for those in the outside world.

For all of these phenomena, the traditional "narcissistic" characterization has been or can be challenged. To take one example, discussed earlier in this chapter, the characterization of the "narcissistic infant" has largely given way to Mahler's "symbiotic infant." (Observational studies have shown that the infant is capable of forming an attachment to another at a much earlier age than was previously thought (see Greenspan, 1979). In recent years there has been a tendency among psychoanalytic writers to retain the term "narcissistic" to describe the young infant, but to shift the meaning of the term so that it conforms to Mahler's observations. This, we think, is confusing, just as it is to retain the term for the other states and conditions that we have listed above: Serious question can be raised as to whether these states and conditions should be characterized as involving excessive self-concern.

We think a better solution is to find other words to describe these states and conditions and to limit the term to its original meaning. Stolorow and Lachmann (1980) have proposed that narcissism be viewed in terms of the function that it serves in maintaining an adequate sense of self. Thus, "mental activity [should] be considered narcissistic to the degree that its function is to maintain the structural cohesion, temporal stability, and positive affective coloring of the self representation" (p. 10).

The kinds of pathological behavior that reflect such mental activity include inappropriate or excessive self-reference in interactions with others; a seeking of tribute; an idealization of people from whom admiration and a mirroring of grandiose self-estimations is anticipated (and, conversely, a depreciation of those who are seen as having inflicted narcissistic hurts); controlling and dominating behavior toward others in the service of enhancing the sense of self; and the experience of certain people as extensions of the self (Kernberg, 1975). Persons who are dominated by the kinds of behavior just described have been designated "narcissistic personalities" or "narcissistic characters."

What role can the search for oneness play in narcissistic

behavior? Before answering this question, let us review the major formulations proposed by psychoanalytic clinicians to account for narcissistic behavior.

First, there is the view of those psychoanalytic clinicians who see all neurosis, including pathological narcissistic behavior, as a regression from (and an expression of) oedipal conflict. Narcissistic behavior, in this view, is simply another way of coping with a universal neurotogenic agent (Tartakoff, 1966; Easser, 1974).

A second group of psychoanalytic clinicians view narcissistic behavior as a reaction to preoedipal conflicts of varying kinds. Kernberg (1975) has offered the following specific formulation. Such behavior (in persons he designates "narcissistic personalities") is a response to intense rage and envy over a sense of having received inadequate oral gratification in infancy. The resulting feeling of being a "have not" leads to a need to devalue those who "have." At times, projection of this envy and rage intensifies the negative view of, and uncaring behavior toward, others. At other times, there is a denial of the envy and rage bolstered by a characterological haughtiness and grandiosity. At still other times, there is a turning toward other people as either narcissistic "suppliers" or extensions of the self.

A third view of narcissistic behavior has been proposed by Kohut (1971, 1977). Considered from a psychoanalytic frame of reference, this view is the most radical of the three in that the underlying problem of narcissism is not seen to involve conflict over unconscious impulses, either oedipal or preoedipal, a notable departure from the traditional psychoanalytic view that such conflict is always at the root of non-psychotic psychopathology. For Kohut, narcissistic behavior (again in persons designated "narcissistic personalities") is the result of deficiencies in the sense of self that are a *direct* result of parental failings. (We emphasize the word "direct" here because psychopathology resulting from a faulty sense of self had been written about before in the psychoanalytic literature, but was understood as a response to intrapsychic conflict; the role of the parents was viewed as a more distal and complex variable.) Kohut's theory will now be presented in some detail. We believe it demonstrates the relevance of oneness fantasies for narcissistic behavior.

According to Kohut, primary disturbances in "self structures" (or what we have referred to as the sense of self) come about in the following way. In normal development, in order to mute the narcissistic disappointments that inevitably accompany living in a world of adults, the infant attempts to regain his or her narcissistic equilibrium in two discrete ways. One involves the development of grandiose and omnipotent fantasies; the other involves the emergence of an idealized view of the parents with whom the infant then merges in order to share their desired qualities. In normal development, the empathic, attuned parent meets the child's need by admiring the child (which Kohut terms "mirroring") and by allowing him or herself to be the object of the child's idealizations. In providing these functions, the parents become "selfobjects" for the child; they function not as discrete objects satisfying the child's needs, but as dimensions of the child's own self-experience, dimensions that are integral to the child's emerging sense of self-cohesion. Kohut and Wolff (1978) recently described selfobjects in the following way:

> Selfobjects are objects which we experience as part of our self; the expected control over them is, therefore, closer to the concept of the control which a grown-up expects to have over his own body and mind than the concept of the control which he expects to have over

others. There are two kinds of selfobjects: those who respond to and confirm the child's innate sense of vigour, greatness, and perfection [with the "mirroring mother" as the prototype]; and those to whom the child can look up to and with whom the child can merge as an image of calmness, infallibility and omnipotence [the idealized father as prototype] [p. 414].

Under optimal conditions, the availability of the parents as selfobjects enables the child to emerge with a cohesive, integrated self. This development, according to Kohut, proceeds from an act of "transmuting internalization" by which the child is able to internalize the parents' selfobject functions and render them constituents of his or her own consolidating self structures. Kohut suggests that relative failures by either parent may be compensated for by the selfobject availability of the other. When both parents are deficient as selfobjects, however, the child will demonstrate vulnerable self structures and will undertake defensive efforts to hide his core weakness. Children subject to such parental selfobject failures mature into adults whose vulnerable self structures cause them to rely on others for self-esteem regulation, lest they feel empty, bored, depressed, or "fragmented." Such individuals (for whom Kohut originally used the term "narcissistic personality disorders") must use others as "archaic selfobjects" who can make good a lack of internalized self structure; for such individuals the reliance on such selfobjects is a frequent rather than occasional occurrence in everyday life. Failures of, disappointments in, or less than the required empathy from selfobjects expose the vulnerability of the self structures and lead to regressive narcissistic mental activity in an attempt to restore self-cohesion. From this standpoint, narcissistic pathology can be seen as an attempt at "self-cure."

Kohut's theory has elicited strong reactions from within the psychoanalytic community, ranging from uncritical acceptance to wholesale rejection. Our own view, like the views of Loewald (1973) and Wallerstein (1981), sees considerable usefulness in some of Kohut's proposals, is critical of others, and attempts to integrate the useful proposals with other formulations about narcissism.

What is the relationship between narcissistic behavior and symbiotic-like oneness fantasies? We propose that one function such behavior can serve is to activate such a fantasy. Whereas we believe that any kind of narcissistic behavior can serve this function, it is in the seeking of selfobjects that this can most clearly be seen. That group of selfobjects patterned after the mirroring mother of infancy would, in our terminology, be viewed as "symbiotic-like objects" with whom the narcissistic person attempts to restore an adequate sense of self by means of a oneness fantasy. The following vignette of a case supervised by one of us (F. M. Lachmann) illustrates this point.

Peter, a young man who had come for treatment because of marital difficulties, had been seen by the same therapist for two years prior to the supervision. In presenting his difficulties, the patient stated that he believed that he had not had enough sexual experience prior to his marriage and consequently wanted his wife to agree to his having extramarital affairs. When she agreed on the condition that she too have affairs, he both objected and became distraught. His therapist understood this to reflect his disappointment in his wife that she was not willing unconditionally to gratify his needs and forgo her own. She was not willing, that is, to be a mirroring selfobject, or, in our terms, an object with whom a state of oneness could be achieved. The need for such an object and his disappointment in not being able to "find" one was further reflected in his generally highly critical and contemptuous attitudes toward other people. Thus, when his wife left him, he felt that none of the girlfriends that followed lived up to his expectations.

For the first two years of treatment, Peter spoke for entire sessions. When the therapist tried to interrupt him, to question or comment upon what he had said, he became furious at her. It was as if he were saying, "Your job is simply to accept and mirror what I say." Conversely, and somewhat ironically, Peter would at other times praise her for all the help she was giving, and let it be known that inactivity on her part was also unacceptable.

These paradoxical reactions were later understood as rooted in the patient's early experience with his mother. There were numerous incidents reported in which his mother was viewed as alternately invading his privacy and ignoring him. This understanding enabled the therapist to accept more comfortably the patient's fluctuating needs for non-intrusive listening, on the one hand, and signs of interest on the other. She would thus, at times, ask Peter to let her know when he felt ready to discuss what he had been describing, as a way of conveying to him both her interest and her respect for his wishes that she not intrude. Retrospectively, the very different earlier interventions by the therapist came to be understood as repetitions of the traumatic intrusions of Peter's mother early in life.

The shift in the therapist's stand was rewarded in that the patient eventually explored the necessity for keeping the therapist at arm's length by talking continuously. Material emerged suggesting that the patient was afraid that if he let the therapist talk, she might say something "stupid." This, in turn, would destroy his fantasy of, in Peter's words, a "blissful union with a perfect being." He further came to understand that his early contempt for and criticism of the therapist expressed his rage over her deficiencies in meeting his symbiotic-like needs for a mirroring selfobject.

Just as in our discussion of masochism and homosexuality, our proposal that a oneness fantasy can underlie narcissistic behavior is not an argument that other dynamics may not sometimes be implicated in narcissistic disturbances alone or in conjunction with symbiotic dynamics. We have seen in our clinical practices material that is consistent with the various views presented. There have been instances in which narcissistic problems seemed rooted in the search for an idealized father selfobject or a mirroring mother selfobject (in our terms, a symbiotic-like object), instances in which other preoedipal dynamics prevailed, and instances in which oedipal dynamics dominated. Often, we believe, these different dynamics operate in the same patient, sometimes jointly contributing to the same behavior. Consider the following two patients (treated by F. M. Lachmann and discussed in Stolorow and Lachmann [1980, pp. 113-114]).

When Sally, a 21-year-old, entered treatment, she described herself as "feeling down, depressed, and uninterested. I feel I am cutting myself off. There is nothing I want to do." It soon became apparent that these symptoms had emerged in response to narcissistic hurts occasioned by minor rebuffs at the hands of contemporaries.

In spite of a notable academic record prior to entering college, Sally had encountered severe difficulties in her studies at a school some distance from her home. Exploration of these difficulties revealed that they were triggered by her separation from her mother, whose presence she needed in order to feel capable. In her first year at college, Sally attempted to compensate for this loss by surrounding herself with the "celebrities" of the school. In their presence her self-esteem and ability to work were briefly revived. It was when she experienced a slight loss of interest on their part that both her academic decline and depressed states began.

When she was four years old, Sally's parents had been divorced. Her father had quickly remarried and, although Sally remained with her mother, she sought to maintain a close relationship with her father. When Sally was 12, her mother began a love affair with a considerably younger married man to which Sally reacted with intense disappointment. It became clear that the mother's lover was viewed by Sally as an intruder who came between her mother and her.

Further clinical material revealed that Sally's problems were primarily rooted in her sense of loss of both her mother and father. The mother was experienced as insufficiently gratifying from infancy on, and especially after she had begun her love affair with the younger man. Sally then felt that her mother was even less available than before.

In adolescence Sally had developed a series of mystical interests—astrology, extrasensory perception, and fortune telling. Her associations indicated that these were important to her because they involved communication unimpeded by conventional restraints. They allowed her to experience what she described as a "feeling of oneness on a cosmic level," compensating for the sense of frustration connected with the "loss" of her parents.

The importance of her father for her became apparent in the unfolding transference. She developed painful headaches during her sessions and when asked what she imagined would soothe her pain, made reference to how calm she felt upon hearing the sound of her analyst's voice. She then recalled how, prior to her parents' separation, she had experienced similar headaches, in response to which her father would sit with her and soothingly rub her head. This memory shed light on the meaning of her analyst's soothing voice and reflected the combined sexual and symbiotic-like yearnings for her analyst currently and for her father earlier in life.

A mixture of oedipal and preoedipal concerns were also expressed in dreams about her analyst, such as those in which she reported, "You were talking to me about the cabala," and "I came to your office and some of your patients were witches." Her associations to the first dream further revealed her need for the analyst/father as both an incestuous and symbiotic-like object, the latter being the more prominently expressed via the revival of her mystical interests in the transference. In the second dream, her associations were both to her oedipal fears (her rivals being viewed in frightening terms) and symbiotic-like oneness fantasies (the witches as having supernatural powers).

Somewhat later in treatment symbiotic-like needs emerged in particularly intense form when her analytic hours had to be changed. She experienced a keen sense of disappointment when, during the subsequent discussion, she had to focus on the fact that her analyst also saw other patients; she started speaking wistfully of the happy years she had spent earlier in analysis. It became apparent that this earlier period represented both the time in her life prior to her parents' separation and the time prior to the arrival of her mother's lover.

During most of her treatment, Sally had, by and large, reacted to her analyst as a symbiotic-like object. In the third year of her analysis, however, there was a shift. She described a new pleasurable sensation that she had experienced during intercourse with her boyfriend—the pressure of his body on her own. This reminded her, she said, of feelings she had recently had toward the analyst in which she wanted him to exert a kind of pressure on her by introducing new ideas, even contradictory ones, rather than clarifying or mirroring what she said. From this and other material that she gave (e.g., a reference to her analyst's words "lying on top of her"), it became clear that a sexual/oedipal transference was coming to the fore. It seemed that her need for a symbiotic-like object had been, to some extent, surmounted so that she could now experience pleasure in differences and a complementarity between herself and others.

Another patient, Sandra, began her analysis at age 25 for feelings of anxiety, shame, and humiliation that inhibited her work as an actress. She complained of stage fright that interfered with her ability to control her voice, and dated this problem to the period in which she had made the transition from gifted amateur to professional. She was also bothered by the fact that others viewed her as a haughty prima donna and difficult to get along with, both of which were extremely painful to her since she was easily offended and much in need of the approval of others.

Sandra's father had been in the army until she was two, during which time her mother, as well as several aunts, had devoted themselves to her care. She had been adored and admired, and recalled feeling special—"like a performer"—a part she played from then on. From her fifth year, her mother actively groomed her to become an actress, pushing her to attain various goals, coaching her, and applauding her considerable talent. Conflict between mother and daughter was rare, with Sandra habitually complying with her mother's expectations. A merger-like tie developed between them as Sandra maintained a sense of herself consistent with her mother's image of her as good, pure, unambitious, and uncompetitive. But all this came at a price. While she was admired and applauded in high school dramatics, her exhibitionistic excesses lost her the company of friends. And as she began to succeed on her own, she began to feel victimized by her mother's controlling and intrusive behavior.

In the analysis of her stage fright, what first emerged was material bearing on an apparent displacement from an anal phase struggle. Associations to being on the stage included references to being observed and overheard on the toilet by her mother. The theater audience had, in effect, replaced her mother, so that Sandra's unconscious dilemma was over whether she should allow the audience/mother to control her and the contents of her body or retain control by withholding—that is, not performing. Significantly, when at first she surrendered the control and complied with the audience's wishes, thereby maintaining a fantasy of symbiotic-like oneness, she was symptom-free.

Two dynamic shifts seemed responsible for the development of her stage fright. For one thing, her wish for autonomy (including the desire to control her bowels) started to assert itself and she became anxious that her mother (represented by the theater audience) would disapprove. Second, her acting had taken on an added, oedipally related meaning: She now feared that her ambitiousness and competitiveness would incur her mother's disapproval all the more. All this threatened the fantasy of oneness with her mother that she still needed to maintain her self-esteem.

In time, as a result of notable success in her acting career, Sandra's tie with her mother and her view of herself as unambitious, uncompetitive, pure, and innocent were increasingly jeopardized. Conscious fantasies during intercourse of being raped and degraded, which had appeared only sporadically in the past, now became frequent. The fantasied rapist emerged, in part, as her father, with the rape expressing incestuous wishes accompanied by pain that served as guilt-relieving punishment. But her associations to the rape image also entailed references to dirt and degradation, with the suggestion of anal wishes as well. Finally (and predominantly), the rapist represented her intrusive mother to whom Sandra had to submit in order to maintain the fantasy of symbiotic-like oneness.

In short, Sandra's symptoms were multidetermined. Whereas in Sally's case, symbiotic dynamics were dominant during most of treatment, for Sandra, oedipal and anal dynamics played more of an equal role with symbiotic dynamics from the start.

MATERNAL BEHAVIOR AND SYMBIOTIC-LIKE PATHOLOGY IN NON-PSYCHOTIC CONDITIONS

Are there any generalizations that can be made about the genesis of symbiotic-like pathology in non-psychotic conditions? If we consider the case vignettes presented in this chapter, the following can be noted. The historical material in each vignette includes allusions to the mother's behavior as interfering in one way or another with the experience of sufficient symbiotic-like gratification. In five of the cases—Judith, Rick, Bychowski's patient, Lorna, and Sally—there was evidence that the mother was insufficiently available: in the first instance because she was generally uncaring, in the second because she was severely depressed, in the third because the father's death when the patient was two forced the mother to go to work, and in the latter two because a man suddenly entered the mother's life, leaving the child feeling displaced. In five other cases—Peter, Sandra, and the patients of Fenichel, Reich, and Socarides—the mother's behavior left the child feeling that to seek symbiotic-like gratification would be dangerous. For Peter and Sandra this was because the behavior was intrusive. For the patients of Fenichel and Reich, the maternal behavior that provided symbiotic-like gratifications was also incestuously stimulating. And for Socarides' patient, the mother's behavior was both intrusive and incestuously stimulating.

All of this, however, can be viewed as no more than suggestive, given the small size of our sample, and there being no precautions that a clinician can take to eliminate bias in viewing his or her material. Thus, what is clearly called for is a study that would allow for a more rigorous test of the hypothesis that symbiotic problems are related to the kinds of maternal behaviors that have been described.[3]

NOTES

1. As we noted in Chapter 6, it is possible that the oneness fantasies that have been activated in some of our research participants are not "symbiotic-like." That is, the "object" in the oneness fantasy may be the post-symbiotic, perhaps oedipal mother or father, or even someone else who is not unconsciously linked with the "symbiotic mother." Similarly, it is possible that post-symbiotic oneness fantasies may be involved in the phenomena we will be discussing in Chapters 7 through 9. We will not pursue such possibilities at this time, though we will pursue the use of symbiotic-like fantasies to ward off post-symbiotic, particularly oedipal conflicts.

2. This "translation" might be questioned, of course, since in discussing the study by Bronstein (1976) in Chapter 4 we distinguished between introjection fantasies and oneness fantasies. Based on Bychowski's data, however, and the fact that the concept of a "oneness fantasy" had not been articulated at the time, we believe it unlikely that Bychowski had this distinction in mind.

3. Such a study could also address two related questions. First, since the maternal behavior alluded to in this chapter had much in common with so-called "schizophrenogenic maternal behavior" (described in Chapter 3), a careful comparison of the two

types of behavior would be edifying. Are the behaviors of mothers of non-psychotic patients with symbiotic-like pathology different (qualitatively or quantitatively) from the behaviors of mothers of schizophrenics? If this turns out *not* to be the case, the difference in outcome as far as the offspring are concerned could be due to the genetic component in schizophrenia, or it could be a function of differential behavior on the part of their fathers. Lidz (1973) has implicated the father's behavior in discussing the environmental contribution to schizophrenia, particularly the father's failure to serve as a buffer against the mother's intrusiveness. Whether paternal behaviors also contribute to symbiotic-like pathology in non-psychotic patients could be investigated in the research on maternal behaviors.

8
ONENESS FANTASIES
IN PSYCHOANALYTIC TREATMENT

Having considered the role of symbiotic-like oneness fantasies in three varieties of non-psychotic behavior, we turn now to a related clinical issue: the role of these same fantasies in the psychoanalytic treatment process itself. In Chapter 9, in the context of a more wide-ranging consideration of oneness fantasies in everyday life, we shall discuss the possible contribution of activated oneness fantasies to the ameliorative effect of several varieties of psychotherapy. We reserve for this chapter, however, a more intensive consideration of the way these fantasies enter into psychoanalytic treatment. As part of this presentation, we shall address several preliminary issues that bear on this topic: (1) the "agents" of therapeutic change in psychoanalytic treatment; (2) the role of gratification in psychoanalytic treatment; and (3) the difference between psychopathology based on "structural conflict" and psychopathology rooted in "developmental arrest."

THERAPEUTIC AGENTS IN PSYCHOANALYTIC TREATMENT

There has been a longstanding controversy among psychoanalytic clinicians as to what should be considered legitimate therapeutic agents of change in psychoanalytic treatment. Is insight the only agent of change or are there other legitimate agents as well? (Friedman [1978] has traced the development of the controversy as to the relative weights given to "understanding" vs. "attachment" in the history of psychoanalysis.) Essentially, we can identify two major trends. One group of psychoanalytic clinicians has maintained that in a properly conducted psychoanalysis insight is the *only* legitimate agent of change, and that if any other therapeutic agent is in evidence it should be subjected to analytic scrutiny for its meaning and thereby neutralized. Another substantial group, on the other hand, would legitimize at least certain other agents of change as long as they do not interfere with the development of insight or otherwise impede the psychoanalytic process.

What are these other proposed agents of change? They include what has been termed "identification with the analyst" (Sterba, 1934), internalization of the analyst as an "auxiliary superego" (Strachey, 1934), "corrective emotional experiences" (Alexander, 1954), the psychoanalytic "atmosphere" as it provides a "holding environment" (Winnicott, 1963; Modell, 1976), and the analyst's function as an "empathic mirroring selfobject" (Kohut, 1971, 1977).

But what is the connection between these therapeutic agents and oneness fantasies? One of us has proposed elsewhere (Silverman, 1979) that the ameliorative process to which terms such as these refer involves the activation of two types of unconscious fantasies, one of which is the fantasy of symbiotic-like oneness.[1] These oneness fantasies, we believe, are particularly implicated in the analytic "holding environment" and in the function of the analyst as empathic mirroring selfobject. We will spell out the link between Kohut's concept and symbiotic-like oneness fantasies later in this chapter. As for the holding environment, Modell (1976) clearly implies that the analyst's behavior that helps create this environment is the behavior of the "good symbiotic mother":

... the analyst is constant and reliable; he responds to the patient's affects; he accepts the patient, and his judgment is less critical and more benign [than is the patient's self-judgment]; he is there primarily for the patient's needs and not for his own; he does not retaliate; and he does, at times, have a better grasp of the patient's inner psychic reality than does the patient himself and therefore may clarify what is bewildering and confusing [p. 291].

Seen from the above perspective, the question as to whether non-insight agents of change in psychoanalytic treatment are legitimate can be rephrased in terms of the question: Is the activation of symbiotic-like oneness fantasies legitimate? Or, in more operational language: (1) What effect does such activation have on the patient's symptoms and other indices of adaptive functioning? (2) What effect will it have on the psychoanalytic treatment process—i.e., will it affect, in one way or another, the patient's ability to gain insight?

The research data presented in Chapters 4 and 5 have some bearing on these questions. In the studies reported, many different kinds of individuals responded to the subliminal activation of oneness fantasies with diminished symptoms and other indicators of enhanced adaptation. And in a few investigations, this same activation also led to an increase in what can be characterized as "treatment-facilitating behavior." That is, the MOMMY AND I ARE ONE condition led to an increased ability to accept responsibility for ideas and feelings expressed (Silverman and C. Wolitzky, 1970), greater involvement in individual counseling (Schurtman, 1978), and more frequent self-disclosures in group counseling (Linehan and O'Toole, 1982). Thus, these findings lend some credence to the view that the activation of oneness fantasies in psychoanalytic treatment can have desirable consequences, though they are very far from decisive. For it cannot be assumed a priori that what held in the various experimental settings will also hold in the psychoanalytic treatment situation. Moreover, even in the subliminal studies there were some participants who were left unaffected by the oneness stimulation or showed negative effects. This raises the possibility that during psychoanalytic treatment different types of patients will respond differently when unconscious oneness fantasies are activated, though here, too, the extrapolation is open to question. Psychoanalytic treatment issues such as the one under consideration require both systematic clinical research (the direct study of the psychoanalytic treatment situation carried out with whatever controls can be instituted) and experimental research, each designed to complement the other.[2]

Until controversial issues such as the current one can be addressed in this manner, a clinican can hardly insist that his or her answer is the correct one. Thus, in outlining our position on the activation of oneness fantasies in psychoanalytic treatment, we claim only that it is based on our collective clinical experience and that it is consistent with the research data that have been cited.

Briefly stated, our position is that the activation of symbiotic-like oneness fantasies can no more be avoided in psychoanalytic treatment (we include here psychoanalysis proper and psychoanalytically oriented psychotherapy[3]) than in any other type of treatment. As we will discuss in Chapter 9, such desirable qualities in a clinician as being accepting of a patient and conveying a sense of understanding and helpfulness can activate these fantasies. Thus, in order to prevent their activation, the psychoanalytic clinician would have to suppress these qualities. This hardly makes sense, as these personal attributes are as desirable in a psychoanalytic therapist as they are in any other kind of therapist, helping to establish and maintain a desirable therapeutic ambience. In our opinion, the expression of such basic human qualities is not incompatible with the traditional psychoanalytic stance (see Stone, 1961). But none of the foregoing considerations eliminate the possibility that the activation of oneness fantasies may also pose problems in psychoanalytic treatment. (Shortly, we will spell out how this can happen.) Thus, remaining alert to this possibility is clearly important. But if this caveat is kept in mind, these fantasies can be a most valuable "resource" for the psychoanalytic clinician. As we shall soon detail, there are ways of activating these fantasies that not only do not impede the psychoanalytic process, but facilitate it for certain patients who might otherwise be inaccessible to psychoanalytic treatment.

FERENCZI AND THE ISSUE OF GRATIFICATION IN PSYCHOANALYTIC TREATMENT

Ferenczi was among the more "experimental" members of Freud's circle, and at different points in his career adopted extreme positions on the issue of the role of gratification in treatment. At one time (1919), he advocated not only that analysts not gratify their patients, but that they go out of their way to make sure that patients not gratify themselves in treatment. He went so far as to attempt to limit a patient's movement on the couch, believing that such movement might gratify "larval and vicarious onanistic activities" (p. 194). On the other hand, later in his career, he changed his position dramatically and advocated "pregenital play such as holding and kissing . . . [for] dried up cases and/or those with early traumata" (Bergmann and Hartman, 1976, p. 49).

Ferenczi's recommendations clearly put him in the camp of those who believe that non-insight agents of change have a place in psychoanalytic treatment. One can thus ask if his innovations allowed the psychoanalytic process to proceed unimpeded. In our judgment, his interventions probably led to notable interference. We suspect that, in his early position, Ferenczi too closely resembled a forbidding (most likely same-sex oedipal) parent, whereas later he too closely resembled a gratifying (preoedipal or opposite-sex oedipal) parent. In both instances, he was acting too much like a fantasy representation of a parent—or an actual parent—behavior which, as one of us has discussed elsewhere (Silverman, 1974), can interfere with the analysis of transference. That is, when transferences emerge in psychoanalytic treatment, it becomes important for the patient to be able eventually to experience them as illusory. To the extent that the patient's perception of the analyst in some kind of parental role is matched by the analyst's actually assuming that role, it can become most difficult, if not impossible, for the patient to experience the illusory quality of his or her perception. This experience is probably a prerequisite for tracing the transference back to its origins.

Moreover, Ferenczi's recommendations were based on erroneous assumptions. The assumption behind his restrictive role was based on a literal reading of Freud's energy theory.[4] The rationale for his later advocacy of gratification in treatment was that for patients who had experienced traumatic deprivations during childhood something special was needed both to alleviate their suffering and to make them accessible to psychoanalytic treatment.

By "traumatic deprivation" Ferenczi can be understood to be referring to those early experiences in the lives of his patients that interfered with their development of a sense of self and that resulted in developmental arrests. In our view, such patients do require "something special" during psychoanalytic treatment, specifically, the gratification involved in the activation of oneness fantasies. But we believe that this gratification is helpful only if these fantasies are activated in a particular way. In adding this qualification, we underscore our view that the adaptation-enhancing affects of oneness fantasies can be lost if they arouse fears related to additional meanings the fantasies have for the person. We suspect that interventions of the sort Ferenczi introduced—holding patients in his lap, kissing and fondling them—often activated oneness fantasies that had these hidden additional meanings, meanings which aroused shame over infantile dependence, guilt over incestuous wishes, anxiety over threats to the sense of self, and so on.

In sum, whereas we think Ferenczi deserves credit for being the first psychoanalyst to recognize that certain patients need something in addition to interpretation if they are to be accessible to analysis, his actual interventions could have posed two kinds of problems. It is likely that they impeded the analytic process, particularly in their interference with the analysis of transference. And it is also possible that his "offerings" threatened his patients at the same time as they gratified them, thereby undermining the purpose they were intended to serve.

DIAGNOSTIC CONSIDERATIONS

In our view, the consequences of the activation of oneness fantasies in psychoanalytic treatment will depend in part on the type of psychopathology the patient exhibits. The relevant diagnostic consideration is founded on the distinction between psychopathology based on structural conflict and that based on developmental arrest. Following Kohut (1971, 1977) and Stolorow and Lachmann (1980), we think it meaningful to distinguish between instances of pathology that follow the traditional psychoanalytic model of unconscious libidinal and aggressive wishes in conflict with superego demands and pathology that reflects a defective sense of self resulting from developmental arrest.

In the first type of psychopathology, the patient can be said to have met certain developmental prerequisites as far as self- and object representations are concerned, most importantly, the prerequisite that these representations be largely differentiated. Put differently, in such persons progress through the symbiotic and separation-individuation phases has resulted in an individual sufficiently differentiated so that others, by and large, are experienced as separate. Libidinal and aggressive wishes can thus be directed toward these others, a prerequisite for the development of structural conflict; and in their treatment, transferences emerge in the sense that Freud originally used the term—the analyst becomes the target for displacements of the patient's early conflicts with significant figures in his or her life.

In contrast, for those individuals with developmental arrests, these early phases have not been traversed successfully, so that self- and object representations are much less firmly demarcated. Consequently, the analyst is not experienced (predominantly) as a separate person, but instead as a symbiotic-like object or some other kind of self-object. Rather than being a "repository" for early conflicts over libidinal and aggressive wishes, he or she is "used" to maintain or restore an adequate sense of self. (As we detail in note 5, we do not maintain that conflict is not involved in developmental arrest pathology, only that *structural* conflict is not involved.)

In drawing the distinction between psychopathology based on structural conflict and that based on developmental arrest, our presentation thus far may have led to the mistaken impression that each type of psychopathology characterizes a distinct kind of patient. Following Stolorow and Lachmann, however, we do not view these pathologies as necessarily mutually exclusive. Instead, we find that they are often mixed, with different weightings of each for different patients. Thus, whereas there are patients whose treatment can focus exclusively on either structural conflict or developmental arrest, there is a larger group of patients whose treatment must focus on both issues. Most often, in this latter group, the early part of treatment is spent addressing the developmental arrest pathology. Then, when a sufficient degree of differentiation of self- and object representations has been attained, structural conflict comes to the fore. But there are also instances when this sequence is reversed and still others when the psychoanalytic clinican moves back and forth from one focus to the other, sometimes even within the same session (see Stolorow and Lachmann, 1980, pp. 100-102, 113-115, for clinical examples of the different possibilities). For convenience, we shall at times refer in what follows to patients who manifest problems involving developmental arrest *or* structural conflict, but it should be understood that the situation is usually more complex, and does not allow for dichotomous categorization.

THE SEARCH FOR ONENESS IN THE TREATMENT OF PATIENTS WITH DEVELOPMENTAL ARRESTS

In our view, developmentally arrested patients (or the developmentally arrested aspects of the more complex kind of patients described above) require something in addition to insight as a therapeutic agent in psychoanalytic treatment. Such a patient needs special help in overcoming his or her developmental deficit—an important therapeutic goal in its own right, but one that is additionally important if the psychoanalytic process is to unfold.

The locus of the arrest has been described by Stolorow and Lachmann as residing in the development of self- and object representations, specifically, in "the differentiation or subjective separation of self representations from representations of . . . primary objects, principally the mother" (p. 3) and in the ability "to integrate or synthesize [self- or object] representations with contrasting affective colorations" (p. 34). This is a developmental task which extends into the puberty years, if not beyond, and to which many factors contribute (see Stolorow and Lachmann, 1980, Chapter 8). But the symbiotic and separation-individuation phases of development remain the most crucial to its resolution. What we believe is often at the basis of this arrest is the absence of sufficient and sufficiently safe symbiotic experiences during these early phases; and it is this deficiency that we are proposing must be addressed in treatment through the activation of non-threatening oneness fantasies.

In the research we reviewed in Chapters 4 and 5, the subliminal exposure of the MOMMY AND I ARE ONE stimulus safely activated symbiotic-like oneness fantasies. What would be the analogue in the psychoanalytic treatment situation? We suggest that it is most frequently the analyst's "empathic response," i.e., that response by which the analyst conveys to the patient that he or she understands what the patient is communicating *within the patient's frame of reference.* (See Winnicott [1963]; Kohut [1971, 1977]; Modell [1976]; and Stolorow and Lachmann [1980] for related concepts.) The empathic response, when it is accurate, allows the patient to feel that the analyst is sharing his or her experience, thereby allowing the patient to perceive the analyst unconsciously as the ideal "symbiotic mother" (or, perhaps, as some other ideal selfobject), at the same time as it permits the analyst to carry out the more traditional analytic role.

It should be noted that the conceptualization of the empathic response is not tantamount to the simple admonition that the analyst strive to be empathic with patients. Traditionally, analysts have resorted to empathy (along with other mental processes[6]) to understand the unconscious motives at work in patients at particular points in treatment. But the recommendation that the analyst cultivate an empathic sensibility has until recently not been translated into actual empathic responsiveness, i.e., analysts have not typically responded verbally with a comment that conveys to the patient the sense that the analyst is viewing matters from the same vantage point as the patient. It is only this type of communication that constitutes empathic responsiveness as we are using the term; and it is this type of responsiveness that is probably more likely than anything else an analyst does to activate unconscious oneness fantasies.[7]

We should like to add that whether or not an analyst is experienced by a patient as empathically responsive, moreover, is dependent on the analyst's tone as well as on the content of the communication. Thus, the same statement may be experienced as empathic or unempathic depending on whether the analyst's tone conveys to the patient the sense that he or she is indeed viewing matters from the patient's perspective.

Some further clarifications are in order if our recommendations with respect to the analyst's empathic responsivity are not to be misunderstood. First, let us clarify what we mean when we refer to the analyst's "sharing" the patient's experience. This typically refers to the analyst's putting him or herself into the patient's subjective world (while maintaining a sense of separateness) so that the tone and content of what is conveyed to the patient reflects that he or she is experiencing at least a modicum of what the patient is feeling—or is on the verge of feeling. The analyst need not become engrossed in the patient's subjective world nor need he or she confirm the patient's appraisal of people or situations. Operating within the patient's frame of reference, for example, an analyst might say empathically "You feel attacked," without conveying a belief that an attack had actually occurred.

Second, we are not advocating that in analyzing instances of developmental arrest the analyst *always* react to a patient's communication with empathic responses (though the analyst should always be empathic in the more traditional way the concept of empathy has been used in the psychoanalytic literature). There are, in our collective experience, times when the analyst *should* speak from the position of an outside observer who is *not* sharing the patient's experience.[8] Just when in treatment empathic responses should be made is a matter of clinical judgment which, we hope, will ultimately be addressed by the kind of clinical research we advocated earlier (see note 2).

Third, the use of oneness fantasies activated by empathic responses does not preclude the analysis of these fantasies. On the contrary, we think it important than at appropriate times in treatment the analyst help the patient understand not only that he or she seeks to feel at one with the analyst, but that the analyst's empathic responsivity has left the patient feeling that this wish has been gratified. (See Silverman [1974, pp. 298-299] for a concrete example.)

The following case vignette highlights the concept of the

empathic response as it relates to the activation of symbiotic-like oneness fantasies in psychoanalytic treatment.

Helen was a 30-year-old woman who entered psychoanalytic treatment complaining of difficulties in maintaining relationships with men. Her mother had been unable to provide Helen with adequate symbiotic gratification during long stretches of her infancy, in part because of her own psychopathology and in part because of situational pressures. Helen had been the first-born child in her family and had been followed by three siblings in a very brief period of time. Soon after Helen's birth, her father had developed a chronic illness and had required care, adding to Helen's difficulties in obtaining adequate mothering. In fact, as the eldest child, Helen became a caretaker herself, in compliance with her mother's wishes. She gradually developed a characterological self-sufficiency as a way of denying her need for symbiotic-like gratification.

By the third year of her analysis, a good deal of time had been spent analyzing this self-sufficiency. These efforts were successful in that for the first time in her adult life Helen began to experience the very yearnings that for so long had been disavowed. Not surprisingly, these yearnings found direct expression in the transference, with Helen voicing a desire to hold her analyst's hand. It soon became evident, however, that what was involved was more than a libidinal wish; what was at first expressed as a simple desire soon evolved into a desperate demand. Helen announced that she would not continue treatment unless the analyst would allow her to hold his hand while she lay on the couch. When Helen continued by saying that if her analyst would not allow this, she would feel weak and vulnerable, she, in effect, revealed the crucial motive behind her demand. For Helen, her analyst, at least at that point in treatment, was a selfobject with whom she needed to merge in order to maintain a cohesive sense of self. Apparently, her previous characterological self-sufficiency, linked as it was to underlying grandiose fantasies, served to mask her "self-vulnerability." When her self-sufficiency gave way in analysis, not only previously unexpressed symbiotic-like longings emerged, but also her vulnerability, intensifying her need for the analyst as selfobject, a need that became concretized in the demand that he hold her hand. At the time this demand was made, Helen could take no distance from it. She had, in effect, issued an ultimatum: "Do as I ask or I will have to find a new analyst," a more accommodating selfobject, one might say. How might an analyst respond under such circumstances? Let us consider several possibilities.

First, the analyst could remain silent, a frequent kind of response during psychoanalytic treatment. In our view, with Helen, and in the situation described, silence would have been inappropriate. If the understanding of Helen's central motive was correct, such a response would constitute an empathic failure. For as the material had been formulated, Helen's unusual demand was most importantly a response to the emergence of her precarious sense of self; thus she desperately needed to counter this by using her analyst as a selfobject. To remain silent would have completely ignored this need. In fact, as we shall soon see from Helen's subsequent associations, it is likely that silence would have intensified the therapeutic stalemate by repeating in the analysis precisely that unresponsive behavior of the mother that had played such an important role in creating the problem that Helen sought to resolve in her treatment.

Other responses addressing other motives underlying her demand would have been equally inappropriate. One analyst in training, under comparable circumstances, commented to her patient, "You are making excessive demands on me, as you do on others. No wonder you are so often rebuffed and rejected by people." And in a similar situation, from another analyst in training: "Let us look at what you are trying to do to me by making this demand. You are trying to control me."

There was evidence that both these interpretations were correct in that the motives referred to were *part* of the patient's motivational state. Yet from the point of view of what was called for at the moment they were off the mark, addressing as they did interpersonal consequences of the patient's behavior. Like a silent response, they did not address the issue that deserved priority—the emergence of the patient's vulnerable sense of self.

Interpretations of this kind can also be faulted because they frequently leave the patient feeling criticized, a particularly undesirable consequence for someone with a defective sense of self. Moreover, the experience of criticism often leads to the suppression of subsequent demanding behavior rather than to its understanding. The patient becomes alert to internal signals of the emergence of such behavior and censors it before it gains expression. These suppressive attempts may even be successful, with the result that the psychological state that produced them remains active, possibly to take its toll in other ways.

Aside from silence and "interpersonal" interpretations, situations like the one we have described have been handled by calling attention to the patient's displacement onto the analyst of feelings originally experienced toward earlier figures. "You are reacting to me as if I were your mother" is the type of interpretation we have in mind here. To work with this, the patient must, at that moment, be able to take some distance from what he or she is experiencing in order to contemplate its origins. But this is not always possible. The urgency of Helen's demand mirrored the urgency of her immediate psychological state. The reality of her experience, in other words, was such that, at least for the moment, reflection was out of the question.

In situations such as the one we are discussing, an empathic response is needed that provides the patient with immediate relief for his or her threatened sense of self but at the same time encourages exploration. In the current instance, the analyst commented to Helen:

> "I can sense you're now on the horns of a dilemma. If I don't give you my hand, you'll feel rebuffed and hurt. But if I do, we'd be doing something that you know to be a radical departure from our accustomed way of working. We'd be enacting something that, at present, we don't understand."[9]

In response to this intervention, Helen calmed down considerably and commented, "You know, I'm acting as though I've known you all my life."

With these words, Helen's capacity for self-reflection was temporarily restored, rescued from its domination by the urgency of her need to recover her sense of self. Psychoanalytic exploration could thus continue. Helen then reported for the first time in treatment an incident from around the age of two in which she screamed in her crib for her mother so long that finally no sound came out. Her mother never came.

How might we understand the preceding course of events? The analysis of Helen's self-sufficiency had reawakened her damaged sense of self, her dependence on her mother as a selfobject and her disappointment at her mother's failure to respond. Holding the analyst's hand meant to her (in part) gaining access to a source of strength that would provide her with the sense of wholeness she needed to function. The analyst would be there "at hand" in a way that her mother was not. Actually, unconscious oneness fantasies had been operative earlier in treatment as suggested by references ascribing idealized qualities to the analyst. Merging with the idealized analyst had then enabled Helen to redress her sense of vulnerability. Putting the self-sufficiency to analytic scrutiny undercut this fantasy of oneness and revived the self-vulnerability and the associated image of the disappointing mother. The demand that the analyst give her his hand was thus an attempt to revive this oneness fantasy in a more concrete, drastic, and urgent form and thereby to restore an adequate sense of self.

We surmise that when the analyst reacted to this demand with an empathic response, a oneness fantasy was activated in a way not likely to be threatening. The empathic response, in other words, served to gratify her need for a symbiotic-like object without arousing undue anxiety, shame, or guilt. Helen, like most of the research participants exposed to the MOMMY AND I ARE ONE subliminal stimulus, thereby became able to accept (rather than disown) the activated oneness fantasy, and consequently responded in an adaptive fashion. Her sense of self was bolstered and the analysis continued with the emergence of an early memory of abandonment by her mother. (The emergence of this memory also testifies to the potential value of activating oneness fantasies, via the empathic response, in furthering the psychoanalytic process: We suspect this memory would not have been forthcoming if the analyst had extended his hand.)

In subsequent sessions, further material emerged that helped Helen work through the feelings stirred up by this memory. In one of these sessions, she said:

"I was caught up in a gust of feeling. I couldn't help

myself. I just now had a fantasy about getting up and walking around. I wanted to go to the window."

This was an allusion to suicidal thoughts that she had had prior to beginning treatment three years earlier. These thoughts had earlier been understood as a desperate attempt to feel separate from and not so dependent on her mother who she feared would abandon her. But now an additional meaning emerged. Through her death she would "disappear," thus abandoning her mother and reversing the roles in the early crib trauma.

This was followed by the revival in the transference of her wish for oneness with her mother. Helen continued: "I thought you would get apprehensive and so I cut the fantasy [of suicide] off." Questioned about this, Helen gave evidence that, at that moment, she needed to experience the analyst as sharing her own apprehensiveness. This questioning, in turn, undercut the oneness fantasy, with Helen then announcing in a tone of disappointment: "You're not going to get apprehensive—you know better."

The analyst focused on her dilemma of wanting to feel that he and she shared common emotions, at the same time as she knew that they were different. He said: "That bothers you. While you are caught on the gust of feelings, I may not be."

In response to this intervention, Helen became visibly upset:

"I don't like the whole idea. I don't like to admit it's so. I've always had a thing about feeling that I'm involved with something that nobody else is involved in."

Helen then continued in pain and rage, ostensibly talking about her boyfriend, but clearly alluding to her analyst as well: "I give, give, give, and give, and all I get back is non-feeling."

Quite clearly, the analyst's response had gone too far in undercutting Helen's oneness fantasy. He had stated: "While you are caught on the gust of feelings, I may not be." That is, he had used the exact language which Helen had used in describing her feelings *before* her fantasy of suicide. And yet he had done so in the context of responding to another matter: Helen's disappointment that he had not shared her apprehensiveness *after* the fantasy of suicide. Thus, rather than conveying to Helen that he was viewing matters from the same vantage point as she was, as he had hoped to do, the analyst's response suggested to her that they were talking about two very different things. While Helen wanted to talk about the apprehensiveness issue, the analyst apparently had raised a much broader issue: Not only that Helen wants him to experience her apprehensiveness in the very specific situation following her suicide fantasy, but that Helen wants him to share *all* her feelings, including the "gust of feeling" that led to the suicide fantasy in the first place. The depth of her subsequent anxiety might then be explained in terms of her unwillingness to accept that this more encompassing sharing is what she had unconsciously wanted all along. In other words, the analyst's response might have suggested to her the very depth of her wishes for oneness, wishes that she was not yet ready to face.[10]

Helen's highly distressed reaction to the analyst's intervention can also be explained in terms of a more general conception of empathy. Aside from the specifics of the intervention having posed a threat for Helen, the intervention did not after all come from within her immediate frame of reference. As a result, Helen could have been left with the feeling that her analyst was not there with her as she needed him to be at that moment. Or, stated somewhat differently, it was as though the analyst's words had been equivalent to his physical presence so that when they did not "make contact" with what Helen had been experiencing at the moment, she felt that she had lost him as a selfobject. This, we might add, we have found to be a general problem with patients for whom developmental arrest pathology is at issue: Interpretations that, although accurate, are not exquisitely close to the patient's immediate experience, interfere with the fantasy of oneness.

Helen began the next session by continuing to express distress to the analyst:

> "There's not one safe topic I can plunge into. I'm becoming afraid. I hope you're not afraid."

Believing that his non-empathic response in the previous session had resulted in Helen's experiencing too much distress to reflect on what was occurring, the analyst attempted to restore the empathic mode. He responded: "You want to be sure I won't be scared so that you will be safe."

Helen's agitation dissipated and the analysis of her vulnerable sense of self continued. Its expressions and its links to the past were further clarified. Later in the session Helen was able to say: "I feel frightened and I want you to be afraid also. But a part of me wants you to stand aside." The analyst commented: "You have wanted very much to feel that we are one, but you also want to feel like a separate person." This time Helen did not react with distress and produced further material bearing on her struggle to achieve separateness.

MORE ON THE DANGERS OF DIRECT GRATIFICATION

In our discussion of Ferenczi earlier, we pointed out that one of the problems of directly gratifying symbiotic-like wishes (rather than providing an empathic response) is that the "offering" can have a hidden meaning for the patient, be perceived as a threat, and defeat the purpose for which it was intended. Material emerged later in Helen's analysis to indicate that this easily could have happened if her analyst had extended his hand. For in one of the sessions in which she alluded to her original demand, the contextual material implied that the extended hand represented her father's erect penis. She remembered that during a recent illness of her father she was the only one in the family whom he permitted to wash him and give him alcohol rubs. His preference for her and the bodily contact she had had with him aroused oedipal wishes. Against this background, the analyst with his outstretched hand recalled the longed-for phallic father, at the same time that he represented her mother in providing symbiotic-like gratifications.

In our experience, requests by patients for direct gratification of symbiotic-like wishes often have these kinds of additional meanings. For example, a hand-holding request from another patient reflected not only symbiotic-like wishes, but also a masochistic desire to reinforce a self-image of being a needy person. Thus, to accede to this patient's request would not so much have created a threat as it would have bolstered a masochistic behavior pattern and a devalued self-representation. (See Langs [1975] on "misalliances" in psychoanalytic treatment.)

Whereas an empathic response could also have unforeseen meaning for a patient—anything a therapist does in treatment can fall prey to this danger (Silverman, 1974)—it is, in our experience, much less apt to happen. And if it should occur, it is easier to analyze, so that the perceived threat can be eliminated and the other maladaptive consequences avoided. Patients typically view the analyst's empathy as congruent with his or her role (which is not the case for direct gratifications) and thus are more able to recognize how their own needs may have colored their perception of the analyst's empathic intervention.

AN ADDED DIVIDEND OF THE EMPATHIC RESPONSE

The analyst's empathic response sometimes does more than safely activate oneness fantasies and allow psychoanalytic treatment to proceed. When it is offered in response to the patient's expression of a symbiotic-like need (as it was in Helen's case), it legitimizes the need and thereby implicitly encourages the patient to bring to the analysis related associations and memories that bear on the developmental arrest. (Helen's memory of screaming in the crib and the subsequent material bearing on oneness and separation are an example of this.) The analysis can continue and the patient is helped to understand the history of the arrest. Stolorow and Lachmann (1980) have discussed just how the analyst facilitates this kind of therapeutic movement:

> The analyst's acceptance of the role of selfobject has several consequences for the conduct and course of treatment. Most important, he does not interfere with the unfolding of the patient's arrested [development]. He therefore avoids a repetition of the traumatic interferences . . . that come about through prematurely ruptured selfobject ties. . . . The analyst's empathic communications will include clarifications of the content, affective nuances, and functions of the selfobject configurations that the patient attempts to revive or maintain in the face of threats [to the sense of self] [pp. 182-183].

THE THERAPEUTIC ALLIANCE, ONENESS FANTASIES, AND THE ANALYSIS OF STRUCTURAL CONFLICT

In our clinical experience, attempts to strengthen the therapeutic alliance—the sharing by patient and analyst of a similar conception of how treatment should proceed (Zetzel, 1956; Greenson, 1967; Lachmann, 1971)—frequently require empathic responses. (In our discussion of Helen's case, the demand that her analyst hold her hand vitiated the therapeutic alliance; thus an empathic response was offered in an attempt to restore the alliance.) According to our thesis, these attempts will therefore often activate unconscious oneness fantasies. Since attention to the therapeutic alliance is generally viewed as warranted for all patients, we are faced with a situation in which oneness fantasies will be activated during the psychoanalytic treatment of patients with structural conflicts as well as patients with developmental arrests. And even in the absence of attempts by the analyst to strengthen the therapeutic alliance, there are inevitably instances in psychoanalytic treatment when these fantasies will inadvertently be activated in patients with structural conflict.

What are the implications of this? We have seen in our clinical work both positive and negative consequences of the activation of oneness fantasies in patients with structural conflict. On the positive side, we have noted instances in which this activation appeared to leave such patients feeling more secure (just as it did for patients with developmental arrests) and thus more willing to face the conflict-laden wishes surging within them. And on the negative side, there have been instances in which these fantasies were used to bolster defensive processes. That is, the fantasy of being one with the good mother masked symptoms, muted anxiety, and warded off conflict-laden libidinal and aggressive wishes.

Vignettes from the treatment of two patients will help illustrate this latter point. Donald, a 33-year-old patient, maintained a sadomasochistic relationship with his wife that reproduced an earlier sadomasochistic relationship with his mother. During his puberty and early adolescence, Donald and his mother fought daily—often physically—about his girlfriends; they were invariably of a religion and social background different from his own. Both the fighting and the choice of girlfriends—whom he unconsciously experienced as the opposite of his mother—allowed him to ward off his incestuous wishes for her. These defensive maneuvers continued to operate in his relationship with his wife and included, prominently, unconscious fantasies of oneness with her. These were reflected in his masochistic tie to her (see our discussion of masochism in Chapter 7) and were particularly clear in his descriptions of "losing himself" in his wife during lovemaking. He had apparently retreated from experiencing his wife as an oedipal object and, instead, defensively experienced her as a symbiotic-like object.

Rhoda, a 29-year-old patient, described how she sacrificed her needs and independence to sustain a relationship with a man whom she unconsciously perceived as a symbiotic-like object. The underlying fantasy of being one with him turned out to be her way of handling oedipal wishes. Specifically, in the image of being merged with the man, she was secretly expressing a wish to replace her mother during intercourse with her father. Her recollection of her parents from her childhood years was that they were "as one—never fighting or disagreeing, always together, and having the same friends and interests." This characterization was later understood as derived from primal scene memories of their "togetherness." By transforming oedipal wishes into symbiotic-like wishes, Rhoda was able to ward off feelings of exclusion, associated outrage, and frustrated incestuous desire. For both Donald and Rhoda, the merger fantasies and wishes were not in the service of reviving an aborted developmental phase, but rather of keeping oedipal conflict in abeyance.

In alerting themselves to the defensive use of oneness fantasies, psychoanalytic clinicians should be particularly cognizant of both their personal contribution and of the contribution of the treatment setting to the activation of these fantasies. In the course of Rhoda's treatment, for example, she reported a dream in which the analytic couch was transformed into a bed, with the analyst sitting near her. In the dream she felt comforted and secure about being understood. She then spoke of her boyfriend (whom she had discussed in the previous session) and how, when she lay in his arms, she felt at peace and comforted. But this occurred too infrequently, she said, and she went on to complain of his "inconstancy," making jealous allusions to his sexual interest in other women. This allowed the analyst to interpret the underlying sexual fantasy in the dream. In the dream, she was able to ward off the sexual fantasy by focusing on the analytic setting (the use of the couch) and her analyst's behavior (his empathic stance) to bolster her defensive use of oneness fantasies.

Rhoda then said that as a child, before going to sleep at night, her father would sit at her bedside. She then had him all to herself and they would speak "intimately and in private." She was able to realize that, at those times too, she focused on nonsexual, childlike satisfactions to ward off sexual feelings toward her father and feelings of competitiveness with her mother. And she could sense in both situations—while on the couch with her analyst and on the bed with her father—momentary feelings of oedipal triumph over her rival.

As in the above example, patients who are using symbiotic-like fantasies defensively should be helped to see what in the treatment situation or the contribution of the analyst is triggering these fantasies; this, we have found, gives patients a more comprehensive understanding of how their defensive needs express themselves. (See Langs [1973], Gill [1979], and Silverman, [1979] for related discussions.)

The above discussion leaves open the following question. Given the potential of empathic responses to activate oneness fantasies, should an analyst, in analyzing instances of structural conflict, make use of these responses? (We remind the reader of our distinction between empathic responses and empathy; we take for granted the usefulness of the latter.) We indicated earlier that in attempting to strengthen the therapeutic alliance, there are times when these responses are clearly useful. But beyond these occasions, is the empathic mode or the more neutral mode of analyst-as-outside-observer more congruent with psychoanalytic goals? We think there is no simple, and for now, clear answer to this question. We suspect that depending on such considerations as the specific conflict being analyzed, the state of the transference, and the personality organization of the patient, either the empathic mode or the neutral mode may prove more productive. But we can only surmise this for now since, in our view, systematic study must first be carried out if a reasonably clear answer to this question is to emerge.

ADDRESSING DIFFERENTIATION PROBLEMS IN PSYCHOANALYTIC TREATMENT

In one particular sense, our presentation has been somewhat one-sided to this point. Whereas we view patients with developmental arrests as needing *both* non-threatening oneness gratifications and help in achieving further self/other differentiation, we have until now focused on the role of the psychoanalytic clinician in meeting the former need. We will now spell out the ways an analyst can help a patient complete the differentiation process.

First, by using empathic responses, the analyst aids the process in two ways. The oneness fantasies that are activated can leave the patient more able to attempt psychological separation. (Recall the study of Bryant-Tuckett [1980] described in Chapter 6 in which the adolescents at the residential treatment center who received the MOMMY AND I ARE ONE stimulus were rated as more capable than the controls of independent classroom functioning.) In addition, by resisting a patient's overtures to provide more direct gratifications (as in Helen's case), the analyst lessens the possibility that the patient will become threatened by loss of the sense of self, a threat that would not at all be conducive to completing the separation process.

Second, where anxiety related to loss of the sense of self arises, the analyst can interpret to the patient both the nature of the anxiety and whatever may have occurred during treatment (including the analyst's interventions) that triggered the anxiety. And third, when a patient shows signs—often tentative and fraught with anxiety—of moving toward a greater degree of separateness, the analyst can interpret what the patient is attempting to achieve. That is, analogous to the interpretation of unconscious wishes when addressing structural conflict, the analyst can verbalize the patient's beginning striving for separateness, the awareness of which often seems to encourage further efforts in this direction (see Stolorow and Lachmann, 1980, 1981).

The following vignette illustrates the interventions referred to above.

Anita (whose treatment is discussed by Lachmann and Stolorow [1980] in more detail) established a selfobject transference of the idealizing type (Kohut, 1971) when she entered treatment at age 37 after two earlier analytic experiences. She sought help because of rapid, and to her, unpredictable fluctuations in self-esteem and in her evaluation of certain people in her life. She alternated between viewing herself as "shit" and as "unassailable" while her husband and certain friends were described at times with contempt and at other times with awe. She then described feeling enthralled by their patience, wisdom, and their capacity to make their own way in the world. So long as Anita viewed these people with reverence, she felt connected to them and valued herself. Quite clearly they were selfobjects for her.

During the third year of treatment, Anita showed signs of having sufficiently overcome her developmental arrest so that indications of structural conflict began to appear in the analytic material. In one session, Anita spoke of an acquaintance from her past who by chance had been referred to "her" analyst. She became preoccupied with fantasies that the analyst would prefer the acquaintance to her. But, concurrently, she referred to the acquaintance in the most derogatory terms. She described her as a shallow person who substituted sentimentality for feelings and talked endlessly about inconsequential things. Anita was convinced that this description was accurate and thus wondered how she could imagine that the analyst would prefer this woman to her.

Additional material suggested that there was a defensive element to Anita's fear of being rejected—that acceptance unconsciously meant oneness for her, which in turn threatened her sense of self. The analyst thus offered the following interpretation:

> "When you start to question that I would prefer Mary [the acquaintance] to you, you in effect are saying that you feel you have a place here and that you feel accepted by me. But to feel accepted seems to have a disorganizing effect on you. You avoid the disorganization by asserting your expectation of rejection."

Anita responded that "When you say something right I have mixed-up feelings. I feel 'Thank God you understand,' but I also envy your ability to connect with people." Further inquiry revealed that the envy Anita referred to was a novel experience for her. It thus seemed as if the interpretation of her fear of acceptance/oneness had allowed her to take a step toward differentiating herself from her analyst so that she could view him as the possessor of a quality that she currently believed she lacked. It is true that her words "Thank God" may have reflected the remainder of the idealizing transference in which awe and reverence for the analyst were partially retained. But her reference to the difference between them and the envy this evoked mirrored a shift from a selfobject transference to a transference toward the analyst as a separate person. To affirm this developmental advance, the analyst commented:

> "You seem better able now than in the past to experience us as separate people. And while this leaves you feeling envious, you are now more willing to tolerate the discomfort."

Further material then followed related to the newly emerging feelings of envy.

In closing, we would offer two points of clarification. First, by emphasizing here the patient's achievement of greater psychological separateness, we do not mean to imply that we view renunciation of symbiotic-like oneness fantasies as a goal of treatment or as an endpoint in development. As we have stressed throughout this book, oneness fantasies and psychological separateness should not be viewed as incompatible. In fact, we believe that both are lifelong psychological currents. A defining characteristic of the psychologically healthy person may well be his or her comfort with both currents, that is, an ability to seek oneness and separateness in ways that do not conflict with each other.

Second, we do not believe there is an incompatibility between the interpretation of structural conflict and the interventions we have described—empathic responses and interpretations of feared threats to the sense of self and strivings for separateness. As we indicated earlier, we believe that structural conflict often coexists with problems of developmental arrest. When this is the case, we believe that interpretations of structural conflict and the interventions we have focused on in this chapter are mutually enhancing. We underscore this point because some psychoanalytic clinicians seem to experience the same discomfort with the idea that these other interventions can aid their treatment that physicians experience when told of the power of placebo effects. (This parallel is particularly apt since we will propose in the next chapter that oneness fantasies are also implicated in placebo effects.) But if the psychoanalytic clinician bears in mind the synergistic potential of these fantasies—the fact that they may well make their specific interventions more effective—it may be possible to view them not as a problem that warrants avoidance but as a resource that deserves to be developed and further researched.

NOTES

1. Also proposed as underlying non-insight agents of change are "sanctioned oedipal fantasies." When the analyst conveys

"a sense of parental authority . . . by exuding an air of direc-
tiveness or an *ex cathedra* sense of certainty," particularly when
this is accompanied by the analyst appearing judgmental—for
example, by frequently using confrontations as an intervention
or by making reference to the analysand "acting out"—the analysand is encouraged to "experience the analyst as the same-sex
oedipal parent" (Silverman, 1979, p. 211). But since this "forbidding" oedipal parent does not directly prohibit the expression
of the unconscious and previously taboo incestuous fantasy, the
analysand unconsciously "reasons" that the fantasy itself is "sanctioned" (p. 211). He can then express it in the course of treatment.

2. In a recent paper, Silverman and D. Wolitzky (1982) have
outlined five "research paradigms" that could be used to address
controversial psychoanalytic treatment issues like the ones under
consideration. These range from most to least "naturalistic," a
continuum that refers to "the degree to which the design departs
from the typical treatment situation" (p. 18). Since each of these
paradigms has specific strengths and weaknesses, ideally all
should be used in tackling controversial questions like the current one, thus providing converging and complementary lines
of evidence. The paradigms suggested include:
Paradigm 1: Naturalistic Design with Interclinician Comparisons.
In this paradigm, the data to be examined come from psychoanalytic treatment in its usual setting conducted by groups of clinicians representing two contrasting approaches. Thus, in terms
of the issue under consideration, treatment results could be compared for clinicians who, from their self-reports, can be judged
to maintain an analytic stance that encourages the activation of
oneness fantasies and clinicians who do not. In order for this
paradigm to substantively advance knowledge: (1) each of the
positions compared should be represented by a substantial number of clinicians; (2) the clinicians representing the two positions
should be equated for years of experience and whatever other
variables are judged pertinent to treatment outcome; (3) in selecting cases for the participating clinicians, an attempt should
be made to equate the groups being compared for relevant patient characteristics. (In the study being proposed, at the very
least such equating should be done for degree of pathology and
the presence of problems involving developmental arrest and/or
structural conflict.); (4) the evaluations made should cover not
only the fate of the problem that brought the person to treatment, but the status of various ego functions as well (object
relations, adequacy of defenses, the capacity to be introspective,

etc.); and (5) evaluations should be carried out by independent clinicians who do not have knowledge of the characteristics of the psychoanalytic treatment that each patient received.

Paradigm 2: Naturalistic Design with Intraclinician Comparisons. This paradigm is the same as the first, except that instead of comparisons being made between two groups of clinicians, they are made between pairs of cases of one group of clinicians, with each clinician conducting treatment from the two vantage points being contrasted. As pointed out by Silverman and Wolitzky, this has an important research advantage over the first paradigm, but poses a practical problem as well. The advantage is that it holds constant (or at least more constant) many aspects of the clinician's behavior that could influence outcome, other than the treatment variable that is being evaluated. That is, it is much more likely that two cases will be handled in a similar way with regard to these extraneous variables if they are treated by the same clinician than if they are treated by two different ones. The practical problem is that the clinicians involved have to be both willing and able to conduct treatment from the two vantage points. A possible solution would entail using neophyte clinicians, not set in their ways, and supervised by a clinician who favors one approach for one case of the pair and a clinician with the opposing viewpoint for the other case.

Paradigm 3: Modified Naturalistic Design with Interclinician Comparisons and *Paradigm 4: Modified Naturalistic Design with Intraclinician Comparisons.* These paradigms are the same as the first two described except that the psychoanalytic treatment sessions are taped, with this comprising the "modification." While some clinicians have expressed discomfort with the taping of treatment sessions, a number of those who have actually taped sessions (e.g., Gill, Simon, Fink, Endicott, and Paul, 1968; Dahl, 1972) report that neither the way treatment proceeds nor the outcome need be adversely affected. Silverman and Wolitzky took no sides on this issue (since only systematic investigation could offer a substantive resolution), but they did suggest that this paradigm has important research advantages. Characterizations of the way a clinician conducts treatment would no longer be dependent on self-reports, but could be judged directly from taped transcripts.

It was further noted that the recording of sessions allows for the objective observation of the immediate reactions of patients to particular kinds of interventions. (See Gill et al. [1968], and Sampson, Weiss, Mlodnosky, and Hause [1972] who have carried out such research.) Observations of this sort supplement and complement observations of the more distal effects observed in evaluations carried out after treatment. Whereas these latter observations bear on the important question of how a particular kind of therapeutic approach influences the way a person emerges from treatment, they leave unclear just what aspects of the approach are having what particular effects. In observing the patient's behavior immediately after the treatment intervention, the observer can be much more certain of its specific short-term consequences. In the study being proposed, questions could be addressed as to whether a comforting tone of voice (as a concrete expression of a "holding environment") or an empathic response allows a patient to address anxiety-arousing material that he or she otherwise avoids. Of course, many instances from the treatment of any one patient would have to be examined before a judgment would be warranted as to the effect of such an intervention on that patient. Similarly, reactions of many patients of a particular type (e.g., those with noteworthy developmental arrests) would have to be assessed before one could judge whether any generalization is warranted about the value of this type of therapeutic intervention for that type of patient.

Paradigm 5: Experimental. In the Silverman and Wolitzky paper, the "experimental" paradigm referred, as it does here, to research in which there is an experimental manipulation designed to affect behavior in a particular way, the impact of which is compared with a control manipulation, with all other variables held constant. In terms of our current discussion, studies with the subliminal psychodynamic activation method could allow for an experimental test of the thesis that the activation of symbiotic-like oneness fantasies can enhance the development of insight. The following is one research design that could be used.

Two clinical interviews could be conducted with research participants (one before and one after a period of subliminal stimulation) in which the clinician probes into various areas of the participant's life. As in interviews that many psychoanalytic clinicians conduct prior to deciding whether a particular person is a good candidate for psychoanalytic treatment, the interviewer could give the participants various opportunities to convey whatever insights they have into their motivations and the relationship between their past and present. These interviews would be taped and the tapes evaluated by experienced clinicians for degree and depth of insight, using criteria developed beforehand. If the research participants are divided into matched groups one of which receives subliminal oneness stimulation and the other subliminal control stimulation, data will emerge that bear directly on the question of how the capacity for insight is affected by the activation of oneness fantasies. If, moreover, the research participants consist both of a subgroup of persons dominated by structural conflict and another dominated by developmental arrest, it would be possible to test experimentally the idea that the effects of oneness fantasies on insight may be different for these two groups of people.

Results from a series of experimental studies such as this would complement the clinical studies referred to above. As was noted in Silverman and Wolitzsky, experimental data, while well controlled, are too artificial and removed from clinical reality to be given heavy weight when considered in isolation. Conversely, clinical data alone are too poorly controlled to be compelling. But when both kinds of data are considered together, the weaknesses of each are compensated for by the strengths of the other so that the conclusions reached can be held with reasonable confidence.

3. Before we attempt to support this proposal, a word is in order about the difference between psychoanalysis and psychoanalytically oriented psychotherapy. Formal distinctions between the two are well known. The sitting-up position of the therapy patient and his or her less frequent visits often emphasize the realistic context of the treatment sessions and thus stem the patient's propensity toward free association, fantasy formation, and regression. This, then, can diminish the depth of possible transference reactions. Psychoanalytic clinicians practicing therapy are therefore frequently limited in their ability to analyze transference reactions to their fullest because they do not have available to them the richer data that usually emerges from an analytic patient.

In our view, the distinction between psychoanalysis and psychoanalytically oriented psychotherapy has been encumbered by unnecessary judgments of value. Beginning with Freud's (1919a) unfortunate metaphor, psychotherapy has been considered the "copper" of treatment and psychoanalysis its "gold." Emendations by later generations of analysts to the effect that copper may be the more difficult ore to mine (e.g., Colby, 1951) have done little to change this bias. Thus, what is often added to the characterization of psychotherapy in contrast to psychoanalysis is that the clinican is more apt to use less desirable interventions—supportive and "educative" comments, for example—that can confound the transference.

Our position is that these "nonanalytic" interventions are not an intrinsic part of psychotherapy so that the transference within it can remain uncontaminated and thus optimally analyzable. True, the less frequent visits and other formal differences may have a profound effect on the depth of the transference material that emerges as well as the material generally. The less frequent visits, in particular, tend to aid the side of the resistances so that often the therapist has to work more exclusively with defenses whereas the analyst more readily obtains material reflecting unconscious wishes and fantasy formations. In turn, the analyst is more often in a better position to apprehend, interpret, and reconstruct crucial childhood events that underlie the patient's conflicts.

These distinctions, however, are only quantitative, affecting the content to which attention is most often directed—the wishful side or the defensive side. The *stance* of the clinician vis-à-vis the patient can remain the same. This is particularly true for the important task of distinguishing between material that reflects structural conflict and material that reflects developmental arrest, a distinction that we shall emphasize throughout this chapter. And we believe that the specific interventions we shall discuss—empathic responses and interpretations related to wishes for and fears of both oneness and separateness—lie within the province of the psychoanalytic clinician whether he or she functions as therapist or analyst.

4. Among the more controversial aspects of psychoanalytic theory *within* the psychoanalytic community are Freud's assumptions about psychic energy, his "economic theory." We refer here to his depiction of psychological activity in terms of quantities of energy "deployed" within a closed psychic apparatus. (See, for example, Holt (1976) and Klein (1969) for critiques of this aspect of psychoanalytic theory). In his early theorizing Ferenczi took the energy theory to heart and applied it to clinical psychological phenomena. He believed that by suppressing what subtle forms of sexual self-gratification the patient might be able to obtain on the couch during the analytic hour, he could force this energy to seek discharge along ideational lines rather than through "acting out." In other words, he hoped to divert the energy from expressions that he viewed as narcissistic and infantile into transference fantasies more accessible to analysis.

But to limit a patient's movement would hardly rule out masturbatory gratification. Such gratification could be obtained through symbolic activity, such as verbalizing thoughts ("playing with words"). Moreover, it is not clear why even within the energy theory framework sexual energy could not be discharged at one point during the session (be it in motor activity or verbalization) and build up again at a later point. Ferenczi's implicit assumption seemed to be that once sexual energy was discharged, sexual motives were no longer operative and thus were not accessible to analysis.

5. Our distinction between "structural conflict" and "conflict" is based on the following considerations. When we use the latter term, we include what we referred to earlier (Chapters 3 and 4) as the schizophrenic's dilemma in both seeking symbiotic-like merger and fearing a loss of the sense of self. This same dilemma characterizes many of the patients we are discussing in this chapter—non-schizophrenics who, like schizophrenics, suffer from developmental arrests. (In current psychiatric terminology, these patients' psychopathology would be referred to as "narcissistic personality disorders" and "borderline states.") Thus, one consequence of developmental arrest in the evolution of the sense of self is that merging wishes are often present—that is, these patients' frequently seek selfobjects to rectify their "self problems." But these merging wishes are often conflictual, arousing threats of different kinds, most prominently the danger of the loss of the sense of self. Thus, a vicious cycle is formed: A defective sense of self stimulates merging wishes which, in turn, can further aggravate the "self problem" (see Modell, 1980).

The conflict over merging wishes does not qualify as structural conflict (1) because superego demands are not involved, and (2) because it is unclear if the wish to merge should be viewed as an id function. See also Sandler (1974).

6. The "other mental processes" we refer to include intellectual understanding and logical inference. Empathy differs from these in that it is less cognitive and more affective. In drawing this distinction, we do not mean to imply that these different processes are mutually exclusive; rather, we think it likely that the analyst's response is often based on the simultaneous operation of these processes.

7. Elsewhere, one of us (Silverman, 1979) has noted other frequent "activators" of symbiotic-like fantasies in the psychoanalytic situation, including the vocalizations "mm" and "mm-hmm" used by many analysts. The link between this sound and symbiotic-like fantasies can be drawn as follows.

In a 1954 paper, Greenson noted that the sound "mm" is the only sound an infant can make during nursing without parting his or her lips and allowing milk to escape. Thus, the sound becomes linked with both oral pleasure ("Campbell's soup is mm mm good") and mother (in fact, in the great majority of languages the word for mother begins with the letter "M"). Since it has been suggested (Pine, 1981) that symbiotic experiences for the infant are most frequently evoked during nursing, we think it reasonable to suppose that the sound "mm" may evoke oneness fantasies. (The link between the "mm" sound and oneness fantasies is currently being studied experimentally at the New York Veterans Administration Research Laboratory.)

8. This is particularly the case when a patient is making strides toward psychological separation. In some instances of this sort, the empathic response is still in order since the activation of oneness fantasies can make this goal more attainable; in others, however, the patient may experience the oneness gratification that it provides as antithetical to what he or she is trying to achieve (see the earlier discussion of Sally in Chapter 7). One might say in such an instance that an empathic *understanding* would lead the analyst to recognize that an empathic *response* would be counterproductive.

9. The "dialogues" presented in this chapter are based on treatment notes and the analyst's (F.M. Lachmann) recollections and reconstructions. The sessions were not tape recorded. We decided to put these renderings in dialogue form since we think it important for the reader to be able to consider the actual wording of the interventions we are proposing. All too often in the psychoanalytic literature, interventions are alluded to or described, rather than concretely rendered.

10. It could be argued that even when the analyst's stance is that of an outside observer, interventions should be limited to those which a patient can accept. While we agree with this in the long-range sense, this need not mean that the patient must immediately accept the interpretation. It is certainly possible that interpretations—correct as far as their content is concerned, but which patients do not react to or react to with distress—facilitate insight at a later point in time. How such interventions compare with those that a patient can meaningfully accept at once, is in our minds, an open question that needs to be researched.

9

EPILOGUE: THE SEARCH FOR ONENESS IN EVERYDAY LIFE

A good friend of one of the authors described an unusual experience he had had while taking a tennis lesson from a female tennis pro. "I have taken lessons before," he said, "but progress was always painfully slow. This time, though, things were very different. For years I have had this ping-pong stroke but now after just one lesson I am really playing tennis."

He went on to describe his metamorphosis, one particular aspect of which caused his friend to perk up his ears. "It's funny, but I could feel myself hitting differently almost before she said anything. It was something about her manner. I never had lessons from a tennis pro before who had that kind of effect on me." "What was it about her manner?" he was asked. "She was low-keyed, smiling, never irritated, and always accepting. She left me with a sense that she was totally with me and for me and with that I started to stroke the ball just as she did. If I could afford it, I would take lessons with her every day."

INTRODUCTION

In our clinical discussions in Chapters 7 and 8, we have considered the search for oneness as it is reflected in psychopathology. We have argued that underlying the pathology of certain non-psychotic patients are symbiotic-like

231

wishes, and that the activation of unconscious oneness fantasies in the psychoanalytic treatment of such patients can facilitate both positive behavioral change and the psychoanalytic process itself. We shall now broaden our perspective in two ways, both of which are exemplified by the introductory tennis vignette. First, we shall propose that the search for oneness is also expressed in a variety of experiences and activities that are found in everyday life and that when these experiences and activities succeed in activating oneness fantasies, without threatening the sense of self, improved adaptation follows. Second, and in keeping with some of the research data presented in Chapter 5 (pp. 108-113), we offer this proposition for people generally and not just those with particular forms of psychopathology.

An early and most interesting account of the expression of the search for oneness in everyday life was written by Hellmuth Kaiser (1965), a psychoanalyst from the Menninger Foundation whose writings attracted considerable interest in the 1950's and 1960's. Putting his reflections in the third person (presumably for literary reasons), Kaiser writes about "G.," a psychoanalyst who discovers the ubiquitous tendency of "loosening one's identity and fusing one's personality with another" (1965, p. 117) while recalling with pleasure a show he had seen a few years earlier:

> It had been an ice skating performance executed by well trained professionals. . . . only one number of the program's rich variety had made a sufficiently deep impression on him. . . .
>
> The act had been performed by two young men. They were dressed . . . in ordinary gray slacks, marine blue street jackets and brown hats. They also wore the same type of ties of the same loud red color. They both stood in a relaxed, casual posture waiting

for the music to start. Then they executed some difficult, complicated figures one after the other with the greatest ease, grace, and precision, well synchronized without ever having to look at each other. The last vigorous arc they described terminated in a nonchalant fashion; it brought them back, as if by chance, to the exact location from which they had started. While the audience applauded the brilliant performance, they both relaxed, looked with an expression of slight fatigue and complete indifference somewhere into space and, to G.'s bewilderment, both lifted their arms lazily and readjusted their ties. G. felt excited without knowing the reason for his excitement.

The music started again, and again the two skaters raced through their complicated arcs and spirals, pirouettes and jumps to wind up as at the end of the first number with their momentum spent in their starting position. While the applause rose louder than before, they again relaxed, looked somewhere into space, indifferent, slightly fatigued, and again, almost simultaneously, raised the left arm with the typical gesture and looked dreamily at their watches. . . . [G. reacted with] rapturous enthusiasm. . . .

It needed this one little piece of memory to call to his attention the significance of untold numbers of experiences, most of them of far greater importance and generality than this small single trick of showmanship which by any objective standard could be called amusing and maybe thrilling but nothing more. His next thought turned to the trick itself and the special excitement which it had aroused. . . . When two ice skaters after performing some vigorous figure skating, feel the need to readjust their ties, this is nothing anybody could get excited about. . . . The

source of [his] excitement must have been . . . a fan-
tastic [notion] . . . which seemed tempting not because of its plausibility—it is neither plausible nor
even possible—but because of its secret fascination,
the assumption that they were not wholly separate
personalities but had only one mind between them.
That means that I too have a secret desire that "fusion" be possible. And not only I, everybody is attracted by . . . almost anything which allows for a
fleeting impression of . . . fusion!

A single well-trained soldier going through the
steps and paces, the turns and halts of his drill may
please the eyes of the training officer; in the eyes of
any outsider he looks ridiculous. If a whole battalion
moves over the parade ground, all in step, breaking
up the large column into smaller groups, all making
the turn at exactly the same moment, turning again
and forming one long straight line and maintaining
this unbroken front, marching and pivoting around
and then, on one short signal, freezes on the spot so
that all the arms and legs, the helmets, canteens, and
rifles are suddenly at rest, all in exactly the same position with not even a single bayonet deviating in direction from all the others, then even an ardent anti-
militarist cannot help being gripped by the spectacle.
And what grips him is certainly not the beauty of right
angles and straight lines, but the image . . . or rather
the idea of the many acting as though animated by
one mind [pp. 118-120].

In addition to the spectator's reaction when viewing performers or soldiers acting in unison, Kaiser describes a
variety of other ways in which oneness fantasies (or in his
term "fusion experiences") are activated in the everyday
world. Three of these can be viewed as time-honored av-

enues for expressing such fantasies, though for some years each seems to have enjoyed diminishing popularity: observance of tradition, the practice of religion, and being in love. It is only the first of these that Kaiser elaborates on, in further describing the musings of "G.":

> If [by tradition we] were referring only to the fact that each generation acquires most of its knowledge and skill from the preceding generations the word would imply no allusion [to fusion]. . . . Yet it is capable of an extended meaning. . . . Where adherence to tradition appears as a motivating force it brings about (or, maybe, presupposes) the . . . softening of personality boundaries. . . .
>
> Tradition! G. is thinking of the time honored formalities which govern many functions of the university in his home town. He remembers especially how it was traditional that doctoral examinations took place in the professor's home on a table, covered with a white table cloth and that wine was served before the questioning started. It was unthinkable that the professor, after having invited his "guest" to sit down and having taken the chair on the other side of the table himself, would open the conversation with anything but the question: "white or red?" This was the tradition. Of course the purpose of the examination was the same as that of any examination at any scientific institution the world over. The candidate's knowledge and achievements had to be tested. And the professor was free to ask whatever questions seemed suitable to him for this task. He could be lenient or strict, content himself with a few easy questions, or go on for hours on the most difficult topics. But in contrast to this freedom where the real purpose of the examination was concerned stood the unshak-

able regularity and conformity as to the unessentials: the black coat, the white table cloth, the red and white wine, and the polite inquiry into "guest's" preference. . . .

Is it not essentially the same desire which makes people repeat, or at least imitate, the past on occasions which we call celebrations? This is a vast field. It seems that wherever people come together, motivated by the sober thought that each one will serve his own interests best by cooperating with others, features are introduced which go beyond what is required for the fulfillment of the original interests but tend to create the image of a group personality. It appears that there is an always present interest in "softening the boundaries of the individual" by establishing the artificial super-individual of the group [pp. 121-122].

Oneness in Religion

In Kaiser's references to the wish for fusion (which together with the terms "merging" and "union" we are considering as synonymous with "oneness"[1]), no reference is made to the "good mother of infancy" as the unconsciously fantasied object of the fusion.[2] The link between the "good mother" and the fantasied oneness object must, here at least, be based on inference. But with regard to oneness in religion, this link is more clearly in evidence (though unconscious fantasies involving father also seem to be involved[3]).

Whereas in Western religions, references to mother, although present, are often obscured,[4] in Eastern religions, such references are more generally apparent. Thus from the Taoist holy book (Feng and English, 1972):

You will be at one with the Tao. Being at one with the Tao is eternal [16].

The Tao begot one [42].

Like a newborn babe before it learns to smile . . . I am nourished by the great mother [20].

From the *Dhammapada* (Lal, 1967), the holy book of Buddhism:

How many births have I known without knowing the builder of this body! How many births have I looked for him.[5] It is painful to be born again and again. But now I have seen you, O builder of this body! All desire is extinct, Nirvana is attained [p. 90].

And from the *Upanishads* of the Hindus a reference to the mother:

I will now speak to you of the mystery of the eternal Brahman; and of what happens to the soul after death. The soul may go to the womb of a mother and thus obtain a new body [Mascaro, 1965, p. 64].

From passages such as these it is understandable why Erikson (1958) has characterized religion as gratifying "the simple and fervent wish for a hallucinatory sense of unity with a maternal matrix" (p. 264).

ONENESS IN LOVE

In addition to religious experience and the observance of tradition, one other time-honored way of finding oneness gratification in everyday life is through the experience of being in love. This point, which appears in the writings of Kaiser (1965) and Fromm (1956), is argued extensively by Bergmann (1971). Here, the author first cites well-

known writings in which the potential of a love relationship
for providing oneness is conveyed. We have already quoted
from one of them in Chapter 1:

> . . .the intense yearning which each of them has to-
> wards the other does not appear to be the desire of
> lover's intercourse, but of something else which the
> soul of either evidently desires and cannot tell, and
> of which she has only a dark and doubtful presenti-
> ment. Suppose Hephaestus, with his instruments,
> [was] to come to the pair who are lying side by
> side . . . and [say] to them . . . "Do you desire to be
> wholly one: always day and night to be in one an-
> other's company? for if this is what you desire, I am
> ready to melt you into one and let you grow to-
> gether . . ." there is not a man who when he heard
> the proposal would deny that this meeting and melt-
> ing into one another, this becoming one instead of
> two, was the very expression of his ancient need [Plato,
> *Symposium,* 192, as quoted by Bergmann, 1971].

And from the Bible: "Therefore shall a man leave his
father and his mother, and shall cleave unto his wife: and
they shall be one flesh" (Genesis 2:24).

Even Freud, who, as we indicated earlier (Chapter 7),
said very little about symbiotic motivations, is quoted by
Bergmann as observing: "At the height of being in love
the boundary between ego and object threatens to melt
away. Against all the evidence of his senses, a man who is
in love declares that 'I' and 'you' are one, and is prepared
to behave as if it were a fact" (Freud, 1930, p. 66).

Then, explicitly drawing upon the formulations of Mahler, Bergmann concludes that "love revives, if not direct
memories, then feelings and archaic . . . states that were
once active in the symbiotic phase" (p. 32).

The Current Wave of Oneness Searches

We agree with Rose (1972) who has noted that people of all kinds, on occasion, "suspend the distinction between self and others and thus momentarily experience a state of mind similar to the early unity with mother" (p. 185). No doubt there are innumerable isolated encounters and activities that each of us engage in that provide these symbiotic-like gratifications, ranging from the tennis lesson described earlier to basking in the sun on a beach to submerging in a hot bath. The resourcefulness of people in finding gratification for the symbiotic-like needs that are part of the heritage of early infancy seems to be as great as their resourcefulness in finding satisfactions for oedipal needs—the main heritage of later infancy.[6] For some individuals, isolated instances of symbiotic-like gratification may be sufficient, but for others, more sustained avenues for activating oneness fantasies seem to be a necessary part of life. In the past such avenues have included the observance of tradition, the practice of religion, and being in love. If, indeed, people now avail themselves of these avenues less than they did in the past, what consequences follow?

Logically, one would anticipate two possibilities. There could be an increase in pathology that involves unmet symbiotic-like needs, or there could be a search for new ways to gratify these wishes in everyday life. While support for the first possibility would be hard to come by, we think that the second possibility is clearly demonstrable. An increasing number of people, since the middle of the 20th century, have turned to new pursuits that offer noteworthy oneness gratifications. We shall now discuss two categories of such pursuits. Within one category we shall include meditation, jogging, the use of mind-altering drugs, and "cult living" (we shall refer to these activities as quasi therapies); within the second category we shall include certain forms of psychotherapy that have emerged during the past three decades.

But first a point of clarification. We are not maintaining that everyone availing him or herself of these new avenues necessarily seeks them out because of unmet symbiotic-like needs. We suspect that this may be the initial unconscious motivation in certain instances, though more usually this motivation will come into play only later. That is, since each of these avenues (to varying degrees) can serve a variety of conscious and unconscious motives, we assume that persons could be drawn to them for reasons unrelated to a search for oneness, but that, because they then activate oneness fantasies, they become all the more attractive and compelling.

QUASI THERAPIES

What do meditation, jogging, drug use, and cult living have in common? In addition to our thesis that they activate symbiotic-like oneness fantasies, they have been used (to varying degrees) to overcome anxiety, depression, and other "mental health" problems. It is for this reason that we refer to them as quasi therapies, even though they serve other functions.

Meditation

Whereas meditation has been practiced in Eastern countries by large numbers of people for many centuries, it has only been in the last 25 years that it has gained popularity in the United States. According to Shafii writing in 1973, there were at that time more than 350 centers in the United States which initiated individuals into the practice of meditation.

There are many meditative-practice methods in the United States, but for our purposes, a consideration of four will suffice. These are Yoga, Zen (Buddhism), Transcendental Meditation, and Benson's "Relaxation Response" method. The first two are practiced here as they are in the East. Transcendental Meditation (TM) is a derivative of Eastern meditation developed by the Maharishi Mahesh Yogi in the United States and is probably practiced by more people in this country than any other kind of meditation. The last of the four is a fully secular meditation method developed by Herbert Benson (1975), a Harvard Medical School cardiologist who was impressed by the ability of TM to reduce blood pressure, but wished to make available an alternative that was without a mystical tradition.

In the first three of these types, individuals learn the technique with the help of a teacher who is called a guru in Yoga, a master in Zen Buddhism, and an instructor in Transcendental Meditation. For Benson's meditation, the reading of his book *The Relaxation Response* is considered sufficient for learning the technique.

The common denominators in all four forms of meditation are that the meditator is alone, sits motionless, and remains silent. Beginners are often encouraged to pay attention to their breathing, which, they are told, should be spontaneous and deep. The meditator is instructed to try to develop a freedom from disruptive thoughts and to experience a sense of calm, peace, and harmony. In order to achieve this, he or she is advised to focus on something: a one-syllable word called a mantra in Yoga and Transcendental Meditation, the word "one" in Benson's technique, and a paradoxical problem (called a Koan) in Zen meditation. In all of these practices, the meditator is instructed neither to suppress intrusive thoughts nor to concentrate on them, but rather to allow them to come to mind and then to "let them go."

What evidence is there that symbiotic-like oneness fantasies are activated during meditation? As Deikman (1973) has noted, many meditators, like religious mystics, report that they "have succeeded in achieving a special state that goes beyond the usual feelings and perceptions of ordinary life. These men and women describe an experience of union, of unity with life or God or the ultimate" (p. 199). One such report read as follows:

> "I really began to feel, you know, almost as though the blue and I were perhaps merging—or that the vase and I were [merging]—it was as though everything was sort of merging" [unknown meditator, quoted by Deikman, 1973, p. 223].

The link between meditation and symbiosis has been forged most explicitly by Shafii (1973) who has written:

> Through meditation . . . a profound but temporary and controlled regression occurs. This deep experience helps the individual regress to the preoedipal level of ego state or to the somato-symbiotic phase of the mother-child relationship. The re-experience of this preverbal phase of union with mother and the environment rekindles temporarily the phase of "basic trust" [p. 442].

How does the practice of meditation stimulate the regression of which Shafii speaks? Or translating his conceptualization into our own framework, what in meditative practices is responsible for the activation of oneness fantasies? Shafii emphasizes the silence and the immobility of the meditator, which, we would point out, are also characteristics of the infant after nursing, a time when oneness experiences with mother have been described as being at their height (Pine, 1981).

We would add, speculatively, another possible way in which symbiotic-like fantasies can be triggered during meditation. The great majority of mantras contain the sound "mm" as in the prototypic mantra "om." This, we suspect, serves as a trigger because of the sound's associative links with oral pleasure and the gratifying mother (see our earlier discussion in Chapter 8, note 7).

Along similar lines, as noted earlier, the English word Benson advised substituting for the mantra is "one," a choice that hardly could be improved upon for semantic content apt to trigger symbiotic-like oneness fantasies.

Jogging

Jogging has become increasingly popular in the United States during the past decade. *Runner's World* (December, 1979) has estimated that, since 1970, the number of joggers in this country has grown from two to 30 million. Whereas the most prevalent reason given for involvement in this activity is the desire to maintain or restore physical health (particularly as a prophylactic for coronary heart disease), joggers frequently speak of jogging as a counter to depression, anxiety, and other negative affects and as a way of creating a state of psychological well-being.

There have been reports from a number of joggers that suggest that this activity can stimulate symbiotic-like fantasies:

> The easy rhythmic activity that characterizes running for the runner who has moved beyond the "staying in shape phase" has a soothing quality, and the accompanying kinesthetic and perceptual sensations are usually pleasant. The sensations we get while running

may be closely related to the sensations we received as infants being caressed and cradled [Anderson, 1979, p. 49].

"Altered states of consciousness and mystical experiences [have been reported by many joggers. One of these is termed] equality ... a perception of oneness everywhere" [Michael Murphy, quoted by Spino, 1976, p. 102].

I felt at the beginning of the run ... a peak feeling. ... I take the universe around me and wrap myself in it and become one with it [Sheehan, 1978, pp. 227, 229].

For Roger Bannister [running produces] a physical sensation that brings with it an effortless feeling of being one with the seashore [Sacks, 1979, p. 132].

These reports have led Sacks (a psychiatrist who has written on the psychodynamics of sports) to conclude:

The current popularity of running may be due, in part, to the relative ease with which the runner after several months of practice can obtain [fusion] experiences. ... In an infant the boundaries of self, body, and non-body-self are not clearly defined. The outside world is not yet recognized as outside but is perceived to be an extension of the self. ... [Joggers and runners] seek to return to this earlier state [1979, pp. 132-133].

Mind-Altering Drugs

In a 1982 report from the National Institute of Drug Abuse (a branch of the National Institute of Health), it was estimated that several million Americans use mind-altering

drugs that are stronger than marijuana. Whereas the most frequent reason given by drug users for taking drugs is that it allows them to achieve a "high," reports of their use for the reduction of anxiety, depression, and other negative affects are common.

There is considerable evidence that "drug experiences" involve the activation of symbiotic-like fantasies. Consider the following self-reports from drug users:

> "I literally felt as strong as I think is possible for me to feel. . . . There was a feeling of oneness with this other person and a oneness with all the world" [unnamed drug user, quoted by Bowers, Chipman, Schwartz, and Dann, 1967, p. 561].

> I spent several minutes—or was it several centuries?—not merely gazing at those bamboo legs, but actually being them—or rather being myself in them. . . [Huxley, 1954, p. 22].

And this from therapists' observations of patients:

> One woman [imagined that she] took her mother's breasts and began to whirl around with her mother in a blue infinity. She was herself, then her mother, then herself [Caldwell, 1968, p. 238].

> Nitrous oxide and ether . . . when sufficiently diluted with air, stimulate the mystical consciousness to an extraordinary degree. Depth beyond depth of truth seems revealed to the inhaler. . . . It is as if the opposites of the world, whose contradictoriness and conflict make all our difficulties and troubles, were melted into unity [James, 1902, pp. 378-379].

It is in the light of such reports that a number of clinicians view drug use as a way of gratifying symbiotic-like wishes. Thus, in discussing a heroin addict, Fine (1972) writes: "The mother-son symbiosis . . . was accentuated here. . . . The injection came to symbolize . . . possible death leading to reunion with her" (p. 604). And Mannheim (1975), discussing an opium addict, writes:

> Her dreams entailed the oceanic longing for sheltered existence and oral satisfaction. . . . What she really wanted was the deepest longing of the addict to be the child, suckled, petted and engulfed in the mother [p. 168].

Finally, Grof (1980) writes of the LSD state as "related to the primal union with the mother—to the original state of intrauterine existence during which the maternal organism and the child form a symbiotic unity" (p. 225).

Cult Living

Finally, let us turn to cult living as a fourth way through which large numbers of people find an institutionalized way of activating symbiotic-like oneness fantasies. Reports such as the following come from people among the three million or more who are currently believed to be members of some one thousand religious cults in the United States.

On becoming a member of a sect known as Pensho, a group that began in Japan and spread to Hawaii, a young woman wrote:

> "I went there after cleansing my body. But my spirit was unclean and my conscience kept me from entering the house. Then I heard a voice from inside saying 'come in I won't scold you.' The moment I saw her face I knew this was what I had been awaiting for a long time. Her face was radiating with overwhelming

compassion, I wished I could rush into her arms" [Almond, quoted by Lebra, 1967, p. 253).

And from another member of the same sect, talking about the woman leader of the group:

> "I want to be with Ogamisama every moment. I could not think of anything else. Whenever I was not with her, I missed her.... I felt as if I were having a reunion with my mother at long last" [unnamed Pen-sho member, quoted by Lebra, 1967, p. 253].

Whereas in the above citations it is evident that the cult leader can represent mother, in the following citation the element of oneness emerges:

> As I clapped and shouted, I could feel my tension slipping away, my sense of involvement growing. In spite of myself, I felt a desire to merge into this family.... I began to sing louder and louder until I was putting one hundred percent—"One-oh-oh!" as the Family called it. Ecstatically, I merged into the mass, tasting the glorious pleasure that accompanies the loss of ego [Edwards, 1979, pp. 31, 41].

On occasion, allusions to both elements appear together:

> The main purpose of the rites [of the goddess cult] was to secure the union of votary with the Great Mother in one or another of her forms ... [through] wild music, frenzied dancing ... in the hope that ... communion with the source of all life and vitality might be obtained [James, 1902, pp. 253-254, describing the Cult of the Mother Goddess].

From such reports and observations, Conway and Sie-gelman (1978) have described the behavior of those who join cults (which they refer to as "snapping") in terms that can easily be translated into a search for oneoness, though a search undertaken at the expense of separateness and individuation:

> Snapping as we have come to understand it . . . is a phenomenon that occurs when an individual stops thinking and feeling for himself . . . and loses his mind to some form of external or automatic control. . . . Individuality is surrendered to some religion, psychology or other recipe for living [p. 225].

For each of the four practices and activities just discussed, there have been reports from mental health workers of both adaptation-enhancing and maladaptive effects. The four, however, have not been viewed as equally likely to produce one or the other kind of outcome. For drug use and cult living, there are frequent accounts of negative effects on mental health, though positive reports can also be found.[7]

For meditation and jogging, on the other hand, positive results are typically cited, but negative outcomes are no longer considered surprising.[8]

Assuming that this differential assessment is valid (an assumption that has not yet been tested systematically), how is it to be understood? In keeping with the thesis we have presented earlier, we would suggest the following: Whereas all four quasi therapies provide ample opportunity for oneness fantasies to be activated, drug use and cult living are more apt to threaten the sense of self than are meditation and jogging.

With regard to drug use, it is the chemical action of the drugs that creates a threat to the sense of self. And as for cult living, the interference with psychological separateness, rather than being chemically induced, is brought about by cult leaders. Typically, they discourage the cult members from expressing autonomy and individuality, conveying the message that this is the price to be paid for acceptance and good favor.

On the other hand, with regard to meditation and jogging, the opportunity to maintain a sense of self is considerably greater. In contrast to cult living, both practices are generally limited each day to demarcated periods of time and are carried out in isolation. Moreover, jogging demands no allegiance, while, in meditation, the allegiance is usually limited both in frequency (to several sessions with a teacher) and in extent (there is usually no instruction as to how one should conduct other aspects of one's life). And finally, the following comment by a meditator (an acquaintance of one of the authors) has some bearing on how meditation, by allowing for psychological separateness, preserves the sense of self. "The mantra," he said, "is always available, but you don't have to use it if you don't want to." These words recall Mahler, Pine, and Bergman's (1975) description of the ideal mother of the separation-individuation phase as one who makes herself available for "refueling" when her child needs it, but still encourages the toddler to take brief sojourns away from her, thus helping him or her to separate psychologically.

PSYCHOTHERAPIES

Our thesis in this section is that the inadvertent activation of symbiotic-like oneness fantasies is a common denominator underlying the therapeutic success of many forms of psychotherapy. We have already considered this thesis for psychoanalytic therapies in Chapters 3 and 8. Here, however, our focus will be on *non*-analytic therapies, particularly group activity therapies, systematic desensitization, and client-centered treatment.

While there is no reason to believe that the search for oneness is a major motive for most people who enter psychotherapy, we think a case can be made that this motive is often activated once *treatment is underway*. In keeping with our discussion in the last section, we would propose that various aspects of the psychotherapy situation activate oneness fantasies and that such activation has two consequences. First, for persons, whose unmet symbiotic-like needs are strong, the activation of these fantasies in therapy draws them closer to the therapist in the hope of obtaining further gratification. And second, these fantasies mediate therapeutic gains.

What are the "activators" of symbiotic-like oneness fantasies in the psychotherapy situation? Certainly, a number of aspects of the therapist's attitude toward his or her patient can be viewed as serving this function. These include the therapist's ability to respond to the patient empathically (see Chapter 8), his or her relatively unconditional acceptance of the patient, and the willingness to subserve his or her needs to the patient's. While these qualities have generally been recognized as characteristic of the effective psychotherapist (Keisler, 1973; Chapters 3 and 4), they are also attributes of the "good symbiotic mother," who, as we described her earlier (Chapter 3), mutes the inevitable painful experiences of infancy—namely, separation anxiety, affective hunger, and a sense of ineffectuality and vulnerability.

The view we advance here is that to the degree these qualities are present in a therapist—and there are data (Keisler, 1973) to indicate that there are wide variations among therapists in this respect—the more likely that the patient will unconsciously perceive the therapist as the good symbiotic mother and, consequently, that gratifying oneness fantasies will be activated. The likelihood of this happening is even greater if there are other qualities of the psychotherapy situation that lend themselves to such a perception; and this, we suggest is precisely the state of affairs as far as certain types of psychotherapy are concerned. Here, we shall cite three therapies for which there is reason to believe that symbiotic-like fantasies are particularly likely to be activated: group activity therapies, systematic desensitization, and client-centered treatment.

Group Activity Therapies

Many of the ideas that we have presented in this chapter were anticipated by Gordon in a 1970 paper that was considerably ahead of its time. Gordon formulated that "a spectrum of activities including psychedelic drugs, zen meditation, sensory awareness expansion games, and other group activities" (p. 261) reflect a yearning for symbiotic-like gratification. (Gordon further suggested that these phenomena of our age have become popular because religious practices and other more traditional ways of obtaining symbiotic-like gratification have fallen out of favor.) Her main focus was on group activity therapies such as those associated with Esalen and Synanon. She notes:

> It is interesting . . . how much repetitious and ritualistic behavior occurs, for example, in such games as circling, rocking, even group bathing (baptism?). Submission to the group . . . rejection of words and communication through touching, acting out and sharing of dreams and fantasies, abandonments of the usual sense of privacy as in nude mixed bathing or group massage, and the prolonged exhaustion of lack of sleep which the marathon produces—these are some of the techniques which have as their effect, in part

at least . . . the experience of symbiotic merging, loss of self in the larger whole.

One of the gratifications which appears to be the common denominator among these various group activities seems to be the longing for regression to the time when words were not necessary for communication, where all experience was intimate, all activity play and where delay of impulse discharge was not necessary [pp. 165-166].

As the above citation implies, Gordon, in contrast to those who seem to view the quest for oneness as independent of infantile wishes (e.g., Kaiser, 1965; Watts, 1966), believes that there is a link. She makes this explicit when she writes:

We can see how closely the feeling of being one with the universe, of timeless existence and a life of play rather than work, the immortal and omnipotent qualities which are experienced, correlates with our understanding of the blissful condition of the infant. This is, indeed, the longed-for return to paradise [p. 167].

Systematic Desensitization

Systematic desensitization is regarded by behaviorists as one of their most effective techniques. It consists of the induction of "deep muscle relaxation" followed by the visualization of scenes involving a phobic object (or situation) graded for its fear-arousing potential. As each scene is visualized, the phobic individual reports the degree to which he or she experiences anxiety (usually on a 100-point scale). If anxiety is above a preselected criterion level, the relaxation response is invoked and the individual then re-rates him or herself on the anxiety scale. If the anxiety level is still high, the relaxation response is invoked once more, but if it goes down below the criterion level, the patient is asked to visualize the scene that had been graded as the next most fear-arousing.

We would suggest that the main symbiotic activator in this form of treatment is the state of deep relaxation, with the patient in a prone position on a couch in a darkened room and instructed by a therapist who often speaks in a soothing tone. This combination provides a powerful pull toward a state of tranquillity and pleasurable passivity that is akin to what an infant must feel after a satisfying nursing experience (which, as we noted earlier, is the time when the experience of oneness with mother is believed to be most intense).

One of us (Silverman, 1974) proposed this formulation some years ago and recently received some interesting corroboration for it in a letter from a behavioristically oriented psychologist who had been a former student:

> Six weeks ago, my wife gave birth to my daughter, Monique, and besides being very happy and busy following this event, I've had many occasions to watch Monique after my wife has nursed her. . . . I have been reminded of a hypothesis you had mentioned in the lectures you gave to my class . . . that deep relaxation stirs up memories of symbiosis and this reassuring experience . . . is "curative." This, in any case, is my recollection of your idea. I had and have my doubts about this idea; nonetheless, I want to share with you a repeated observation of mine of my daughter.
>
> After Monique nurses, her arms fall to her side, her legs droop toward the floor, and her head lies limply back. She appears, in short, to be in a state of pro-

found relaxation. Indeed on seeing her like this, my first association was to my own physical experience of the relaxation training exercises I had practiced some years ago. Her facial muscles seem almost without tonicity. . . . The surprising thing is the depth of the relaxation. I had thought one needed to learn the response. Perhaps. But my infant daughter, whatever its origin, has it.

Incidentally, it follows a period of heightened whole body tension. Both the responses of tension (before feeding) and relaxation (after feeding) are global. I mention this only because, while not exactly analogous, the training exercises [for] relaxation follow a similar pattern. First one tenses a given muscle in order to learn how to relax it.

As I understood your idea, the experience of symbiosis was triggered through relaxation by the cognitive "letting go" of boundaries. As I now understand it, relaxation would "recall" . . . early experiences when the self-world was profoundly satisfied. These "memories" stir . . . experiences of the self and world as safe and better than previously thought [Schumacher, personal communication].

Client-Centered Treatment

We include under this heading "non-directive therapy" as developed by Rogers (1951) over three decades ago and Gendlin's (1968) more recent "experiential psychotherapy." In both, the emphasis is on the therapist's continually conveying to the patient ("client" in their terminology) his or her sense of the patient's underlying experiential state. As one of us has proposed earlier (Silverman, 1974), this kind of explicitly empathic focus parallels the empathy of

the good symbiotic mother, an empathy explicitly conveyed by means of touch and such expressions as "Little
baby is frightened," "Sweetie is hungry," "You want your
mommy," and so on.[9]

In one technique that has developed out of this client-
centered approach we can see, with particular clarity, how
symbiotic-like fantasies are inadvertently activated. The
technique is called "focusing" and was developed by Gendlin (1968, 1978). It consists of a series of "experiential
steps" that patients are taught and that are designed to
help them make contact with the "felt sense" of what is
motivating them affectively. Gendlin indicates that for people to focus effectively it is critical that they maintain a
proper stance toward themselves while carrying out these
steps. This stance, in our view, is clearly that of the good
symbiotic mother. Consider the following instructions:

> [It] is important to accept every feeling that comes,
> not argue with it, not challenge it with preemptory
> demands that it explain itself. You don't talk back to
> the feeling like an angry parent demanding that the
> feeling justify itself. You don't say "what do you *mean*
> such and such would be awful? That's nonsense. Just
> why would it be awful?" Instead you approach the
> feeling in an accepting way. . . . the best way is to go
> to the feelings and say quietly, "OK, fine, it's as you
> say, it's thus and so. But why is that?" And you gently
> stay until it answers [pp. 30-31].

> [In] the first movement of focusing . . . you smile at
> yourself, hold out your hand to yourself. "Hello
> there," you say. "How are you feeling now?" [p. 80].

And finally, consider the advice Gendlin gives to the
focuser if he or she senses fright as inhibiting a focusing
response:

> Think of a little girl that is very scared. She stands petrified, only her eyes move. You walk up and say "honey are you scared?" There is the barest little bit of a nod. . . . "It's OK to feel whatever you feel; we'll see what we can do. Has it been scary?" The little girl might then practically melt in your arms. . . [pp. 99-100].

THERAPEUTIC EFFICACY, SPECIFIC AND NON-SPECIFIC TREATMENT EFFECTS, AND THE ACTIVATION OF SYMBIOTIC-LIKE ONENESS FANTASIES

There have been reports attesting to the therapeutic efficacy of the therapies and quasi therapies that we have just discussed.[10] That is to say, when assessments have been made of people who have been in these "treatments," positive findings have often been reported (though, not surprisingly, in the light of our discussion of quasi therapies, there has been considerable variation among the different treatments as to the *frequency* of positive outcomes). Two related questions, however, remain to be answered.

First, these studies have only rarely asked the question as to whether new pathology has replaced the old. It is true that a number of studies have investigated whether new *symptoms* have appeared (and, typically, this has been found *not* to be the case), but hardly any study has checked on whether ego-syntonic "behavioral pathology" has been the price paid for symptom remission. The following example, which was originally reported elsewhere (Silverman, 1974), illustrates what we have in mind:

> During an initial period of psychotherapy, a patient reported that he no longer felt depressed, the symptom that originally brought him into treatment. How-

ever at the same time, he gave evidence of manifesting hostile and even sadistic behavior toward women which could be understood psychoanalytically as the result of impulses emerging that had been internalized while he was depressed. Although this behavior disturbed his heterosexual relationships, he hardly would have reported [had he been asked] that he had developed . . . new [pathology]—since he hid from himself the connection between the disruption of these relationships and his own behavior [p. 304].

We are not suggesting that, in cases in which the treatments under discussion ameliorated pathology, negative changes must necessarily result, but only that without a comprehensive assessment of change, such a possibility cannot be ruled out. (See our parallel recommendation in Chapter 8, note 2, regarding the assessment of different psychoanalytic treatment approaches.)

The second question that has not been resolved is the extent to which each of these treatments produces *specific* therapeutic effects—effects due to the particular "ingredients" or defining characteristics of the treatment. The converse question is the degree to which ameliorative effects may be due to something more general—for example, the dedication or the charisma of the therapist, to mention two of the "non-specific effects"[11] that have often been proposed. (See Silverman and D. Wolitzky [1982] for a related discussion of psychoanalytic treatment.)

In order to answer this question, studies are needed in which the treatment under consideration is compared with a control condition that does not contain specific interventions that are viewed as therapeutic, but which provides an opportunity for non-specific effects to operate. Then, to the extent that the treatment condition produces greater effects than those produced by the control, one can maintain that specific effects have contributed to the therapeutic outcome.

It would be ideal if the treatment and control conditions could be "administered" in double-blind fashion, as they have been in drug studies. For when they are not, a more positive reaction to the treatment condition may be a function of the patient's or therapist's own expectations that the treatment will work rather than the specific properties of the treatment intervention. In such a case, non-specific effects would be contributing to the outcome, an obviously undesirable state of affairs in a study investigating whether non-specific effects can be ruled out.

Whereas double-blind conditions can be maintained in studies investigating the effectiveness of drug medication, they are generally not feasible in studies of psychological interventions. (Studies involving subliminal stimulation are the exceptions to the rule.) The best that can be done—and this is generally considered a reasonably acceptable substitute—is to institute as a control condition an intervention that both interventionist and patient *believe* to be as potent as the treatment intervention.[12] If this is done and the treatment condition produces superior results, one can assume (though with less certainty than in double-blind studies) that neither the investigator nor the patient have artifactually affected the impact of the two conditions.

In the studies that have attested to the therapeutic efficacy of the treatments under discussion, it is rare for there to have been a condition that met this criterion.[13] Thus, to date, it remains unclear as to what degree the improvements reported for the therapies and quasi therapies under consideration are due to specific treatment effects.

The final point that we wish to make in considering non-specific treatment effects is that such effects can be understood, in part, as linked to the same symbiotic-like oneness fantasies that we have been discussing. Therapist characteristics that are viewed as capable of producing non-specific effects (e.g., dedication) can be seen as silent activators of symbolic-like fantasies, while the patient's expectation of cure may reflect the fact that these fantasies have already been activated.

PLACEBO EFFECTS IN MEDICINE AND THE ACTIVATION OF ONENESS FANTASIES

In a recent paper Shapiro (1978) writes that "the history of medical treatment [is] largely [the] history of the placebo effect" (p. 449). Later in the same paper he makes reference to the "very powerful therapeutic potential of the placebo effect" (p. 459). Before pursuing our thesis in relation to the placebo effect, it is important to clarify its meaning as used by Shapiro. "Placebo effect" refers to what in the last section we termed "non-specific treatment effects," effects which, in a medical context, usually refer to the therapeutic benefits of an ingested substance (such as a pill) that are not due to the specific chemical action of the substance but to the psychological impact of its ingestion. "Placebos" include both chemically active medications which do not affect the illness for which they are taken and inert substances that are used as "controls" in studies testing the efficacy of a particular medication. It should further be borne in mind that, for Shapiro, the term does not necessarily have negative connotations, it remaining an empirical question, in his view, as to how substantive is the therapeutic impact of the placebo and how long it will last. Finally, the question as to whether a particular medication *is* producing placebo (or non-specific) effects (as opposed to "specific effects" due to its chemical prop-

erties) is also decided empirically— by comparing the medication with an already established placebo under "double-
blind" conditions. (While we are using the terms "placebo
effects" and "non-specific effects" interchangeably here,
we deliberately spoke only of non-specific treatment effects
in the previous section. Our decision was based on the fact
that the term "placebo," rooted as it is in medical usage,
has come to have certain connotations that obfuscate and
confuse issues when applied to psychological disorders.[14])

Shapiro (1978) was making two important and interre-
lated points in the quotes cited above. First, that up until
relatively recently (about the past 40 years) there was very
little that physicians administered that produced more
than placebo effects—that would have shown up to advantage if tested in controlled double-blind studies. And
second, that, despite this fact, these treatments often produced powerful therapeutic benefits. Of course, placebo
treatments often had no effect, and occasionally negative
effects, but they produced positive effects often enough
to justify Shapiro's conclusion that they had a "very powerful therapeutic potential."

These points had been made dramatically some 30 years
earlier by Houston in a paper entitled "The Doctor Himself
as a Therapeutic Agent" (1939). Shapiro cites the following
passage from that paper:

> In the early history of medicine, [the relationship be-
> tween doctor and patient] comprised all that the doc-
> tor had to offer the patient. It is only very recently
> that medicine has had more to give. . . . Historians
> sentimentalize the practical values of ancient medi-
> cine. One scans the pages of Hippocrates in vain for
> any treatments of specific value. The pages of medical
> history read like the log of an old-fashioned voyage,
> in which it is noted that on such a day a whale spouted,

on such a day a flying fish was sighted, or a bit of driftwood, but in which no mention is made of the huge prevailing fact that what was constantly seen day by day, almost to the exclusion of other sights, was the unending green waste of water. And this inevitable circumambient ocean is, by analogy, in medical history the personal relationship between doctor and patient.

In a word, the medicines used were placebos. . . . The great lesson, then, of medical history is that the placebo has always been the norm of medical practice, that it was only occasionally and at great intervals that anything really serviceable, such as the cure of scurvy by fresh fruits, was introduced into medical practice. . . . The medical historian is apt to mislead us when he speaks of the learned and skillful doctors of the past. . . . Their skill was a skill in dealing with the emotions of men. They themselves were the therapeutic agents by which cures were effected. Their therapeutic procedures, whether they were inert or whether they were dangerous, were placebos, symbols by which their patients' faith was sustained.

The history of medicine is a history of the dynamic power of the relationship between doctor and patient . . . [quoted by Shapiro, 1978, p. 442].

But what is it in the physician-patient relationship that produces the "dynamic power . . . by which cures [are] effected?" To no reader's surprise, we would propose that this power derives, in part, from the activation of symbiotic-like oneness fantasies in the physician-patient relationship. If religious figures, cult leaders, and psychotherapists are capable of unwittingly activating such fantasies, physicians should be eminently more capable of activating them. With their bodily touching (Stone [1961, p. 82] has referred to the physician as the unconsciously perceived "mother of bodily care") and their prescription of medications to be orally ingested, they are in an ideal position to activate such fantasies. (Consistent with our discussion in note 3, we would propose that there are other aspects of the physician-patient relationship that activate unconscious fantasies involving the father.)

In support of this thesis we would cite certain characteristics of patients and physicians that have been proposed to be correlated with placebo effects. For patients, these are suggestibility, faith, and hope; for physicians, interest in and liking of the patient and investment in the treatment. Each of these can be seen as either signaling that symbiotic-like oneness fantasies are active or encouraging the activation of such fantasies. With regard to the latter, consider, for example, the physician's investment in treatment and, in particular, Shapiro's description of the specific kind of behavior that comes under this heading:

> A physician with [a particular interest in a form of] therapy usually has considerable knowledge about such treatment. He will be interested in the symptoms and the differential response of the patient to various drugs and will be careful to observe side effects, especially those that may be dangerous. He may encourage the patient to call at any time if side effects develop. A new drug with inadequately evaluated indications, contraindications, and side effects will elicit even more interest, and promote in the physician using it a greater intellectual and emotional investment. This may explain, in part, the reports of almost universal effectiveness accompanying the introduction of new therapies [1978, p. 468].

It is easy to envision how such behavior could lead a

patient to feel that he or she is being treated very specially indeed, thereby encouraging the fantasy of being one with the good mother of infancy.

The two-pronged hypothesis that we present here—that many therapeutic gains achieved in both psychotherapy and medicine are attributable to placebo (or non-specific) effects and that such effects are, in part, attributable to the activation of unconscious oneness fantasies—has noteworthy theoretical and therapeutic implications. It is thus a hypothesis that invites controlled experimental studies that could provide data more convincing than the circumstantial evidence and logical arguments we have adduced. The following proposal, which makes use of the method of subliminal psychodynamic activation, represents one experimental design that could be used to test the posited relationship between the placebo effect and the activation of symbiotic-like oneness fantasies.

Miltown is a minor tranquillizer that was widely used during the 1950's and 1960's for relief from anxiety. Serious question has been raised, however, as to whether Miltown contains anything of value as an anti-anxiety agent beyond a name that people associate with anxiety reduction. Thus, in an extensive review of studies in which the effects of Miltown (or, more accurately, meprobamate, the drug contained in Miltown) were compared with those of inert-substance placebos, Greenblatt and Shader (1971) pointed out that while some findings argued for Miltown having more than placebo effects, other findings argued strongly against it. Greenblatt and Shader were more persuaded by the latter studies (which outnumbered the former) and concluded that Miltown's effectiveness was largely as a placebo.

A study designed in the following way would shed further light on whether Miltown is capable of more than

placebo action and, more importantly, whether this action
is rooted in the activation of unconscious oneness fantasies.
Six groups of hospitalized patients with anxiety symptoms
(matched for severity, psychiatric diagnosis, and other pertinent variables) would participate. The first two groups
would be administered capsules which they would be told
"might" reduce their anxiety, with the first group receiving
an inert substance and the second Miltown. A third group
would also receive Miltown but would be told both the
name of the medication and that "thousands of people
have reported Miltown to be a highly effective drug for
reducing anxiety." The fourth, fifth, and sixth groups
would be given Miltown under the same conditions as the
third, but would also receive subliminal stimulation each
time the tablets were administered. The fourth group
would receive a neutral control stimulus, the fifth group
MOMMY AND I ARE ONE, and the sixth a stimulus designed to interfere with oneness fantasies, perhaps I AM
WHOLLY ON MY OWN. Assuming (1) that the first two
groups showed no difference in degree of anxiety reduction (thus demonstrating that Miltown does not have specific effects), (2) that the third group manifested greater
anxiety reduction than the first two (thus demonstrating
the placebo effect), and (3) that the fourth group showed
the same anxiety reduction as the third (indicating that the
introduction of a subliminal neutral stimulus had no effect
on the action of Miltown), we would be in a position to test
our hypothesis that oneness fantasies underly placebo effects. For if the fifth group then showed greater anxiety
reduction than the fourth, we would have demonstrated
that activating unconscious oneness fantasies enhances the
placebo effect. But while such a finding would be consistent
with the hypothesis, it would not directly support it—that
is, it would not necessarily argue that placebo effects in-

volve oneness fantasies to begin with. Only if the sixth group reacted with *less* anxiety reduction than the third and fourth, would we have data that directly supported the hypothesis. Such a loss of effectiveness for the placebo-inducing characterization of Miltown could only be attributed to the fact that the I AM WHOLLY ON MY OWN message had muted the impact of the characterization. And in the absence of any other plausible explanation as to why that message should have had such a negative effect, it would be reasonable to say that the message had contradicted existing fantasies of oneness.

If these were indeed the results of such a study, follow-up investigations would be very much in order. One such investigation could involve three groups, one of which would be given Miltown with a placebo-inducing characterization (as in the third group above). This group's anxiety reduction would be compared with two groups both of which received subliminal stimulation in large doses (see Chapter 6) but without Miltown or any other ingested substance. The subliminal stimulus for one of these groups would be MOMMY AND I ARE ONE and for the other PEOPLE ARE WALKING. If the former subliminal group (but not the latter) showed as much anxiety reduction as the Miltown group, this finding, in conjunction with the findings from the first study, would argue compellingly that unconscious oneness fantasies underly placebo effects. This, in turn, would allow us to say that the reason why, in a number of studies, the subliminal exposure of oneness stimuli notably strengthened adaptation-enhancing behavior was that this laboratory intervention made possible the harnessing of the considerable power of the placebo effect.

So we have come full circle. In returning to the method of subliminal activation in the context of experiments exploring the placebo effect, we return as well to the methodological vantage point from which we initially conceptualized the "search for oneness": that theory-building in psychoanalysis requires, wherever possible, controlled experimental study. Have we been premature in attempting to extrapolate from laboratory experiments to the clinical situation and beyond in Chapters 7-9? We believe that our undertaking has been a reasonable one, consistent with the experimental data cited in Chapters 2-6, plausible from the standpoint of contemporary knowledge of child development, and convergent with the views expressed in a number of clinical commentaries. Each reader, of course, will have his or her opinion on this question. Perhaps, though, we can agree that if we are to move from opinion to confident judgment, answers can only come through systematic and continuing investigations that are as well controlled as the study of any particular area permits. Thus, if certain formulations that we have offered prove insufficient or incorrect, such continuing study makes it likely that more complete and valid explanations will be forthcoming. We look forward to these future investigations, and the theory building and clinical applications that follow upon them, with great anticipation.

NOTES

1. The equating of these terms should, however, eventually be tested empirically. Would the messages MOMMY AND I ARE MERGED and MOMMY AND I ARE UNITED produce the same experimental effects as MOMMY AND I ARE ONE? Perhaps not, since the word "one" also implies wholeness that the words "merged" and "united" do not. If the new messages did not elicit the adaptation-enhancing effects that MOMMY AND I ARE ONE has elicited, it would then imply that the latter stimulus has been effective because it addresses the need for a firm sense of self at the same time that it addresses the need for symbiotic-like gratifications.

2. It is to be noted that although Kaiser's training and back

ground were psychoanalytic, his clinical writings are devoid of a genetic perspective. His focus is entirely on attempting to elucidate the meaning of behavior in terms of "here-and-now" motives.

3. Unconscious fantasies involving father, as they are implicated in religious experiences and practices, can express either preoedipal or oedipal dynamics. In the former, father has replaced mother as the good symbiotic object of infancy (see our discussion in Chapter 4 of Cohen's [1977] and Jackson's [1981] experimental findings in relation to Lidz's [1973] clinical observations).

In the latter, "father fantasies" can involve forgiveness for transgressions and internalizations of the "oedipal father's" strength, power, and phallus (see Silverman and Fishel [1981] for a review of experimental data bearing on the effects of subliminally activating unconscious oedipal fantasies involving father).

4. Fromm (1956) has written:

> In the Jewish religion, the mother aspects of God are reintroduced especially in the various currents of mysticism. In the Catholic religion, mother is symbolized by the Church and by the Virgin. Even in Protestantism, the figure of mother has not been entirely eradicated, although she remains hidden. . . . [For example] the Lutheran doctrine . . . in spite of its manifest patriarchal character carries within it a hidden matriarchal element. Mother's love cannot be acquired; it is there, or it is not there; all I can do is to have faith. As the Psalmist says, "thou hadst let me have faith unto my mother's breast and to transform myself into the helpless powerless child" [pp. 66-67].

5. The allusion to "him" in the context of references to birth may reflect a kind of condensation of unconscious fantasies involving both mother and father.

6. Disguised satisfactions for oedipal wishes are particularly in evidence in participation in sports, vocational accomplishment, and heterosexual activity (see Silverman [1979, p. 201] for an elaboration).

7. For a chilling account of the deleterious impact of many cults on youth, see Conway and Siegelman (1978). On the other hand, for a report of symptom reduction in members of one cult, see Galanter (1978).

A wide-ranging survey of the harmful physiological and psychological consequences of continued use of mind-altering drugs can be found in Jaffe (1975). But see Caldwell (1968) for a report on the use of L.S.D. as a psychotherapy adjunct.

8. The positive impact on mental health of jogging can be found in Sacks (1979) and of meditation in Benson (1975). Observations of negative effects of each of these activities in a small minority of those so engaged have been reported by Morgan (1979; jogging) and Otis (in press; meditation).

9. See Stolorow (1976) for a discussion of some interesting similarities in the theorizing and treatment recommendations of Rogers and Kohut.

10. Systematically collected data bearing on therapeutic effectiveness are cited by Rogers (1951) for client-centered therapy, by Kazdin and Wilcoxon (1976) for systematic desensitization, by Lieberman, Yalom, and Miles (1973) for encounter groups, by Benson (1975) for meditation, by Sacks (1979) for jogging, and by Galanter (1978) for cult living.

11. See Grunbaum (1981) for an apt critique of the illogicality of using the term "non-specific effects" to refer to effects that are indeed specific (as well as related terminological issues).

12. This is determined by obtaining ratings of the potential usefulness of the treatment and control interventions from either the participants in the study or a different sample from the same population.

13. See Kazdin and Wilcoxon (1976) who cite a few attempts to pit systematic desensitization against control interventions that met the aforementioned criterion. Overall, the data that emerged did not show systematic desensitization to be of greater effectiveness.

14. Placebo effects in medicine are typically viewed negatively by physicians, who frequently either deny their existence or see them as something to be nullified (Shapiro and Struening, 1973a, b). In one sense this is understandable, since any professional might feel uncomfortable with the thought that the specific interventions he or she has been trained in might not be accomplishing what they are supposed to accomplish. But, finally, this is a short-sighted view, as evidenced not only by the fact that placebo effects have had a remarkably powerful impact on patients, but also because it overlooks the possibility that these effects can operate synergistically. That is, placebo effects in medicine (and the same can be said for non-specific effects in psychotherapy) may enhance the potency of specific effects and thus make a clinician's interventions more effective than they would have been by themselves. (See also our discussion in Chap-

ter 8 [p. 222] of synergistic possibilities in psychoanalytic treatment.)

REFERENCES

Alexander, F. (1954), Some quantitative aspects of psychoanalytic technique. *J. Amer. Psychoanal. Assn.*, 2:685-701.

—— French, T. M., & Pollock, G. H. (1968), *Psychosomatic Specificity*. Chicago: University of Chicago Press.

Alpert, A. (1959), Reversibility of pathological fixations associated with maternal deprivation. *The Psychoanalytic Study of the Child*, 14:169-185. New York: International Universities Press.

Anderson, R. (1979), Running: A road to mental health. *Runners World*, 14:49-52.

Angel, K. (1967), On symbiosis and pseudo symbiosis. *J. Amer. Psychoanal. Assn.*, 15:294-316.

Argyris, C. (1968), Some unintended consequences of rigorous research. *Psychol. Bull.*, 70:185-197.

—— (1975), Dangers in applying results from experimental and social psychology. *Amer. Psychol.*, 30:469-485.

Ariam, S. (1979), *The Effects of Subliminal Symbiotic Stimuli in Hebrew on Academic Performance of Israeli High School Students*. Unpublished doctoral dissertation, New York University School of Education. (Article accepted for publication, *J. Abnorm. Psychol.*)

Arieti, S. (1974), *Interpretation of Schizophrenia*. New York: Basic Books.

Bak, R. C. (1954), The schizophrenic defense against aggression. *Internat. J. Psychoanal. Psychother.*, 35:129-133.

Beebe, B., & Stern, D. (1977), Studies of mother-infant interactions. In: *Communicative Structures and Psychic Structures*, ed. N. Freedman & S. Grand. New York: Plenum, pp. 35-56.

271

Benson, H. (1975), *The Relaxation Response*. New York: Morrow.

Bergmann, M. S. (1971), On the capacity to love. In: *Separation-Individuation: Essays in Honor of Margaret S. Mahler*, ed. J. B. McDevitt & C. S. Settlage. New York: International Universities Press, pp. 15-40.

———— & Hartman, F. (1976), *The Evolution of Psychoanalytic Technique*. New York: Basic Books.

Bernstein, D. (1980), Female identity synthesis. In: *Career and Motherhood: Struggle for New Identity*, ed. A. Roland & B. Harris. New York: Human Sciences Press, pp. 103-123.

Beskind, H. (1972), A hypothesis regarding some psychogenic aspects of depersonalization symptoms. *Bull. Phil. Assn. Psychoanal.*, 22:42-59.

Bettelheim, B. (1972), Regression as progress. In: *Tactics and Techniques in Psychoanalytic Therapy*, ed. P. L. Giovacchini. New York: Jason Aronson, pp. 189-199.

Blatt, S. J., & Wild, C. M. (1976), *Schizophrenia—Developmental Analysis*. New York: Academic Press.

Bowers, M., Chipman, A., Schwartz, A., & Dann, O. T. (1967), Dynamics of psychedelic drug abuse. *Arch. Gen. Psychiat.*, 16:560-566.

Brenner, C. (1975), Affect and psychic conflict. *Psychoanal. Quart.*, 44:5-28.

———— (1976), *Psychoanalytic Technique and Psychic Conflict*. New York: International Universities Press.

Bronstein, A. (1976), *An Experimental Study of Internalization Fantasies in Schizophrenic Men*. Unpublished doctoral dissertation, Yeshiva University.

Bryant-Tuckett, R. (1980), *The Effects of Subliminal Merging Stimuli on the Academic Performance of Emotionally Handicapped Students*. Unpublished doctoral dissertation, New York University.

Burnham, D. L., Gladstone, A. I., & Gibson, R. W. (1969), *Schizophrenia and the Need-Fear Dilemma*. New York: International Universities Press.

Bychowski, G. (1950), On neurotic obesity. *Psychoanal. Rev.*, 37:302-329.

———— (1959), Some aspects of masochistic involvement. *J. Amer. Psychoanal. Assn.*, 7:248-273.

Caldwell, W. V. (1968), *L.S.D. Psychotherapy*. New York: Grove Press.

Cohen, R. (1977), *The Effects of Four Subliminally Introduced Merging Stimuli on the Psychopathology of Schizophrenic Women*. Unpublished doctoral dissertation, Columbia University.

Colby, K. M. (1951), *A Primer for Psychotherapists*. New York: Ronald Press.

Conway, F., & Siegelman, J. (1978), *Snapping*. New York: Delta.

Dahl, H. (1972), A quantitative study of a psychoanalysis. In: *Psychoanalysis and Contemporary Science*, Vol. 1, ed. R. R. Holt & E. Peterfreund. New York: Macmillan, pp. 237-257.

Dauber, R. (1979), *The Effects of Subliminal Stimulation on the Affect of Depressively Prone College Students*. Unpublished masters thesis, Loyola University of Chicago.

―――― (1980), *An Investigation of Guilt, Loss and the Separation-Individuation Process in Depression*. Unpublished doctoral dissertation, Loyola University of Chicago.

Deikman, A. (1973), Deautomatization and the mystic experience. In: *The Nature of Human Consciousness*, ed. R. Ornstein. San Francisco: W. H. Freeman, pp. 216-233.

Dement, W. C., & Fisher, C. (1960), Studies in dream deprivation and satiation (Abstract). *Psychoanal. Quart.*, 29:671.

Des Lauriers, A. M. (1962), *The Experience of Reality in Childhood Schizophrenia*. New York: International Universities Press.

Deutsch, H. (1932), On female homosexuality. In: *The Psychoanalytic Reader*, ed. R. Fliess. New York: International Universities Press, 1948, pp. 208-230.

Dixon, N. F. (1971), *Subliminal Perception: The Nature of a Controversy*. New York: McGraw-Hill.

Eagle, M. (1959), The effects of subliminal stimuli of aggressive content upon conscious cognition. *J. Personal.*, 27:578-600.

―――― (1962), Personality correlates of sensitivity to subliminal stimulation. *J. Nerv. Ment. Dis.*, 134:1-17.

Easser, B. R. (1974), Empathic inhibition and psychoanalytic technique. *Psychoanal. Quart.*, 43:557-581.

Edwards, C. (1979), *Crazy for God.* Englewood Cliffs, N.J.: Prentice-Hall.

Ekstein, R., & Caruth, E. (1972), Keeping secrets. In: *Tactics and Techniques in Psychoanalytic Therapy*, ed. P. L. Giovacchini. New York: Jason Aronson, pp. 200-215.

Eriksen, C. W. (1960), Discrimination and learning without awareness: A methodological survey and evaluation. *Psychol. Rev.*, 67:279-300.

Erikson, E. (1958), *Young Man Luther.* New York: Norton.

Erlenmeyer-Kimling, L. (1968), Studies on the offspring of two schizophrenic parents. In: *The Transmission of Schizophrenia*, ed. D. Rosenthal & S. Kety. New York: Pergamon, pp. 65-83.

Fairbairn, W. R. D. (1952), *Psychoanalytic Studies of the Personality.* London: Tavistock.

Farber, S. (1981), *Twins Reared Apart: A Reanalysis.* New York: Basic Books.

Federn, P. (1952), *Ego Psychology and the Psychoses.* New York: Basic Books.

Fenichel, O. (1925), The clinical aspect of the need for punishment. In: *Collected Papers.* New York: Norton, 1953, pp. 71-92.

Feng, G., & English, J., Trans. (1972), *Tao Te Cheng.* New York: Vintage.

Ferenczi, S. (1919), Technical difficulties in the analysis of a case of hysteria. In: *Further Contributions to the Theory and Technique of Psychoanalysis.* New York: Basic Books, 1952, pp. 189-197.

Fine, R. (1972), The psychoanalysis of a drug addict. *Psychoanal. Rev.*, 59:585-608.

Fisher, C. (1960), Introduction. In: *Preconscious Stimulation in Dreams, Associations, and Images: Classical Studies*, by O. Pötzl, R. Allers, & J. Teler. [*Psychological Issues*, Monogr. 7.] New York: International Universities Press, pp. 1-40.

Florek, W. (1978), *Effects of Subliminal Stimulation of Anxiety and Cognitive Adaptation.* Unpublished manuscript, St. John's University.

Forest-Letourneau, M., (1974), *The Effect of Subliminal Stimulation of Aggressive and Symbiotic Wishes on the Thought Processes of Chronic Schizophrenics*. Unpublished doctoral dissertation, University of Montreal.

Frank, S. J., McLaughlin, A. M., & Crusco, A. (1981), Merging fantasies, eye shift patterns and intuitive judgments: Dynamic and cognitive factors in the disruption of empathic abilities. Unpublished manuscript, Illinois Institute of Technology.

Freedman, N., Cutler, R., Englehart, D. M., & Margolis, R. (1967), On the modification of paranoid symptomatology. *J. Nerv. Ment. Dis.*, 144:29-36.

Freeman, T., Cameron, J. L., & McGhie, A. (1958), *Chronic Schizophrenia*. New York: International Universities Press.

Freud, A. (1969), *Difficulties in the Path of Psychoanalysis*. New York: International Universities Press.

Freud, S. (1900), *The Interpretation of Dreams. Standard Edition*, 4 & 5. London: Hogarth Press, 1953.

——— (1905), Fragment of an analysis of a case of hysteria. *Standard Edition*, 7:3-122. London: Hogarth Press, 1953.

——— (1909a), Analysis of a phobia in a five-year-old boy. *Standard Edition*, 10:3-149. London: Hogarth Press, 1955.

——— (1909b), Notes upon a case of obsessional neurosis. *Standard Edition*, 10:153-318. London: Hogarth Press, 1955.

——— (1911), Psycho-analytic notes on an autobiographical account of a case of paranoia. *Standard Edition*, 12:3-82. London: Hogarth Press, 1958.

——— (1915), The unconscious. *Standard Edition*, 14:166-215. London: Hogarth Press, 1958.

——— (1918), From the history of an infantile neurosis. *Standard Edition*, 17:3-122. London: Hogarth Press, 1955.

——— (1919a), Lines of advance in psychoanalytic therapy. *Standard Edition*, 17:158-168. London: Hogarth Press, 1955.

——— (1919b), 'A child is being beaten': A contribution

to the study of the origin of sexual perversions. *Standard Edition*, 17:177-204. London: Hogarth Press, 1955.

——— (1920), The psychogenesis of a case of homosexuality in a woman. *Standard Edition*, 18:147-174. London: Hogarth Press, 1955.

——— (1924), The economic problem of masochism. *Standard Edition*, 19:157-170. London: Hogarth Press, 1961.

——— (1930), Civilization and its discontents. *Standard Edition*, 21:59-145. London: Hogarth Press, 1961.

Fribourg, A. (1981), The effect of fantasies of merging with a good mother on schizophrenic pathology. *J. Nerv. Ment. Dis.*, 169:337-347. (Originally reported in a doctoral dissertation entitled *The Effect of Fantasies of Merging with the Good Mother Figure on Ego Pathology of Schizophrenics*, New York University, 1979.)

Friedman, L. (1978), Trends in the psychoanalytic theory of treatment. *Psychoanal. Quart.*, 47:524-567.

Fromm, E. (1956), *The Art of Loving*. New York: Harper.

Galanter, M. (1978), The "relief" effect: A sociobiological model for neurotic distress and large group therapy. *Amer. J. Psychiat.*, 135:588-591.

Gendlin, E. (1968), The experiential response. In: *The Use of Interpretation in Treatment*, ed. E. F. Hammer. New York: Grune & Stratton, pp. 208-227.

——— (1978), *Focusing*. New York: Everest House.

Gill, M. M. (1979), The analysis of the transference. *J. Amer. Psychoanal. Assn.*, 27(suppl.):263-288.

——— Simon, J., Fink, G., Endicott, N. A., & Paul, I. H. (1968), Studies in audio-recorded psychoanalysis: I. General considerations. *J. Amer. Psychoanal. Assn.*, 16:230-244.

Gillespie, W. H. (1964), Symposium on homosexuality. *Internat. J. Psycho-Anal.*, 45:203-209.

Giovacchini, P. L. (1972), The symbiotic phase. In: *Tactics and Techniques in Psychoanalytic Therapy*, ed. P. L. Giovacchini. New York: Jason Aronson, pp. 137-169.

Goldberger, L., & Holt, R. R. (1961), Experimental interference with reality contact (perceptual isolation): Individual differences. In: *Sensory Deprivation and Isolation*, ed. P. Solomon, P. Kubzansky, P. Liederman, J. Mendelsohn, R. Trumbull, & D. Wexler. Cambridge, Mass.: Harvard University Press, pp. 130-142.

Goldfarb, W. (1943), Infant rearing and problem behavior. *Amer. J. Orthopsychiat.*, 13:249-265.

—— (1961), *Childhood Schizophrenia*. Cambridge, Mass.: Harvard University Press.

Gordon, L. (1970), Beyond the reality principle. *Amer. Imago*, 27:160-182.

Gottesman, I. I., & Shields, J. (1972), *Schizophrenia and Genetics—A Twin Study Vantage Point*. New York: Academic Press.

Greenacre, P. (1957), The childhood of the artist: Libidinal phase development and giftedness. *The Psychoanalytic Study of the Child*, 12:22-72. New York: International Universities Press.

Greenberg, N. (1977), The effects of subliminal neutral and aggressive stimuli on the thought processes of schizophrenics. *Canad. J. Behav. Sci.*, 9:187-196.

Greenblatt, D. J., & Shader, R. I. (1971), Meprobamate: A study of irrational drug use. *Amer. J. Psychiat.*, 127:1297-1303.

Greenson, R. (1954), About the sound "Mm. . . ." *Psychoanal. Quart.*, 23:234-239.

—— (1967), *The Technique and Practice of Psychoanalysis*. New York: International Universities Press.

Greenspan, S. I. (1979), *Intelligence and Adaptation*. [*Psychological Issues*, Monogr. 47/48.] New York: International Universities Press.

Grof, S. (1980), *L. S. D. Psychotherapy*. Pomona, Cal.: Hunter House.

Grunbaum, A. (1981), The placebo concept. *Behav. Res. Ther.*, 19:157-167.

Guntrip, H. (1969), *Schizoid Phenomena, Object Relations, and the Self*. New York: International Universities Press.

Heston, L. L. (1966), Psychiatric disorders in foster home reared children of schizophrenic mothers. *Brit. J. Psychiat.*, 112:819-825.

Hines, K. (1977), *Subliminal Psychodynamic Activation of Oral*

Dependency Conflicts in a Group of Hospitalized Male Alcoholics. Unpublished doctoral dissertation, Memphis State University.

Hobbs, S. (in preparation), *The Effects of Activated Oedipal and Symbiotic Fantasies on Prejudiced Attitudes.* Unpublished doctoral dissertation, New York University.

Holt, R. R. (1969), Manual for scoring of primary process manifestations in Rorschach responses, Draft 10. Research Center for Mental Health, New York University (mimeographed).

—— (1976), Drive or wish? A reconsideration of the psychoanalytic theory of motivation. In: *Psychology versus Metapsychology,* ed. M. M. Gill & P. Holzman. [*Psychological Issues,* Monogr. 36.] New York: International Universities Press, pp. 158-197.

Houston, W. R. (1939), The doctor himself as a therapeutic agent. *Annals of Internal Medicine,* 11:1416-1425.

Huxley, A. (1954), *Doors of Perception.* New York: Harper & Row.

Jackson, J. (1981), *The Effects of Fantasies of Oneness with Mother and Father on the Ego Functioning of Male and Female Schizophrenics.* Unpublished doctoral dissertation, New York University.

Jacobson, E. (1964), *The Self and the Object World.* New York: International Universities Press.

—— (1967), *Psychotic Conflict and Reality.* New York: International Universities Press.

Jaffe, J. H. (1975), Drug addiction and drug abuse. In: *The Psychopharmacological Basis of Therapeutics,* ed. L. S. Goodman & A. Gilman. New York: Macmillan, pp. 284-324.

James, W. (1902), *The Varieties of Religious Experience.* New York: The Modern Library, 1959.

Jones, E. (1927), The early development of female sexuality. In: *Papers on Psychoanalysis.* Boston: Beacon Press, 1961, pp. 438-451.

—— (1959), *The Life and Work of Sigmund Freud.* New York: Basic Books.

Kaiser, H. (1965), *Effective Psychotherapy—The Contribution of Hellmuth Kaiser,* ed. S. Fierman. New York: Free Press.

Kallman, F. J. (1938), *The Genetics of Schizophrenia*. New York: J. J. Augustin.

—— (1946), The genetic theory of schizophrenia: An analysis of 691 Schizophrenic Twin Index families. *Amer. J. Psychiat.*, 103:309-322.

Kanner, L. (1949), Problems of nosology and psychodynamics of early infantile autism. *Amer. J. Orthopsychiat.*, 19:416-426.

Kaplan, L. J. (1978), *Oneness and Separateness*. New York: Simon & Schuster.

Kaplan, R. (1976), *The Symbiotic Fantasy as a Therapeutic Agent: An Experimental Comparison of the Effects of Three Symbiotic Elements on Manifest Pathology in Schizophrenics*. Unpublished doctoral dissertation, New York University.

Kaye, M. (1975), *The Therapeutic Value of Three Merging Stimuli for Male Schizophrenics*. Unpublished doctoral dissertation, Yeshiva University.

Kazdin, A. B., & Wilcoxon, L. A. (1976), Systematic desensitization and non-specific treatment effects: A methodological evaluation. *Psychol. Bull.*, 83:729-758.

Keisler, D. J. (1973), *The Process of Psychotherapy*. Chicago: Aldine.

Kernberg, O. (1975), *Borderline Conditions and Pathological Narcissism*. New York: Jason Aronson.

Key, W. B. (1973), *Subliminal Seduction*. New York: Signet.

—— (1976), *Media Sexploitation*. New York: Signet.

Kidd, K., & Cavalli-Sforza, L. (1973), An analysis of the genetics of schizophrenia. *Soc. Biol.*, 20:254-265.

Klein, G. S. (1969), Freud's two theories of sexuality. In: *Psychology versus Metapsychology*, ed. M. M. Gill & P. Holzman. [*Psychological Issues*, Monogr. 36.] New York: International Universities Press, pp. 14-70.

—— Spence, D. P., Holt, R. R., & Gourevitch, S. (1958), Cognition without awareness: Subliminal influences upon conscious thought. *J. Abnorm. Soc. Psychol.*, 57:255-266.

Knowlton, P. (1954), Some principles of psychotherapy with atypical children. *Amer. J. Orthopsychiat.*, 24:789-796.

Kohut, H. (1971), *The Analysis of the Self.* New York: International Universities Press.

—— (1977), *The Restoration of the Self.* New York: International Universities Press.

—— & Wolff, E. (1978), The disorders of the self and their treatment: An outline. *Internat. J. Psycho-Anal.,* 59:413-426.

Kringlen, E. (1967), *Heredity and Environment in the Functional Psychoses: An epidemiological and Clinical Twin Study.* London: University Press.

—— (1968), An epidemiological-clinical study on schizophrenia. In: *The Transmission of Schizophrenia,* ed. D. Rosenthal & S. Kety. New York: Pergamon, pp. 49-63.

Kris, E. (1952), *Psychoanalytic Explorations in Art.* New York: International Universities Press.

Lachmann, F. (1950), The modern interpretations of Bach. *Choir Guide,* 3:40-43.

—— (1971), A recent development in the technique of psychoanalysis: The therapeutic alliance. *The Clinical Psychologist,* 25:6, 10-11.

—— (1975), Homosexuality: Some diagnostic perspectives and dynamic considerations. *Amer. J. Psychother.,* 29:254-260.

—— (1982), Narcissistic development. In: *Early Female Development: Current Psychoanalytic Views,* ed. D. Mendell. New York: Spectrum, pp. 227-248.

—— & Stolorow, R. (1980), The developmental significance of affective states: Implications for psychoanalytic treatment. In: *The Annual of Psychoanalysis,* Vol. 8, ed. The Chicago Institute for Psychoanalysis. New York: International Universities Press, pp. 215-229.

Lal, P., Trans. (1967), *Dhammapada.* New York: Farrar Straus & Giroux.

Langs, R. (1973), *The Technique of Psychoanalytic Psychotherapy,* Vol. 1. New York: Jason Aronson.

—— (1975), Therapeutic misalliances. *Internat. J. Psychoanal. Psychother.,* 4:77-105.

Lebra, T. (1974), *Japanese Culture and Behavior.* Honolulu: University Press of Hawaii.

Leiter, E. (1973), *A Study of the Effects of Subliminal Activation of Merging Fantasies in Differentiated and Non-Differentiated Schizophrenics.* Unpublished doctoral dissertation, New York University. (Article accepted for publication, *Psychol. Res. Bull.*)

Lidz, R. W., & Lidz, T. (1952), Therapeutic considerations arising from the intense symbiotic needs of schizophrenic patients. In: *Psychotherapy with Schizophrenics,* ed. E. B. Brody & F. C. Redlich. New York: International Universities Press, pp. 168-178.

Lidz, T. (1968), *The Person.* New York: Basic Books.

——— (1973), *The Origin and Treatment of Schizophrenic Disorders.* New York: Basic Books.

Lieberman, M. A., Yalom, I. D., & Miles, M. B. (1973), *Encounter Groups: First Facts.* New York: Basic Books.

Limentani, D. (1956), Symbiotic identification in schizophrenia. *Psychiatry,* 19:231-236.

Linehan, E., & O'Toole, J. (1982), The effect of subliminal stimulation of symbiotic fantasy on college students' self disclosures in group counseling. *J. Counsel. Psychol.,* 29:151-157. (Originally reported by Linehan in a doctoral dissertation with the same title, St. John's University, 1979.)

Little, M. (1960), On basic unity. *Internat. J. Psycho-Anal.,* 41:377-384.

Litwack, T. (1972), *A Study of Certain Issues Concerning the Dynamics of Thinking and Behavioral Pathology in Schizophrenics through the Use of Subliminal Stimulation.* Unpublished doctoral dissertation, New York University.

——— Wiedemann, C. F., & Yager, J. (1979), The fear of object loss, responsiveness to subliminal stimuli and schizophrenic psychopathology. *J. Nerv. Ment. Dis.,* 167:79-80.

Loewald, H. (1973), Review of *The Analysis of the Self* by Heinz Kohut. *Psychoanal. Quart.,* 42:441-451.

Lomangino, L. (1969), *Depiction of Subliminally and Supraliminally Presented Aggressive Stimuli and Its Effects on the Cognitive Functioning of Schizophrenics.* Unpublished doctoral dissertation, Fordham University.

Loveland, L. K. (1977), *The Effects of Subliminal Aggressive and Symbiotic Stimulation on Ego Functioning in Two Sub-types of Schizophrenics.* Unpublished master's thesis, William and Mary College.

Luborsky, L. (1967), Momentary forgetting during psychotherapy and psychoanalysis: A theory and research method. In: *Motives and Thought: Psychoanalytic Essays in Honor of David Rapaport,* ed. R. R. Holt. [*Psychological Issues,* Monogr. 18/19.]. New York: International Universities Press, pp. 177-217.

Lyketsos, G. C. (1959), On the formation of mother-daughter symbiotic relationship patterns in schizophrenia. *Psychiatry,* 22:161-166.

Maccoby, E. E., & Jacklin, C. N. (1974), *The Psychology of Sex Differences.* Palo Alto: Stanford University Press.

Mahler, M. S. (1952), On childhood psychoses and schizophrenia: Autistic and symbiotic infantile psychoses. *The Psychoanalytic Study of the Child,* 7:286-305. New York: International Universities Press.

———— (1968), *On Human Symbiosis and the Vicissitudes of Individuation.* New York: International Universities Press.

———— Furer, M., & Settlage, C. F. (1959), Severe emotional disturbances in childhood psychosis. In: *American Handbook of Psychiatry,* Vol. 1, ed. S. Arieti. New York: Basic Books, pp. 816-839.

———— Pine, F., & Bergman, A. (1975), *The Psychological Birth of the Human Infant.* New York: Basic Books.

Mannheim, J. (1975), Notes on a case of drug addiction. *Internat. J. Psycho-Anal.,* 36:166-173.

Martin, A. (1975), *The Effect of Subliminal Stimulation of Symbiotic Fantasies on Weight Loss in Obese Women Receiving Behavioral Treatment.* Unpublished doctoral dissertation, New York University.

Mascaro, J., Trans. (1965), *Upanishads.* New York: Penguin.

Mendelsohn, E. (1979), *Responses of Schizophrenic Men to Subliminal Psychodynamic Stimuli.* Doctoral dissertation, Yeshiva University.

———— (1981), The effects of stimulating symbiotic fantasies on manifest pathology in schizophrenics: A revised formulation. *J. Nerv. Ment. Dis.*, 169:580-590. (Originally reported in Mendelsohn [1979].)

Milich, R. (1976), *A Study of the Effects of Symbiotic Gratification Stimuli and Aggressive Fantasizing on the Psychopathology of Chronic Hospitalized Schizophrenics.* Unpublished doctoral dissertation, Columbia University.

Miller, J. (1973), *The Effects of Aggressive Stimulation upon Young Adults Who Have Experienced Death of a Parent during Childhood and Adolescence.* Unpublished doctoral dissertation, New York University.

Modell, A. (1976), The holding environment and the therapeutic action of psychoanalysis. *J. Amer. Psychoanal. Assn.*, 24:285-308.

———— (1980), Comments at a panel on "Focus on Developmental Defects: Self Psychology vs. Conflict Psychology" at the Annual Scientific Conference of the Council of Psychoanalytic Psychotherapists, New York, May.

Morgan, W. P. (1979), Negative addiction in runners. *Physicians and Sports Medicine*, 7:57-70.

Nacht, S. (1964), Silence as an integrative factor. *Internat. J. Psycho-Anal.*, 45:299-308.

National Institute of Drug Abuse (1981), *Population Projections Based on the National Survey on Drug Abuse, 1979.* Rockville, Md.: National Institute of Drug Abuse.

Nissenfeld, S. (1979), *The Effects of Four Types of Subliminal Stimuli on Female Depressives.* Unpublished doctoral dissertation, Yeshiva University.

Ostrander, S., Schroeder, L., & Ostrander, N. (1979), *Superlearning.* New York: Delacorte.

Otis, L. S. (in press), Adverse effects of Transcendental Meditation. In: *The Science of Meditation*, ed. D. H. Shapiro, Jr. New York: Aldine.

Packer, S. (in preparation), *The Effects of Subliminal Psychodynamic Activation on Behavior Assertiveness Training in Women.* Unpublished doctoral dissertation, New York University.

Palmatier, J. R., & Bornstein, P. H. (1980), The effects of subliminal stimulation of symbiotic merging fantasies on behavioral treatment of smokers. *J. Nerv. Ment. Dis.*, 168:715-720. (Originally reported by Palmatier in a doctoral dissertation with the same title, University of Montana, 1980.)

Parker, K. A. (1977), *The Effects of Subliminal Merging Stimuli on the Academic Performance of College Students.* Doctoral dissertation, New York University.

—— (1982), The effects of subliminal symbiotic stimulation on academic performance: Further evidence for the adaptation-enhancing effects of oneness fantasies. *J. Counsel. Psychol.*, 29:19-28. (Originally reported in Parker [1977].)

Paul, I. H. (1959), *Studies in Remembering.* [*Psychological Issues*, Monogr. 2.] New York: International Universities Press.

Pine, F. (1961), Incidental versus focal presentation of drive related stimuli. *J. Abnorm. Soc. Psychol.*, 60:68-75.

—— (1979), On the pathology of the separation-individuation process as manifested in later clinical work: An attempt at delineation. *Internat. J. Psycho-Anal.*, 60:225-242.

—— (1981), In the beginning: Contributions to a psychoanalytic developmental psychology. *Internat. J. Ment. Health*, 1:63-75.

Pious, W. L. (1949), The pathogenic process in schizophrenia. *Bull. Menn. Clin.*, 13:152-158.

Podall, J. (1979), *The Effect of Subliminal Perception on Cooperative Choices in a Prisoner's Dilemma Game.* Unpublished masters thesis, New York University.

Rapaport, D. (1960), *The Structure of Psychoanalytic Theory: A Systematizing Attempt.* [*Psychological Issues*, Monogr. 6.] New York: International Universities Press.

—— Gill, M. M., & Schafer, R. (1968), *Diagnostic Psychological Testing.* Chicago: Year Book Publishers. [Rev. Ed., 1968, ed. R. R. Holt. New York: International Universities Press.]

Rapaport, J. (1963), A study of the influence of the normal heartbeat sound on a group of autistic girls. *J. Amer. Women's Med. Assn.*, 18:982-984.

Reich, W. (1933), *Character Analysis*. New York: Touchstone.

Reichard, S., & Tillman, C. (1950), Patterns of parent-child relationships in schizophrenia. *Psychiatry*, 13:247-257.

Reyher, J. (1958), *Hypnotically Induced Conflict in Relation to Subception, Repression, Antisocial Behavior and Psychosomatic Reactions*. Unpublished doctoral dissertation, University of Illinois.

Rogers, C. (1951), *Client-Centered Therapy*. Boston: Houghton-Mifflin.

Rose, G. (1972), Fusion states. In: *Tactics and Techniques in Psychoanalytic Therapy*, ed. P. L. Giovacchini. New York: Jason Aronson, pp. 137-169.

Rosen, J. (1953), *Direct Analysis: Selected Papers*. New York: Grune & Stratton.

Rosenthal, D. (1972), Three adoption studies of heredity in the schizophrenic disorders. *Internat. J. Ment. Health*, 1:63-75.

Rudin, E. (1916), *Zur Vererbung und Neuenstehung der Dementia Praecox* (On the Inheritance and Fresh Occurrence of Dementia Praecox). Berlin: Springer Verlag.

Rutstein, E. H., & Goldberger, L. (1973), The effects of aggressive stimulation on suicidal patients: An experimental study of the psychoanalytic theory of suicide. In: *Psychoanalysis and Contemporary Science*, Vol. 2, ed. B. Rubinstein. New York: Macmillan, pp. 157-174. (Originally reported by Rutstein in a doctoral dissertation with the same title, New York University, 1970).

Sacks, M. (1979), A psychodynamic overview of sports. *Runners World*, 9:13-22.

Salk, L. (1962), Mothers' heartbeat as an imprinting stimulus. *Transactions of the N.Y. Academy of Sciences*, 24:753-763.

——— (1973), The role of the heartbeat in the relations between mother and infant. *Scient. Amer.*, 28:24-31.

Sampson, H., Weiss, J., Mlodnosky, L., & Hause, E. (1972), Defense analysis and the emergence of warded-off mental contents. *Arch. Gen. Psychiat.*, 26:524-531.

Sandler, J. (1974), Psychological conflict and the structural model: Some clinical and theoretical implications. *Internat. J. Psycho-Anal.*, 55:53-62.

Savitt, R. A. (1963), Psychoanalytic studies on addiction: Ego structure in narcotic addiction. *Psychoanal. Quart.*, 32:43-57.

Schafer, R. (1948), *The Clinical Application of Psychological Tests*. New York: International Universities Press.

——— (1968), *Aspects of Internalization*. New York: International Universities Press.

Schmidl, F. (1955), The problem of scientific validation in psychoanalytic interpretation. *Internat. J. Psycho-Anal.*, 36:105-113.

Schur, H. (1966), An observation and comments on the development of memory. *The Psychoanalytic Study of the Child*, 21:468-482. New York: International Universities Press.

Schurtman, R. (1978), *The Effect of Psychodynamic Activation of Symbiotic Gratification Fantasies on Involvement in a Treatment Program for Alcoholics*. Unpublished doctoral dissertation, New York University. (Article accepted for publication, *Internat. J. Addict.*)

Schwartz, F., & Rouse, R. O. (1961), *The Activation and Recovery of Associations*. [*Psychological Issues*, Monogr. 9.] New York: International Universities Press.

Searles, H. F. (1951), Data concerning certain manifestations of incorporation. In: *Collected Papers on Schizophrenia and Related Subjects*. New York: International Universities Press, 1965, pp. 39-69.

——— (1959), Integration and differentiation in schizophrenia. In: *Collected Papers on Schizophrenia and Related Subjects*. New York: International Universities Press, 1965, pp. 304-348.

Sechehaye, M. (1951), *Symbolic Realization: A New Method of Psychotherapy Applied to a Case of Schizophrenia*. New York: International Universities Press.

Seitz, F. D. (1966), The consensus problem in psychoanalytic research. In: *Methods of Research in Psychotherapy*, ed. L. A. Gottschalk & A. H. Auerbach. New York: Appleton-Century-Crofts, pp. 209-225.

Shafii, M. (1973), Silence in the service of the ego: Psychoanalytic study of meditation. *Internat. J. Psycho-Anal.*, 54:431-443.

Shapiro, A. K. (1978), The placebo effect. In: *Principles of Pharmacology*, ed. W. G. Clark & J. del Guidice. New York: Academic Press, pp. 441-459..

—— & Morris, W. (1978), The placebo effect. In: *Handbook of Psychotherapy and Behavior Change*, ed. S. L. Garfield & A. E. Bergin. New York: Wiley, pp. 369-410.

—— & Struening, E. L. (1973a), The use of placebos: A study of ethics and physician's attitudes. *Psychiatry and Medicine*, 4:17-29.

—— & Struening, E. L., (1973b), Defensiveness in the definition of placebos. *Comprehen. Psychiat.*, 14:107-120.

Sheehan, G. (1978), *Running and Being.* New York: Simon & Schuster.

Silverman, L. H. (1965), A study of the effects of subliminally presented aggressive stimuli on the production of pathological thinking in a non-psychiatric population. *J. Nerv. Ment. Dis.*, 141:443-455.

—— (1966), A technique for the study of psychodynamic relationships: The effects of subliminally presented aggressive stimuli on the production of pathological thinking in a schizophrenic population. *J. Consult. Psychol.*, 30:103-111.

—— (1967), An experimental approach to the study of dynamic propositions in psychoanalysis: The relationship between the aggressive drive and ego regression—initial studies. *J. Amer. Psychoanal. Assn.*, 15:376-403.

—— (1970), Further experimental studies on dynamic propositions in psychoanalysis: On the function and meaning of regressive thinking. *J. Amer. Psychoanal. Assn.*, 18:102-124.

—— (1972), Drive stimulation and psychopathology: On the conditions under which drive-related external events evoke pathological reactions. In: *Psychoanalysis and Contemporary Science*, Vol. 1, ed. R. R. Holt & E. Peterfreund. New York: Macmillan, pp. 306-326.

———— (1974), Some psychoanalytic considerations of non-psychoanalytic therapies: On the possibility of integration and related issues. *Psychother. Theory, Res. & Pract.*, 11:298-306.

———— (1975), On the role of laboratory experiments in the development of the clinical theory of psychoanalysis. *Internat. Rev. Psycho-Anal.*, 2:43-64.

———— (1976), Psychoanalytic theory: The reports of my death are greatly exaggerated. *Amer. Psychol.*, 31:621-637.

———— (1977), *Ethical Considerations and Guidelines in the Use of Subliminal Psychodynamic Activation.* Unpublished manuscript, Research Center for Mental Health, New York University.

———— (1979), The unconscious fantasy as therapeutic agent in psychoanalytic treatment. *J. Amer. Acad. Psychoanal.*, 7:189-218.

———— (1982a), The subliminal psychodynamic activation method: Overview and comprehensive list of studies. In: *Empirical Studies in Psychoanalysis*, Vol. 1, ed. J. Masling. New York: Erlbaum.

———— (1982b), A comment on two subliminal psychodynamic activation experiments. *J. Abnorm. Psychol.*, 91:126-130.

———— (1982c), Rejoinder to Allen and Condon's and Heilbrun's replies. *J. Abnorm. Psychol.*, 91:136-138.

———— Bronstein, A., & Mendelsohn, E. (1976), The further use of the subliminal psychodynamic activation method for the experimental study of the clinical theory of psychoanalysis: On the specificity of relationships between manifest psychopathology and unconscious conflict. *Psychother. Theor. Res. & Pract.*, 13:2-16.

———— & Candell, P. (1969), *The Effects of Subliminal Drive Stimulation on Schizophrenic Functioning: A Further Report.* Unpublished manuscript, Manhattan Veterans Administration Hospital.

———— ———— (1970), On the relationship between aggressive activation, symbiotic merging intactness of body boundaries and manifest pathology in schizophrenia. *J. Nerv. Ment. Dis.*, 150:387-399.

—————— Pettit, T. F., & Blum, F. A. (1971), Further data on the effects of aggressive activation and symbiotic merging on the ego functioning of schizophrenics. *Percept. Mot. Skills,* 32:93-94.

—————— & Fishel, A. (1981), The Oedipus complex: Studies in adult male behavior. In: *Review of Personality and Social Psychology,* Vol. 2. Beverly Hills: Sage, pp. 43-68.

—————— & Frank, S. (1978), Aggressive stimulation, aggressive fantasy and disturbances of ego functioning: Some heretofore unexplored considerations on the effects of aggressive film viewing. In: *Psychoanalytic Perspectives on Aggression,* ed. D. S. Milman & G. D. Goldman. Springfield, Ill.: Charles C. Thomas, pp. 121-139.

—————— —————— & Dachinger, P. (1974), Psychoanalytic reinterpretation of the effectiveness of systematic desensitization: Experimental data bearing on the role of merging fantasies. *J. Abnorm. Psychol.,* 83:313-318.

—————— & Goldweber, A. M. (1966), A further study of the effects of subliminal aggressive stimulation on thinking. *J. Nerv. Ment. Dis.,* 143:463-472.

—————— & Gordon, D. (1969), *Further Data on the Effects of Subliminal Aggressive Stimulation on Schizophrenics.* Unpublished manuscript, Research Center for Mental Health, New York University.

—————— & Grabowski, R. (1982), *The Effects of Activating Oneness Fantasies on the Anxiety Level of Male and Female College Students.* Unpublished manuscript, Research Center for Mental Health, New York University.

—————— Klinger, H., Lustbader, L., Farrell, J., & Martin, A. (1972), The effect of subliminal drive stimulation on the speech of stutterers. *J. Nerv. Ment. Dis.,* 155:14-21.

—————— Kwawer, J. S., Wolitzky, C., & Coron, M. (1973), An experimental study of aspects of the psychoanalytic theory of male homosexuality. *J. Abnorm. Psychol.,* 82:178-188.

—————— Levinson, P., Mendelsohn, E., & Ungaro, R. (1975), A clinical application of subliminal psychodynamic activation: On the stimulation of symbiotic fantasies as an adjunct in the treatment of hospitalized schizophrenics. *J. Nerv. Ment. Dis.*, 161:379-392.

———— Martin, A., Ungaro, R., & Mendelsohn, E. (1978), Effect of subliminal stimulation of symbiotic fantasies on behavior modification treatment of obesity. *J. Consult. Psychol.*, 46:432-441.

———— Ross, D., Adler, J., & Lustig, D. (1978), A simple research paradigm for demonstrating subliminal psychodynamic activation. *J. Abnorm. Psychol.*, 87:341-357.

———— & Silverman, D. K. (1964), A clinical-experimental approach to the study of subliminal stimulation: The effects of a drive-related stimulus upon Rorschach responses. *J. Abnorm. Soc. Psychol.*, 69:158-172.

———— & Silverman, S. E. (1967), The effects of subliminally presented drive stimuli on the cognitive functioning of schizophrenics. *J. Proj. Tech.*, 31:78-85.

———— & Spiro, R. H. (1967), Some comments and data on the partial cue controversy and other matters relevant to investigations of subliminal phenomena. *Percept. Mot. Skills*, 25:325-338.

———— ———— (1968), The effects of subliminal, supraliminal and vocalized aggression on the ego functioning of schizophrenics. *J. Nerv. Ment. Dis.*, 146:50-61.

———— ———— Weisberg, J. S., & Candell, P. (1969), The effects of aggressive activation and the need to merge on pathological thinking in schizophrenia. *J. Nerv. Ment. Dis.*, 148:39-51.

———— & Wolitzky, C. (1970), *The Effects of the Subliminal Stimulation of Symbiotic Fantasies on the Defensiveness of "Normal" Subjects in Telling TAT Stories.* Unpublished manuscript, Research Center for Mental Health, New York University.

———— Wolitzky, D. (1982), Toward the resolution of controversial psychoanalytic treatment issues. In: *Curative Factors in Dynamic Psychotherapy*, ed. S. Slipp. New York: McGraw-Hill, pp. 321-348.

Silverman, S. E. (1970), *The Effects of Subliminally Induced Drive Derivatives on Ego Functioning in Schizophrenics.*

Unpublished doctoral dissertation, New York University.

Silverstein, R. (1978), *The Effects of Tachistoscopic Oedipal Stimulation on Competitive Dart Throwing*. Senior honor's thesis, Brown University.

Slater, R. (1953), *Psychotic and Neurotic Illnesses in Twins*. London: Her Majesty's Stationery Office.

Socarides, C. (1969), Psychoanalytic therapy of a male homosexual. *Psychoanal. Quart.*, 38:173-190.

―――― (1978), *Homosexuality*. New York: Jason Aronson.

Spino, M. (1976), *Beyond Jogging*. Milbrae, Cal.: Celestial Arts.

Spiro, R. H., & Silverman, L. H. (1967), Effects of body awareness and aggressive activation on ego functioning of schizophrenics. *Percept. Mot. Skills*, 28:575-585.

Spiro T. (1975), *The Effects of Laboratory Stimulation of Symbiotic Fantasies and Bodily Self-Awareness on Relatively Differentiated and Non-Differentiated Schizophrenics*. Unpublished doctoral dissertation, New York University.

Spitz, R. A. (1965), *The First Year of Life*. New York: International Universities Press.

Sterba, R. (1934), The fate of the ego in analytic therapy. *Internat. J. Psycho-Anal.*, 15:117-126.

Stierlin, H. (1959), The adaptation to the "stranger" person's reality: Some aspects of the symbiotic relationship of the schizophrenic. *Psychiatry*, 22:143-152.

Stolorow, R. (1976), Psychoanalytic reflections on client-centered therapy in the light of modern conceptions of narcissism. *Psychotherapy*, 13:26-29.

―――― & Atwood, G. (1979), *Faces in a Cloud: Subjectivity in Personality Theory*. New York: Jason Aronson.

―――― & Lachmann, F. (1980), *Psychoanalysis of Developmental Arrests: Theory and Treatment*. New York: International Universities Press.

―――― ―――― (1981), Two psychoanalyses or one? *Psychoanal. Rev.*, 68:307-319.

Stone, L. (1961), *The Psychoanalytic Situation*. New York: International Universities Press.

Strachey, J. (1934), The nature of the therapeutic action

of psycho-analysis. *Internat. J. Psycho-Anal.*, 15:127-159.

Sundberg, N. D. (1966), A method of studying sensitivity to implied meaning. *Gawein J. Psychol.* (Nymegen: University of Netherlands), 15:1-8.

Tartakoff, H. H. (1966), The normal personality in our culture and the Nobel Prize complex. In: *Psychoanalysis—A General Psychology*, ed. R. M. Loewenstein, L. M. Newman, M. Schur, & A. J. Solnit. New York: International Universities Press, pp. 222-252.

Thass-Thienemann, T. (1967), *The Subconscious Language.* New York: Washington Square.

Varga, M. (1973), *An Experimental Study of Aspects of the Psychoanalytic Study of Elation.* Unpublished doctoral dissertation, New York University.

Waldhorn, H. (1951), Notes taken at a meeting of the New York Psychoanalytic Society on "Clinical Observations on the Treatment of Manifest Male Homosexuality, since Freud." *Psychoanal. Quart.*, 20:337-338.

Wallerstein, R. S. (1981), The bipolar self: Discussion of alternative perspectives. *J. Amer. Psychoanal. Assn.*, 29:337-394.

——— & Sampson, H. (1971), Issues in research in the psychoanalytic process. *Internat. J. Psycho-Anal.*, 52:11-50.

Watts, A. (1966), *This Is It.* New York: Pantheon.

Wender, P., Rosenthal, D., & Kety, S. (1968), A psychiatric assessment of the adoptive parents of schizophrenics. In: *The Transmission of Schizophrenia*, ed. D. Rosenthal & S. Kety. New York: Pergamon, pp. 235-250.

Wiedeman, G. (1962), Survey of the psychoanalytic literature on overt male homosexuality. *J. Amer. Psychoanal. Assn.*, 10:386-409.

Wiener, M., & Schiller, P. H. (1960), Subliminal perception or perception of partial cues. *J. Abnorm. Soc. Psychol.*, 61:124-137.

Wilson, K., & Bixenstine, E. (1962), Forms of social control in two-person two-choice games. *Behav. Sci.*, 7:92-102.

Winnicott, D. W. (1960), A theory of the parent-infant relationship. In: *The Maturational Processes and the Fa-*

cilitating Environment. New York: International Universities Press, 1965, pp. 37-55.

——— (1962), Ego integration in child development. In: *The Maturational Processes and the Facilitating Environment*. New York: International Universities Press, 1965, pp. 56-63.

——— (1963), Psychiatric disorder in terms of infantile maturational processes. In: *The Maturational Processes and the Facilitating Environment*. New York: International Universities Press, 1965, pp. 230-241.

——— (1965), *The Family and Individual Development*. New York: Basic Books.

Wisdom, J. O. (1967), Testing an interpretation within a session. *Internat. J. Psycho-Anal.*, 48:44-52.

Zetzel, E. (1956), The concept of transference. In: *The Capacity for Emotional Growth*. New York: International Universities Press, 1970, pp. 168-181.

——— (1966), An obsessional neurotic: Freud's Rat Man. In: *The Capacity for Emotional Growth*. New York: International Universities Press, 1970, pp. 216-228.

Zuckerman, M. (1960), The effects of subliminal and supraliminal suggestion on verbal productivity. *J. Abnorm. Soc. Psychol.*, 60:404-411.

Zuckerman, S. (1980), *The Effects of Subliminal Symbiotic and Success-Related Stimuli on the School Performance of High School Underachievers*. Unpublished doctoral dissertation, New York University School of Education.

NAME INDEX

SUBJECT INDEX